THE COMPLETE IDIOT'S GUIDE® TO

Robert's Rules

by Nancy Sylvester, PRP, CPP-T

ALPHA

A member of Penguin Group (USA) Inc.

To my family, Jim, Marcy, and Holly, my greatest supporters; my parents,
Marge and Leonard Jochim, for raising me in a family in which rules were honored;
and my clients, for all you taught me.

Standard Book Number: 1-59257-163-8
Library of Congress Catalog Card Number: 2003113807

06 05 04   8 7 6 5 4 3 2 1

Interpretation of the printing code: The rightmost number of the first series of numbers is the year of the book's printing; the rightmost number of the second series of numbers is the number of the book's printing. For example, a printing code of 04-1 shows that the first printing occurred in 2004.

Printed in the United States of America

Most Alpha books are available at special quantity discounts for bulk purchases for sales promotions, premiums, fund-raising, or educational use. Special books, or book excerpts, can also be created to fit specific needs.

For details, write: Special Markets, Alpha Books, 375 Hudson Street, New York, NY 10014.

Publisher: *Marie Butler-Knight*
Product Manager: *Phil Kitchel*
Senior Managing Editor: *Jennifer Chisholm*
Senior Acquisitions Editor: *Renee Wilmeth*
Development Editor: *Jennifer Moore*
Production Editor: *Megan Douglass*
Copy Editor: *Michael Dietsch*
Illustrator: *Chris Eliopoulos*
Cover/Book Designer: *Trina Wurst*
Indexer: *Julie Bess*

Contents at a Glance

Contents

Foreword

Congratulations on your purchase of this book. You've already shown one thing—you're no idiot! *The Complete Idiot's Guide to Robert's Rules* is the most comprehensive guide available on meeting procedures, running effective meetings, and the world of parliamentarians.

The start of my own interest in parliamentary procedure may sound familiar. Some 20 years ago, I attended a meeting where an important proposal was being considered. I decided to say something and went to a microphone. Before I was called on, another member made a motion, it was seconded, there was a vote, and the whole matter was resolved—all before I had a chance to speak! At that instant, I decided to learn enough about meeting procedure so that would *never* happen again.

Unfortunately, as I tried to learn about parliamentary procedure, there wasn't a lot to help me. There were rule books, like *Robert's Rules of Order*, but most of these were overwhelming. There were books on organizing meetings, but most of these didn't even mention parliamentary procedure or how to make proposals and express views in a meeting. I don't recall *any* book that listed parliamentary organizations or where to go for further study.

Oh how *The Complete Idiot's Guide to Robert's Rules* could have helped! This book has it all. You'll find information on parliamentary authorities (like *Robert's Rules*), tips for planning and running effective meetings, differences between board meetings and other kinds of meetings, listings of parliamentary organizations, and much more. If you need it, it's in here!

To get started, just jump right in. Sure, the best idea is to read this book from start to finish. But you might not have that much time before your meeting! Whether you're pretty sure of yourself or a novice, start with Chapter 1, Chapter 2, and Chapter 4. Then, if you're new to parliamentary procedure, you may want to read Part 2. On the other hand, if you will soon have to run a meeting yourself, you may want to jump to Chapter 15 and Chapter 16. Wherever you start, you'll learn valuable tips about effective meetings.

Best of luck as you start your *Robert's Rules* journey. You're likely to find that knowing meeting procedure makes a big difference. Those who know the rules can get their ideas across and often quickly assume leadership positions. If you're already in a leadership role, proper procedure can help turn long, confrontational meetings into short, painless ones. As a result, you should make every effort to learn the essentials of this guide.

Time to get started! As Henry M. Robert (yes, *the* Robert of *Robert's Rules*) once stated:

> It is difficult to find another branch of knowledge where a small amount of study produces such great results in increased efficiency in a country where the people rule, as in parliamentary law.

I couldn't have said it better!

—Jim Slaughter

Jim Slaughter is the most active parliamentary consultant in the country. He is a practicing attorney, Certified Professional Parliamentarian-Teacher and a Professional Registered Parliamentarian. Jim has served as Parliamentarian to hundreds of national and state conventions, including many of the largest trade and professional associations in the country. His articles on procedure have been published in many magazines, including the *American Bar Association Journal*, CAI's *Common Ground*, and ASAE's *Association Management*.

Introduction

Parliamentary procedure is all about helping people run meetings efficiently and fairly. It's important stuff for any group that wants to make sure that it doesn't violate the rights of its members and that wants to get its business done as quickly and efficiently as possible.

People often mistakenly view parliamentary procedure only as a set of rules. When looked at this way, I can understand why people approach the subject with dread—for those rulebooks are capable of curing the most severe cases of insomnia! But parliamentary procedure is so much more than a set of rules. It is a process for conducting business.

The approach I have taken in this book is to explain that process and the foundation upon which the rules are based. Then, when you find yourself without this book and you need to decide the proper way to handle the situation, you can fall back on that understanding of the process instead of trying to recall some long-forgotten rule.

My goal in writing this book was to take this very technical subject and explain it in plain English so that at your next meeting, you'll understand what's going on, what you can do, and what you can't do. Toward that end, I've divided this book into five parts.

You've probably heard the term *parliamentary procedure* before, but do you really know what it's all about? In **Part 1, "What Is Parliamentary Procedure and What Can It Do for Me?"** I'll fill in the background information on this subject. It will help you understand the concepts that Robert's Rules are based on so that you can use your judgment instead of memorizing rules.

Motions introduce business to meetings; without them, parliamentary procedure would be meaningless. **Part 2, "Let's Get Moving: The Motion-Making Process,"** will help you move, debate, and vote on motions efficiently and fairly. It is a process that is best understood when broken down into the six easy-to-understand steps.

In **Part 3, "Motions for (Almost) Any Occasion,"** I explain approximately 25 motions. I've also included a script—a guide of what to say when processing a motion—for most of the motions in this book. In addition to allowing you to see each motion in action, these scripts will help you to sound like a pro when you use them during your next meeting.

Part 4, "Let's Get to Order," helps you prepare for your meeting, say the right things during the meeting, and make sure that you handle those all-important elections properly. The information in this part is for all members of the group, but leaders will really love it!

In **Part 5, "Officers, Committees, and Meetings"** you'll learn all about minutes and hopefully find that they are much easier to prepare than you thought. You will also learn about the responsibilities of officers and committees and the purposes of their respective reports. In addition, you'll find a chapter devoted to conventions and their unique requirements and another chapter introducing you to using parliamentary procedure to run electronic meetings.

Since parliamentary procedure has its own language, I have prepared an extensive glossary, Appendix A, for your quick reference. And finally, while this isn't a rulebook, I did want to include the rules. Appendix B is the abridged text of the last rulebook Henry M. Robert wrote before his death.

Sidebars

You'll find the following sidebars scattered throughout the book:

> **Parliamentary Pearls**
>
> These parliamentary tips will help you implement Robert's Rules.

> **Robert's Says**
>
> Here you'll find easy to understand definitions for those technical terms that plague parliamentary procedure.

> **Gavel Gaffs**
>
> Follow these warnings to avoid making parliamentary blunders.

> **Point of Information**
>
> In these boxes I expand on key parliamentary points.

Acknowledgments

A special thank you goes to my family: Jim, Marcy, and Holly. They have been incredibly supportive during the time of the writing of this book and throughout my entire career. They have not only allowed me to get lost in writing for days at a time, but each of them has taken on a different, yet very active role in helping me prepare this book. Jim, my husband, read each chapter to give me the perspective of a non-parliamentary person reading the book. Jim's favorite statement about *Robert's* is that the rulebook is the greatest cure for insomnia. The good news is that he stayed awake while reading this book. My daughters, Marcy and Holly, each contributed—Marcy's wit and Holly's attention to detail were appreciated.

Thank you also to Rhonda Arends, my dear friend and fellow trainer. Years of writing training manuals with her has helped me develop my writing skills, and her dedication to helping me proof this book was invaluable.

Thank you to Dr. Otis J. Aggertt, my college parliamentary procedure professor who got me hooked, and all of the parliamentarians I have had the pleasure to learn from. This book is payback because now I can pass that wonderful knowledge on to others. I also appreciate all of my clients who have helped me learn more about parliamentary procedure than even I sometimes wanted.

Special Thanks to the Technical Reviewer

The Complete Idiot's Guide to Robert's Rules was reviewed by an expert who double-checked the accuracy of what you'll learn here, to help us ensure that this book gives you everything you need to know about the rules of parliamentary procedure. Special thanks are extended to Jim Slaughter, J.D., CPP-T, PRP.

Trademarks

All terms mentioned in this book that are known to be or are suspected of being trademarks or service marks have been appropriately capitalized. Alpha Books and Penguin Group (USA) Inc. cannot attest to the accuracy of this information. Use of a term in this book should not be regarded as affecting the validity of any trademark or service mark.

Part 1

What Is Parliamentary Procedure and What Can It Do for Me?

I like to call parliamentary procedure the rules of the road for meetings. When driving, you need to know whether you can turn right on red, who goes first at a four-way stop, and how fast you can go. In a meeting, you need to know when you can introduce an item of business, who gets to speak first on the issue, and how long each person can speak on it.

This first part is designed to give you an overview of parliamentary procedure. First of all, you will finally get an answer to those questions you have been wondering about for a long time: What *is* parliamentary procedure? Who is this Robert guy? And why do I need to follow his rules?

Robert's Rules 101

In This Chapter

- ◆ Parliamentary procedure, defined
- ◆ Other parliamentary authorities besides *Robert's*
- ◆ How *Robert's Rules* have changed
- ◆ Why *Robert's* still rules

Imagine the following scenario: As an active member of your community, you attend a meeting about an issue that is important to you. During the discussion, you want to make a point, but you have no idea how to phrase it or even when it's acceptable to speak up. You try once, but are ruled out of order by the chair! Embarrassed, you sit quietly during the rest of the meeting and never share your idea with the rest of the group.

Sound familiar? Unfortunately, a lot of people are scared off by parliamentary procedure, when in reality it's meant to allow all members to participate fairly and equally.

So What Is Parliamentary Procedure?

Parliamentary procedure is a system of conducting business when working in a group (that group is sometimes also called a *deliberative assembly*).

Simply stated, it's an organized system that allows a group of people to come together and make a decision. The system is made up of basic principles and rules that determine how the group will proceed through the decision-making process.

Parliamentary procedure is about helping the group come to a decision; it is not about helping any one individual get his or her way, and it is certainly not intended to prevent members from participating in the group.

Robert's Says

Deliberative assembly—A group of people meeting together to openly discuss issues and make decisions that then become the decision of the group.

Parliamentary procedure also helps the group stay focused on a single issue until the members resolve it. This technique helps groups make better, more logical decisions—they have the advantage of many minds working together using a systematic approach to problem-solving.

In many respects parliamentary procedure is the "rules of the road" for meetings, but I hope you will see that it's not simply a set of rules. Rather, you should think of it as a set of guidelines by which to conduct meetings.

Getting Down to Basics

The following are the foundational concepts upon which parliamentary procedure is based:

- **One thing at a time.** Only one main motion is allowed on the floor at a time, but there is a system to put that motion aside if something more urgent comes up.

- **One person, too.** Only one person may talk at a time.

- **And only one time per meeting.** The same motion, or practically the same motion, can not be made more than once per session (the only exception is if a member changes his or her mind).

- **Enough of us have to be here to decide.** The group determines the minimum number of people (called a quorum) that must be present to make a decision for the whole group.

- **Protected even if absent.** The rights of the members who are absent are protected.

- **Vote requirements are based on members' rights.** The determination of what kind of vote is needed (such as majority, two thirds, and so on) is based on members' rights. If an action gives rights to the members, it requires a majority vote to pass. If an action takes away rights from members, it requires a two-thirds vote to pass.

♦ **Silence = consent.** If a member chooses to abstain from voting, that member is giving his or her consent to the decision made by the group.

♦ **Everybody is equal.** All voting members have equal rights. The majority rules but the minority has the right to be heard and to attempt to change the minds of the majority.

Make the Rules Meet Your Needs!

Because each group is different, parliamentary procedure is designed to be the basis for the rules, which groups can then adapt to their own needs. So in a deliberative assembly, you have the rules that are determined by your parliamentary authority, and you have the rules that are determined by your particular organization (bylaws, special rules, and so on, which I discuss in Chapter 4).

Other Parliamentary Authorities

What do I mean by *parliamentary authority?* That is the set of rules that a group adopts as the rules that will govern them. Although this book is about *Robert's Rules of Order,* it is only one, albeit the most popular, parliamentary authority that a deliberative assembly might choose to use. Other parliamentary authorities include the following:

♦ *The Standard Code of Parliamentary Procedure,* originally by Alice Sturgis, is in its fourth edition. The author's aim was to write a concise book based on common sense and parliamentary principles. She got away from the more technical language used in *Robert's.* Sturgis is most popular in the medical profession. Alice Sturgis is dead, and the American Institute of Parliamentarians authored the current edition.

Parliamentary Pearls

You can find the parliamentary authority for your organization in your bylaws. If the bylaws are written following the format prescribed in *Robert's,* you will find an article titled "Parliamentary Authority." That article should be one of the last articles in the bylaws.

♦ *Demeter's Manual of Parliamentary Law and Procedure,* by George Demeter, was first published in 1948 and has been revised a few times. The differences between *Demeter's* and *Robert's* are very minor. *Demeter's* is usually considered to be more user-friendly than *Robert's*.

Gavel Gaffs

Don't let people tell you that *Robert's Rules* is outdated and therefore not needed anymore! Although following correct parliamentary procedure might seem outmoded and over-fussy in today's informal, fast-paced world, it's actually more crucial now than ever. As long as large groups make decisions, we will need parliamentary procedure.

♦ *Mason's Manual of Legislative Procedure* is used by more than half of all legislative bodies. It was written by Paul Mason, first published in 1935. The latest revision in 1989 was written by the National Conference of State Legislatures.

♦ *Cannon's Concise Guide to Rules of Order*, by Hugh Cannon, was published in 1992. Although not used as a parliamentary authority per se, this book is frequently looked to by presiding officers to help simplify *Robert's*.

While these other parliamentary authorities have gained a small following, *Robert's* still rules when it comes to parliamentary procedure.

Robert's Revisions

When people refer to *Robert's Rules*, they are referring to a lot of different books. Since the first edition came out in February 1876, nine subsequent editions—many of them with substantial revisions—have been published. Here's a list of all of the revisions, their dates, and the key changes:

♦ **First Edition, February 1876.** The complete title of this first book was *Pocket Manual of Rules of Order for Deliberative Assemblies*. Robert had 4,000 copies printed thinking that would last for at least two years. However, he sold all 4,000 copies in six months!

♦ **Second Edition, July 1876.** Robert added a few pages and quickly got out the second edition because of the surprising success of the book.

Point of Information

Henry Martyn Robert (1837–1923) was a general in the United States Army. Robert began researching the subject of parliamentary procedure after he was elected chairman of a group. There were only a few technical books available on the topic, and he soon became frustrated with the lack of information available. Making matters worse, the books that were available contained conflicting information.

♦ **Third Edition, 1893.** Robert's plan from the very beginning was to get the first book out to the public, receive feedback on it and, once the printing plates were worn out, revise the book, taking the feedback into consideration. The 1893 edition was that revision.

♦ **Fourth Edition, 1915.** Robert himself best explained this edition when he wrote, "The constant inquiries from all sections of the country for information ... that is not contained in *Rules of Order* seems to demand a revision and an enlargement of the manual. To meet this want, the work has been thoroughly revised and enlarged, and to avoid confusion with the old Rules, is published under the title of *Robert's Rules of Order Revised.*"

♦ **Fifth Edition, 1943.** Henry M. Robert died in 1923, and the 1943 edition of *Robert's Rules of Order Revised* was based on notes that he wrote before his death.

♦ **Sixth Edition, 1951.** This was published as the Seventy-Fifth Anniversary Edition.

♦ **Seventh Edition, 1970.** This 594-page revision almost doubled the size of the previous edition. The principles are the same, but in addition to rules it includes many examples and explanations of the rules. This revision was written by Sarah Corbin Robert, the wife of Henry's only son, Henry M. Robert Jr., with the assistance of Henry M. Robert III, James W. Cleary, and William J. Evans.

♦ **Eighth Edition, 1981.** The changes in this edition were so minor that they were able to make them within the same pages, sometimes referred to as an in-pagination revision. So if you find something on page 365 of the seventh edition, it will be on page 365 of the eighth edition.

♦ **Ninth Edition, 1990.** *Robert's Rules of Order Newly Revised*, 1990, is a whopping 706 pages long. The authors of this edition made many changes and enhancements, which are described in the preface to the book.

♦ **Tenth Edition, 2000.** This edition (written by Henry M. Robert III, William J. Evans, Daniel H. Honemann, and Thomas J. Balch) maintains the basic rules but clarifies and updates them. The specific changes and clarifications are listed in the preface to the book.

Parliamentary Pearls

The object of Rules of Order is to assist an assembly to accomplish in the best possible manner the work for which it was designed. To do this it is necessary to restrain the individual somewhat, as the right of an individual, in any community, to do what he pleases, is incompatible with the interests of the whole. Where there is no law, but every man does what is right in his own eyes, there is the least of real liberty.

—Words of Wisdom from Henry M. Robert, December, 1875.

Everybody Loves *Robert's*

Robert did not set out to be the leading authority in parliamentary procedure. He simply envisioned a need for a set of rules that were consistently followed everywhere. That was the beginning of what is today the most recognized authority on parliamentary procedure.

More than five million copies of *Robert's*, in its various editions, have been sold. While it is impossible to verify exactly, approximately 90 percent of the organizations in the United States that follow parliamentary procedure use some form of *Robert's* as their parliamentary authority. Sturgis is the second most popular parliamentary authority, and the other authorities have been adopted by only a small number of organizations.

Because it has been distributed so widely and used by so many people and groups, if you understand *Robert's*, you understand parliamentary procedure.

The Least You Need to Know

◆ Parliamentary procedure is a system of conducting business when working in a group. It helps groups to conduct business efficiently and ensure that the rights of individuals are protected while the will of the group is achieved.

◆ *Robert's* has undergone many revisions since it was first published in 1876. It is currently in its tenth edition.

◆ Other books on parliamentary procedure have been written, but none have surpassed *Robert's* in popularity.

Chapter 2

What *Robert's Rules* Can Do for You and Your Meeting

In This Chapter

- ◆ Shorten your meetings
- ◆ Protect the minority voice
- ◆ Avoid getting sued (or at least from losing if you do get sued!)
- ◆ The importance of a quorum
- ◆ Kinds of meetings and acceptable levels of formality
- ◆ Revised rules for small meetings

Imagine playing a baseball game in which the umpire makes random calls. Or imagine driving in a country where there are no rules of the road. Both situations would result in instant chaos! The same is true for meetings. Almost any group activity—and meetings fall into this category—must follow a set of rules and guidelines to be successful.

When you walk into a meeting and you know and understand the rules, you are empowered to participate actively. In this chapter, we examine what knowing the rules can do for you and your organization and how you can adapt them to various kinds of meetings.

How *Robert's* Helps You Manage Your Meeting

Whether your group's meetings regularly have 5 or 5,000 attendees, you can hold an orderly meeting. To do so, however, requires adopting parliamentary procedure. Parliamentary procedure gives meetings structure, which aids in meeting management.

Point of Information

The main purposes of parliamentary procedure are ...

- ◆ To expedite business.
- ◆ To ensure legality.
- ◆ To protect the rights of the minority.

Gavel Gaffs

Just saying that you are following parliamentary procedure doesn't shorten the meeting. It is the discipline of actually following the procedures that makes the meetings shorter.

Keep It Short and Sweet

I've never met anyone who wished that meetings lasted longer. One of the greatest advantages of parliamentary procedure is that if it is followed properly, it makes for shorter meetings. Over the years, I have observed large groups following parliamentary procedure make major decisions in a relatively short period of time. I have also witnessed smaller groups, not using any formal procedure, take a half a day to make a minor decision.

As you review the later chapters on processing a motion (Chapters 5–9), you will encounter many tools that you can use to keep the meeting short and to the point. For instance, *Robert's* limits the length (10 minutes) and number of times (2 times) that each member can comment on an issue. In addition, it limits discussion to the specific motion that is on the floor. When people are forced to focus their remarks, it is amazing how much time everyone saves!

Preserve the Rights of the Minority

Although the majority rules in parliamentary procedure, the rights of the minority are protected. For instance, everyone is given the same amount of time to speak on an issue, and the rules strictly prohibit making personal verbal attacks.

It's important to protect the rights of the minority because often the minority point of view, over time and with proper discussion, becomes the majority point of view. This is particularly true when it comes to social issues. For example, when I was a college student, no one ever even thought about the dangers of drinking and driving, and the people who pushed for stricter drinking and driving laws were clearly in the minority. Today, few people oppose strict drinking and driving laws. The minority point of view has turned into the majority point of view.

Defend Yourself Against Lawsuits

As I'm sure you know, we live in a litigious society. People file lawsuits all of the time and over almost anything imaginable (Remember the lady who sued McDonald's because her coffee was too hot?). Just as you can get into legal trouble for not following the rules of the road while driving, you can get in legal trouble for not following the governing documents when you are meeting as a member of a group. The governing documents serve as a contract between and among the members. You can even be 100 percent right and still get slapped with a lawsuit that costs you precious time and money, so it's important that you protect yourself by following the rules that your organization adopts.

Gavel Gaffs

Lawsuits over improper use of parliamentary procedures have involved not giving proper notice, improperly calling of adjourned meetings, violating a member's right to speak or vote, failing to establish or maintain a quorum, using an improper method of nomination, and on and on.

There Must Be a Quorum

Since parliamentary procedure is based on each group deciding its own rules, it is the group itself (or a higher authority governing the group, such as the national organization) that decides how many members are necessary to come together to make a decision on behalf of the entire group. In the parliamentary world, we call that number a *quorum*.

Once a quorum has made a decision, the whole group should accept this decision.

Robert's Says

A **quorum** is the number of voting members who must be present in order that business can be legally transacted.

Quorum = Majority

The most frequent quorum requirement is a majority of the members. If your bylaws don't specify how many members constitute a quorum, the quorum is a majority of the entire membership. However, your group can choose any number it wants as the quorum number.

Be careful not to set the quorum number too low. If, for example, you have an organization of 100 members and your quorum is 20 percent, 20 people constitutes a quorum. Do you really want 20 people deciding issues on behalf of the entire group?

Count the Warm Bodies

To determine whether a quorum is present, you count the number of voting members in attendance, not the number of people who vote. In other words, members who choose not to vote on an issue are still counted in the quorum.

For example, let's say that your organization has a membership of 100 and the bylaws indicate the quorum is a majority of the membership, which would be 51 members. At a meeting there is a motion and the vote is 20 yes, 19 no, and 12 abstentions (meaning that the members are present but not voting). Is there a quorum?

Simply adding the number of yes and no votes together gives a total of 39, so if you only counted votes, there is no quorum. But there are also 12 members who are present but who did not vote, bringing the total number of members present to 51. In this case, there is a quorum and business can be legally transacted. However, if an hour into the meeting two of the members leave, you no longer have a quorum and you must stop conducting business, unless you have a rule to the contrary.

What You Can Do Without a Quorum

In the absence of a quorum, the group is severely limited in the kinds of actions it can take. Permissible actions are as follows:

◆ Set the time for another meeting—using the motion to *fix the time to which to adjourn* (see Chapter 11)

◆ End the meeting—using the motion to *adjourn* (see Chapter 11)

◆ Take a short break—using the motion to *recess* (see Chapter 11)

◆ Take measures to obtain a quorum. In other words, go out and beat the bushes to try to find enough members to have a quorum.

Taking Action Without a Quorum

If the group believes that they must take a particular action, even though a quorum is not present, they can do so, but it is not considered to be an action of the group until it is ratified at the next meeting in which a quorum is present.

For instance, let's say that your group can get some unexpected money if you send in a proposal for a grant by Friday. It is Thursday, your regular meeting, and you don't have a quorum. The members who are in attendance are absolutely certain that the rest of the members would think that applying for the grant money is a great idea.

The treasurer reminds the group of how helpful this money would be. The members present see no downside to proceeding, so they vote on a motion to send in the proposal.

At your next meeting a member must make the motion to ratify the action taken at the previous meeting. If that motion passes, you legitimize the action taken at the meeting without a quorum. If not, the individuals attending the previous meeting are responsible for the action taken without a quorum.

> **Gavel Gaffs**
>
> Don't overuse or abuse taking actions without a quorum and then ratifying those actions at the next meeting. Remember, you are taking the action individually until it is ratified by the group with a quorum present! Save such actions for emergency situations.

Types of Meetings

Robert's defines a *meeting* as an assembly of members gathered to conduct business during which there is no separation of the members except for a short recess. A *session* is a meeting or a series of connected meetings, as in a convention.

If your organization meets regularly (for example, monthly, weekly, and so on) the distinction between meeting and session will probably not matter to you. For example if you meet each month, your February meeting is a meeting that is also a session. But if you attend a convention, which has a series of connected meetings, the distinction will matter. Each of those meetings held at the convention is just that, a meeting. The collection of all of those meetings at a single convention is referred to as a session. Why does it matter? Sometimes the rules depend on whether it is a meeting or a session.

> **Robert's Says**
>
> A **meeting** is an assembly of members gathered to conduct business during which there is no separation of the members except for a short recess.
>
> A **session** is a meeting or a series of connected meetings as in a convention.

Robert's distinguishes between several different kinds of meetings, each serving a particular parliamentary purpose:

♦ **Regular meeting.** A business meeting of a permanent group that is held at regular intervals (weekly, monthly, quarterly, and so on). Each meeting is a separate session. The meetings are held when prescribed in the bylaws, the standing rules, or through a motion of the group that is usually adopted at the beginning of the administrative year.

- **Special meeting.** A meeting called at a specific time for a specific purpose. The time, place, and purpose of the meeting must be included in the information sent to all of the members regarding the meeting—referred to as the call of the meeting. Only business that was specified in the call of the meeting can be transacted at the meeting. A group cannot hold a special meeting unless it's authorized in the bylaws. Special meetings are usually held for emergency purposes, things that were not, nor could be, planned for in advance.

- **Annual meeting.** A meeting held yearly, usually for the purpose of electing officers and receiving the annual reports of current officers. The annual meeting is usually specified in the bylaws.

- **Adjourned meeting.** A meeting that is a continuation of a previous meeting. It occurs when the work wasn't completed at a regular or special meeting and there was a motion to continue the meeting at a different time (called a motion to fix a time at which to adjourn, discussed in Chapter 11). The original meeting and the adjourned meeting make up a single session. Because it is a continuation of a previous meeting, special notice of the meeting doesn't need to be sent out to the membership. The adjourned meeting begins where the meeting it is continuing left off.

Point of Information
An organization's board of directors can be known by several different names, including board of governors, board of managers, executive board, and board of trustees. Whatever they're called, they still need to follow the rules.

- **Mass meeting.** An open meeting of a group of people with a common interest but not formally organized.

- **Board of directors meeting.** A meeting of a specified group of members who make decisions on behalf of the organization. The membership, authority, and limitations of this group are specified in the bylaws. Meetings of the board are usually only open to members of the board and their invitees.

- **Convention.** An assembly of delegates usually chosen for one session. The participants frequently attend as representatives of a local, state, or regional association. The convention participants come together to make decisions on behalf of the entire organization. Because conventions are unique in several ways, I discuss them in detail in Chapter 21.

- **Committee meeting.** A meeting of a group of members who have been elected or appointed to carry out a task. They have only the power given to them by the body that created them (members, board, president, bylaws).

◆ **Executive session.** A meeting or a portion of a meeting in which the proceedings are secret and the only attendees are members and invited guests. All or part of any of the other meetings in this list may be held in executive session. Deliberations of an executive session are secret and all attendees are honor bound to maintain confidentiality. Meetings of boards of directors are usually held in executive session.

Level of *Robert's* to Use

One of the reasons that some people don't like parliamentary procedure is that they think it must be all or nothing—they believe that you have to use all of it or you should ignore it completely.

Even Henry M. Robert recognized that it's important to adapt his rules to meet the needs of the group. Keep in mind, however, that the rules are intended to protect the rights of the members. If your adaptation of the rules infringes upon any members' rights (not just those members who agree with you), the adaptation is unacceptable.

Point of Information

If you are ever in a meeting and can't remember the parliamentary rule that applies, ask yourself the following three questions:

◆ What is the fairest thing to do in this situation? Be sure to consider what is fairest to all, not just to you.

◆ What is the most logical answer to this problem? *Robert's* is a very logical system, so the most logical answer is probably the correct one.

◆ What is the most efficient way of doing this? If you can get there in two steps, don't take three!

Formal vs. Informal

How formal should your meeting be? Only you and your organization can answer that question. You have to look at what you are doing presently and how effective it is.

The size of the group plays a large part in determining how formal it needs to be. As a general rule, the larger the group, the greater the amount of formality there should be. A meeting of 10 committee members can be conducted very casually (see the next

Gavel Gaffs

Not all meetings should be conducted with the same level of formality. Three things you might consider in determining the level of formality of your group are ...

◆ The size of the group.

◆ The purpose of the meeting.

◆ The cost in time and money of the meeting.

section for revised rules for small meetings). A meeting of 100 at the same level of informality could be highly ineffective. A meeting of 1,000 at the same level of informality could be an out and out disaster.

The meeting's purpose should also be taken into account when determining how formal or informal to make it. If you are getting together with some committee members simply to discuss an issue, an informal approach might be your best bet. If you have very difficult and controversial issues to resolve, a more formal format might help keep the group focused on the issues.

How much time and money you want to spend are other factors that you should consider when establishing your level of formality. If members live just a few miles apart and get together on a regular basis, informality may be the answer. But if members must travel long distances, must pay for lodging and other travel-related expenses, and have a limited amount of time to spend together, the more formal format would probably be the more time and money saving approach.

Parliamentary Pearls

Henry M. Robert gives great advice to the presiding officer about adapting the meeting:

Use your judgment; the assembly may be of such a nature through its ignorance of parliamentary usages and peaceable disposition, that a strict enforcement of the rules, instead of assisting, would greatly hinder business; but in large assemblies, where there is much work to be done, and especially where there is liability to trouble, the only safe course is to require a strict observance of the rules.

No More Than a Dozen: Rules for Small Boards and Committees

Henry M. Robert realized that you need different rules for a board or committee of 5 and a convention of 5,000. Therefore, he established less stringent rules when there is a meeting of a board with no more than 12 members present or a committee. Those rules include:

◆ It's not necessary to rise in order to make a motion or when seeking recognition by the chair.

- There is no limit on the number of times a person may speak.

- The presiding officer does not have to leave the chair when making a motion or when participating in debate.

- Motions to close or limit debate are not allowed.

- Motions do not need to be seconded.

- A motion can be reconsidered, regardless of when the motion was made.

- A motion can be reconsidered by anyone who did not vote on the losing side (so a member who was not present can move to reconsider, as can a member who abstained).

- If the motion to reconsider is made at a later meeting, it requires a two-thirds vote without notice, or a majority vote with notice.

The Least You Need to Know

- *Robert's* is all about protecting the rights of the minority, ensuring legality, and expediting business.

- Various meetings serve different parliamentary purposes. All of them should follow parliamentary procedure, however.

- It is essential to establish a quorum before any meaningful business is conducted.

- The level of formality that you use at your meeting depends on how many people are involved, the purpose of the meeting, and how much time and money is available.

- *Robert's* provides for less stringent rules for meetings with 12 or fewer members.

Who's Who?

In This Chapter

♦ The power of the bylaws

♦ The various leadership roles in an organization

♦ The position of executive director

♦ Where professional parliamentarians fit in

Leadership is always an important aspect of an organization's success. This chapter reviews each of the leadership positions of an organization. However, it's not the title that gives someone power—a person holding a leadership position only has the power that is given to the position in the bylaws, which are the primary rules governing an organization (for more on bylaws, see Chapter 4).

When you take on a leadership role in your organization, you should always review the governing documents to see what roles, duties, and responsibilities are outlined there. You are responsible for performing those duties, whether or not the person who held the office before you did.

The President: Facilitator, Not Dictator

The roles of the president vary according to the organization and, as with everyone else's duties, should be clearly spelled out in the bylaws. Some of the common duties of the president are as follows:

♦ Preside at all meetings (see Chapter 16 for tips on presiding at meetings).

♦ Serve as official representative of the organization.

♦ Report at each meeting and prepare an annual report (see Chapter 20 for more on reports).

♦ Sign documents on behalf of the organization.

♦ Make position appointments as specified in the bylaws.

♦ Serve as ex officio member of committees as specified in the bylaws. *Ex officio* means a person is a member by nature of the office held. (While we're on the topic of ex officio members, it's worth pointing out that many people believe that an ex officio member doesn't have the right to vote. Not so! An ex officio member has all of the rights of membership, unless the bylaws say otherwise.)

♦ Work with the secretary to prepare the agenda for meetings (see Chapter 15 for information on the agenda).

Robert's Says

The **presiding officer** is the person—often the president—who is in charge of the meeting. The term is interchangeable with the terms **chair** and **chairman** (some organizations opt for the more gender neutral **chairperson**). When addressing the presiding officer, *Robert's* recommends the following: Mr. Chairman or Madam Chairman.

Parliamentary Pearls

Henry M. Robert gave some wonderful advice to the presiding officer: "Know all about parliamentary law, but do not try to show off your knowledge. Never be technical, or more strict than is absolutely necessary for the good of the meeting."

Presiding at Meetings

Most people find that presiding at meetings, including board and general membership meetings, is the most challenging part of the president's job. While presiding, the chair has many responsibilities, some of which include …

♦ Calling the meeting to order on time.

♦ Announcing the business before the assembly in the order prescribed in the agenda.

- Determining the presence of a quorum.

- Recognizing members who are entitled to the floor.

- Processing all motions.

- Expediting business.

- Ruling on any points of order (motions made by members when they feel that the rules are not being followed).

- Conducting the meeting in a fair and equitable manner.

Because the president is presiding over the meeting, he or she should maintain an aura of neutrality and refrain from making any motions. In addition, the president should vacate the chair if he or she wishes to debate on any motions. (In Chapter 8, I explain the process for vacating the chair; in Chapter 16, I offer many more tips for presiding at a meeting.)

The President-Elect: Lady/Gentleman in Waiting

Some organizations choose to have an office of the president-elect. When this is the case, the organization doesn't elect a president. Instead the election is for president-elect, who serves one term as president-elect, and then automatically becomes president the following term. And if the organization has the position of immediate past president, the president automatically becomes immediate past president after his or her term as president is over. Thus, it's possible to have one election for up to three terms, one in each of the three offices.

As with any other position, that of president-elect does not exist unless it is specified in the bylaws. Organizations' bylaws usually specify that the president-elect is to preside in the absence of the president and to fill a vacancy in the office of president.

The Pros and Cons of Having a President-Elect

When someone knows one full term ahead of time that he or she will be the next president of the organization, the transition is usually much smoother. The president-elect can give careful thought to his or her appointments and will have plenty of time for training and mentoring. If the organization has a heavy travel schedule for the president, the year advance notice makes scheduling much easier.

Some of the advantages are also disadvantages. For example, when you know one year ahead of time that you are the next president, you just might start doing that job a little bit too early. Also, if members aren't getting their way with the current president, they might begin working on the next president! If that occurs, it unfairly erodes some of the president's effectiveness.

Because the move to president from president-elect is automatic, if the person does not rise to the occasion as president-elect and it becomes clear that he or she will not be a good president, you are stuck with him or her. The only way to have that person not become president is to remove them from office, which is usually not a pretty sight!

An organization should give serious consideration to the decision of whether or not to have a president-elect. If you choose to have a president-elect and that position succeeds the president in case of a vacancy in the office of president, some of the responsibilities that are listed in the section for vice president, discussed in the following section, apply to the president-elect.

The Vice President: Second, Third, or Fourth in Command

If there is no president-elect and only one vice president, the position of vice president is straightforward—the vice president presides when the president is absent or must vacate the chair and fills a vacancy in the office of president. Once we add a president-elect or more than one vice president to the mix, things get a bit more complicated. For example, if your organization has a position of president-elect, and the bylaws *do not* specify that the president-elect presides when the president is absent and fills a vacancy in the office of president, the vice president does those tasks. If the bylaws *do* specify the president-elect fulfills those duties, obviously the president-elect, *not* the vice president, does them. That's why some organizations that have a president-elect don't have any vice presidents—the positions are somewhat redundant. You have to read your bylaws to know what applies in your organization's situation.

From this point on in the discussion of vice president, we will assume that there is no position of president-elect.

The main job of the vice president is to be familiar with the president's duties so that, if the president becomes unable to serve, the vice president is prepared to step in and take over. Many organizations assign other duties to the vice president, such as oversight of specific committees. I encourage people to think of the vice president as a support system for the president.

Sometimes there is more than one vice president. In that situation, the vice presidents should be numbered first vice president, second vice president, third vice president, and so on. When there are multiple vice presidents and the positions are not numbered it creates uncertainty. When they are numbered, and there is a vacancy in the office of president, the first vice president becomes president, and the second vice president becomes first vice president, and so on.

Gavel Gaffs

One of the main duties of the office of vice president is to be prepared to take over for the president should he or she become unable to fulfill the duties of president. Therefore, it is inappropriate to accept the position of vice president if you are not willing to become the president should there be a vacancy in the office of president.

Should the vice president be unwilling to perform the duties of the president, the only choice the vice president has is to resign.

When the Veep Fills In for the President

When presiding at a meeting in the absence of the president, the vice president should refer to himself or herself as the "chair" or the "presiding officer," not as the "vice president" and certainly not as the "president."

When the vice president assumes the authority of the president only for a particular meeting, his or her authority is limited. For example, if the bylaws require that the president appoint all committees, when the vice president presides over a meeting for the president and a committee needs to be appointed, the vice president cannot appoint the committee members. The vice president should only assume those duties that are prescribed in the bylaws, which usually means conducting the meeting. In addition, if the bylaws indicate that the president is an ex officio member of all committees, the vice president does not attend those meetings for the president.

Parliamentary Pearls

A vice president should always be prepared to take over for the president. Some ways of doing that include discussing with the president the agenda before each meeting; having an agenda, the bylaws, and the parliamentary authority for all meetings; and arriving at the meeting early enough to be prepared for the start of the meeting. If a vice president prepares in that manner, then in an emergency that delays the president, attendees won't have to sit around wasting time waiting for the president. The vice president can start the meeting on time. You would be surprised how popular this can make a vice president!

The Secretary: More Than Minutes

People often overlook the importance of the office of secretary, but they shouldn't. The secretary is the official record keeper of the organization. This position goes far beyond keeping the minutes—it includes keeping an accurate list of members, the roll-call list, the governing documents, delegate information, committee membership, and so much more!

Although the most common name for this office is secretary, it might also be called clerk, recording secretary, recorder, or scribe. In large organizations that have a full staff, this position, or sometimes simply the work of this position, is done by a staff member. Some of those same large organizations have the executive director serve as corporate secretary and have no elected secretary.

As we review the position of secretary, it is helpful to examine it from the perspective of duties and responsibilities before, during, and after the meeting.

Before the meeting:

- Work with the president to prepare the agenda.

- Distribute to the members before the meeting the packet of material needed for the meeting, including the agenda (see Chapter 15 for more on preparing an agenda).

- Send out the call of the meeting (the official notice of a meeting given to all members of the organization).

- Before the annual meeting, prepare an annual report.

> **Point of Information**
>
> Some organizations choose to split the secretary position into two positions: recording secretary and corresponding secretary. When that is done, the bylaws should specify the responsibilities of each position. Usually the recording secretary takes the minutes and the corresponding secretary sends out notices of meetings and handles the general correspondence of the organization.

During the meeting:

- In the absence of the president and vice president the secretary calls the meeting to order and immediately conducts the election for the chairman pro tem (the temporary chairman).

- Have access to the minutes book.

- Have access to all of the governing documents of the organization.

- Have a list of the current membership as well as the current committees and committee members.

- Have ballots in case of a ballot vote.

- Maintain the official list of members and the official attendance list, if there is one.

- Keep notes of what occurred at the meeting.

- Sit near the president and serve as a resource to the president.

After the meeting:

- If any governing documents were amended at the meeting, the secretary should make the changes in the governing documents and distribute new copies to the appropriate parties.

- Maintain the file of committee reports.

- Prepare the minutes from the meeting.

- Distribute the minutes to the members.

- Give each committee any information that has been referred to them.

- Notify officers, delegates, and committee members of their election or appointment.

The Treasurer: The Buck Stops Here

The size and kind of organization has a large bearing on the duties of the treasurer, which, as with all of the other offices, should be spelled out in the bylaws. Basically, the treasurer is the custodian of the funds of the organization.

The treasurer receives all incoming money and disperses that money according to instructions from the organization. In large organizations it is the treasurer's job to oversee the income and expenditure of funds, but the actual tasks are performed by staff members. In that situation, it is the treasurer's job to make sure funds are handled correctly.

In addition, the treasurer is usually involved in preparing the organization's budget, making sure that the books are audited, and filling out

Parliamentary Pearls

If the treasurer handles large sums of money, he or she should be bonded. Bonding is a form of insurance that protects the organization in case of financial loss. The bonding should be paid for by the organization, not the person serving as treasurer.

appropriate tax forms. Once the board or the members have adopted the budget, it is the treasurer's responsibility to make sure that the organization spends within the established budget.

The treasurer needs to keep accurate records and report regularly to the membership. For more on the treasurer's reports, the audit, and the budget, see Chapter 20.

The Executive Director: Working Behind the Scenes

While not an official member of the leadership team of the organization, the executive director is a very important leader nonetheless. The executive director is a salaried position in charge of the association headquarters and staff. Just like other positions, the bylaws should specify the responsibilities of the executive director and to whom the executive director reports.

The position has many names. Years ago, the position was most frequently referred to as executive secretary. Now you will see it referred to as the chief executive officer (CEO), the chief operating officer (COO), and even the president (in which case the title chairman of the board is given to the position usually referred to as president).

The responsibilities of the executive director vary according to the size and needs of the organization. In many organizations the position is a full-time job with a full staff reporting to it. In some smaller organizations the position of executive director is part-time and the organization has no additional staff.

Besides the fact that the executive director is salaried, as opposed to volunteer, the executive director is also usually involved in the leadership of the organization for longer than most other leaders. One executive director will usually be in that position throughout many administrations.

The advantage of that longevity is that the executive director becomes the consistent force behind the organization. The disadvantage, at least for the executive director, is that each term he or she reports to a different board. It requires a fair bit of flexibility.

Your organization's bylaws should specify who is in charge of hiring and firing the executive director. It is then the executive director's responsibility to hire and fire the remainder of the staff.

There are Professional Parliamentarians!?!

When I tell people that I'm a professional parliamentarian, they look at me like I just told them I have some strange, incurable disease. After I assure them that being a parliamentarian is not a disease, I proceed to explain the profession. Just in case you didn't know there are such creatures as professional parliamentarians out there, let me explain my profession to you.

What Is One?

A professional parliamentarian is an expert in parliamentary procedure and is hired by a person or an organization to give advice on matters of parliamentary law and procedure. A professional parliamentarian is qualified to assist the organization or the individual in the application of parliamentary procedure, thus improving the effectiveness of their meetings.

A professional parliamentarian can help ensure that your convention, membership meeting, board meeting, or stockholder meeting is conducted smoothly and efficiently. As a consultant, the professional parliamentarian can advise the presiding officer, the organization, and the individual members on the application of parliamentary procedure for the orderly conduct of the business of the association. Since the professional parliamentarian is not a member of the association, the appearance of bias is not an issue.

Just like other professionals, parliamentarians belong to one or more professional organizations and are bound by a code of ethics. They come to your organization as an objective expert, thus assisting the group in a way that no member of the organization can.

Parliamentary Designations

Behind the name of a professional parliamentarian you will see some letters. Those letters indicate the level of professional designation that person holds. There are two national organizations and each has multiple designations.

The National Association of Parliamentarians (NAP) has two levels of parliamentary proficiency, thus two levels of designations, as follows:

- ◆ *RP* stands for Registered Parliamentarian. An RP must pass an examination consisting of multiple choice questions that are based on the current edition of *Robert's*.

- ◆ A *PRP* is a Professional Registered Parliamentarian. In addition to passing the RP, this person has also completed a course of lectures and hands-on training in the skills necessary for a professional parliamentarian. To maintain the PRP designation a member must successfully complete a Professional Development Course every six years and participate in additional professional activities.

The American Institute of Parliamentarians (AIP) has three levels of designations.

♦ A *CP* is a Certified Parliamentarian and has successfully passed a written examination that is based not only on the current edition of *Robert's*, but also on other authorities.

♦ A *CPP* is a Certified Professional Parliamentarian and has successfully completed an oral examination before a panel of Certified Professional Parliamentarians. The examination is based on the same books as the CP examination. Additionally points are needed that demonstrate an active participation in the profession.

♦ A designated Teacher of Parliamentary Procedure (*CP-T* or *CPP-T*) is a specialized certification offered by AIP. To attain this designation a member must have successfully completed a teacher education course offered by Education Department of the American Institute of Parliamentarians and must show evidence of at least 15 hours of successful teaching experience.

To maintain the CP and CPP designations a member must, every 7 years, complete approved continuing education requirements.

Role of Parliamentarian

Professional parliamentarians should be impartial advisors. They should avoid getting into the issues being debated and instead focus on the procedure of that debate. Because the rules are the same no matter which "side" you are on, good parliamentarians are able to advise both "sides" on an issue.

In addition, because professional parliamentarians are focusing on the parliamentary procedure, attendees are free to focus on the issues.

CAUTION

Gavel Gaffs

Don't ask about the ruling of the parliamentarian! The parliamentarian does not rule. The parliamentarian is an advisor and therefore makes no final decisions. The parliamentarian may give an interpretation of a rule, an opinion on a rule, or even be ask to cite a rule, but never rules!

The only person who can rule is the chair of the meeting. If you disagree with the ruling of the chair, then you have an avenue to deal with that disagreement, it is called the motion to appeal from the decision of the chair. Notice there is no motion to appeal from the decision of the parliamentarian. That is because the parliamentarian does not make decisions.

What a Professional Parliamentarian Can Do for You

A parliamentarian assists the organization before, during, and after meetings. A parliamentarian also may be of assistance to the organization throughout the entire year, not just at convention time.

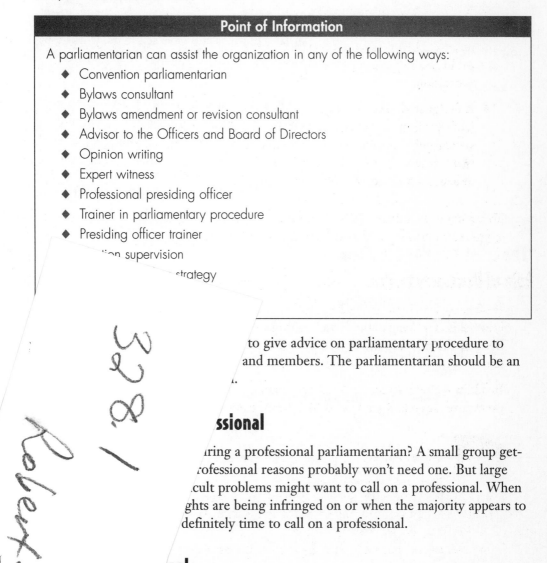

Point of Information

A parliamentarian can assist the organization in any of the following ways:

- ◆ Convention parliamentarian
- ◆ Bylaws consultant
- ◆ Bylaws amendment or revision consultant
- ◆ Advisor to the Officers and Board of Directors
- ◆ Opinion writing
- ◆ Expert witness
- ◆ Professional presiding officer
- ◆ Trainer in parliamentary procedure
- ◆ Presiding officer trainer
- ◆ ⁀ion supervision
- ◆ ⁀trategy

to give advice on parliamentary procedure to
and members. The parliamentarian should be an
.

ssional

.ring a professional parliamentarian? A small group get-
.rofessional reasons probably won't need one. But large
.cult problems might want to call on a professional. When
.ghts are being infringed on or when the majority appears to
definitely time to call on a professional.

nal

.nentarian organizations—the National Association of Parlia-
.nd American Institute of Parliamentarians (AIP)—will refer you

Point of Information

National Association of Parliamentarians
213 South Main Street
Independence, MO 64050-3850
Tel: 1-888-NAP-2929 or 816-833-3892
www.parliamentarians.org

American Institute of Parliamentarians
P.O. Box 2173
Wilmington, DE 19899-2173
Tel: 888-664-0428 or 302-762-1811
www.parliamentaryprocedure.org

to professional parliamentarians in your area free of charge. The major difference between NAP and AIP is that NAP's primary emphasis is on *Robert's* as the parliamentary authority, while AIP emphasizes knowledge of other parliamentary authorities as well.

Both organizations train and register and/or certify parliamentarians and have seminars, workshops, local organizations, written materials, and quarterly publications.

If you're considering hiring a parliamentarian, be sure that the person you select has skills and talents that match the needs of your organization. And if, once you've finished reading this book, you'd like to learn more about parliamentary procedure, contact NAP or AIP for more information on their training courses.

The Least You Need to Know

- Be sure to read the rules of the organization after taking an office—you need to know what you are expected to do.

- The president should use his or her powers to facilitate, not to dictate.

- The executive director is often the stabilizing force in the whirlwinds of position changes.

- Professional parliamentarians can help you keep your meeting running smoothly.

Chapter 4

The Law's the Law

In This Chapter

- ◆ The order of governing documents
- ◆ Which state's statutes to follow
- ◆ The typical order of bylaws
- ◆ How to change an organization's bylaws

How do you think that a judge would react if you tried to avoid paying a ticket for driving 70 mph in a school zone by pleading ignorance of the speed limit? Any judge worthy of his or her black robe would probably inform you that it's your responsibility to know the rules of the road if you are going to drive on them, and then order you to pay your ticket. Just as ignorance is no excuse for violating traffic laws, it's not an acceptable excuse for violating your organization's "rules of the road," either.

This chapter examines the different rules that govern your organization. In the parliamentary world, all these laws and rules are collectively referred to as governing documents.

The Hierarchy of Governing Documents

Any number of laws and documents govern an organization, but certain of them take priority over others. For instance, your organization's bylaws can't be in violation of federal or state laws, and the governing documents of a parent organization trump the constitution of any branch of that organization.

Generally, the hierarchy of governing documents looks like this:

- Federal laws
- State statutes
- Articles of incorporation
- Governing documents of parent organization
- Constitution
- Bylaws
- Special rules of order
- Parliamentary authority
- Standing rules
- Policies and procedures

Federal Laws and State Statutes

Most of the time people don't give much thought to the federal and state laws that affect their organizations. Whether you think about them or not, however, you are still responsible for knowing them.

Federal Laws

Federal tax laws govern many of the procedures of nonprofits, unions, and many other organizations. For instance, federal Internal Revenue Code has specific requirements for an organization to be chartered as a charitable (tax exempt) organization. The tax code where this exemption is found is IRC 501(c). Not-for-profit organizations must apply for and receive from the IRS a "Tax-exempt determination letter" which will state under which IRS 501(c) code section the organization qualifies. For example, nonprofit voluntary health and welfare organizations are identified as 501(c)-3 organizations; trade organizations are 501(c)-6; social clubs are 501(c)-7.

State Statutes

In addition, each state has laws that govern not-for-profit and for-profit organizations, as well as governmental bodies and community associations. If you are on a board of a local business, you will be governed by the for-profit statutes; if you are on a board of, say, your local United Way chapter, you would be governed by the not-for-profit statutes.

Your organization is required to follow the statutes of the state in which your organization is incorporated—even if your meetings aren't always held in that state. The state of incorporation can be found in the articles of incorporation and is often mentioned in the bylaws.

Because each state's laws vary, it is important that your attorney be familiar with the state statutes that affect your organization. Check with the governing state body (such as the attorney general's office or secretary of state's office) to determine what filing or audit requirements exist, since the state requirements can be different than the requirements of the IRS.

Parliamentary Pearls

You can find state statutes that govern organizations on the Internet (all statutes are available online), and through the office of the attorney general or the secretary of state in the state of incorporation. Always check to make sure that all such statutes are up-to-date.

Governing Documents of the Parent Organization

Some groups are local branches of a state, national, or international organization. In those cases, the very existence of the local organization is authorized in the governing documents of what is referred to as the *parent organization*. In those situations, the local organization exists at the will of the national organization.

Just like in real life, the parent can tell the child what to do and what not to do. Because bylaws of the parent organization are a higher body of authority for the local organization than its own bylaws, the bylaws of the local organization can't conflict with the bylaws of the parent organization.

This gets to be a touchy situation. The bylaws of the local organization can't conflict with the

Robert's Says

A national organization that has in its bylaws a system to charter local, state, or regional associations is referred to as the **parent organization**.

bylaws of the parent organization (unless the parent organization's bylaws specifically allow them to), but they don't have to mirror the bylaws of the parent organization either. Although each situation is unique, some examples will help illustrate this point:

- **Membership qualifications.** Membership qualification at the local level cannot conflict with the membership qualification specified in the national bylaws, unless the national bylaws specifically allow them to.

  Let's say that the national bylaws of the Association of Complete Idiots (the ACI) require that all members be complete idiots. There is nothing in ACI's national bylaws that give local associations the right to have members who are not complete idiots. Because local organizations are limited by national bylaws, the local association's bylaws can't require that its members be dummies or dunces; it can only require that they be complete idiots.

- **Officers.** The set of officers at the local level do not have to mirror the officers at the national level. For example, if there is a president-elect at the national level, you do not have to also have a president-elect at the local level. That is, unless the parent organization's bylaws specify the set of officers at the local level.

The parent organization's bylaws can affect all levels of your rules. It's important that you become familiar with them.

Articles of Incorporation

The articles of incorporation must conform to state and federal laws. The articles are the legal instrument required to incorporate the organization. An organization usually hires a lawyer to write its articles of incorporation. They must be filed with the state of incorporation.

Incorporation may be necessary or advisable for an organization to own property, enter into contract, hire employees, and so on. An attorney can advise an organization on whether or not it should become incorporated. The need for incorporation depends upon the state of incorporation and the activities of the organization.

> **Point of Information**
>
> Different states have different names for the articles of incorporation. In some states they are referred to as articles of organization; other states refer to them as a corporate charter.

The articles of incorporation are the highest legal document of a particular organization. In other words, you can't have things in your bylaws, constitution, or policies that contradict the articles of incorporation. Usually this document is very skimpy and only contains a few rules, but they are the law of the land, so to speak, for your group. If, for example, you want to change the name of your organization, you probably have to change your articles of incorporation, because the name of your organization is usually contained in that document.

The articles of incorporation should include a method for amending them.

Constitution

For most of the last century, parliamentary authorities have recommended not to have both a constitution and bylaws but to combine them into a single document. The main reason for combining the constitution and bylaws is ease—it's easier for members to look up information when there is only one document to refer to.

Some organizations believe that having two separate documents is best for their organization, for whatever reason. In addition, old habits die hard—if an organization has always had a constitution and bylaws, and no one wants to change them, that's fine.

If you choose to have a constitution for your organization, make sure that it doesn't contain any rules that are procedural in nature. The constitution is where you define the primary characteristics of the organization, not its policies. Make sure this document only contains the highest level of rules, in the form of articles, as follows:

- **Name**. The full name of the organization, properly punctuated, should be included here.

- **Object**. A concise statement of the objective of the organization.

- **Members**. The classes of members; qualifications of membership; method of becoming a member; and the duties, rights, and obligations of members.

- **Officers**. The officer titles, terms, nomination and election process, duties that are different from those stated in *Robert's*, and the method of filling vacancies.

- **Meetings**. Information on regular, annual, and special meetings as well as how meetings are called; the quorum for a meeting and any information on changing the meeting in case of emergency.

- **Method of amendment**. How the constitution can be changed, who can change it, what kind of vote and notice is required, and so on.

Bylaws

Bylaws are rules that, for the most part, cannot be suspended (unless the bylaws themselves provide for a method of suspending them, which is somewhat self defeating). So your organization's bylaws should include all of the rules that the group considers to be so important that they cannot be changed at the whim of the members present at a single meeting and cannot be suspended.

Gavel Gaffs

In Henry M. Robert's day the word *bylaws* was hyphenated: *by-laws*. The hyphen has since been dropped, and the acceptable spelling is *bylaws*.

The rights and responsibilities of members when they meet together as a group and of individuals as members of the organization should be included in the bylaws. This is a basic concept of bylaws. It helps to think of the bylaws as a contract between the members and the organization. If a responsibility is not spelled out in the bylaws, members cannot be held to that responsibility.

For instance, suppose that the Association of Complete Idiots has been having some legal problems lately, and the legal fees have put a huge strain on the finances of the organization. At a meeting of the membership, a motion is adopted to assess all members $50. If ACI's bylaws do not authorize an assessment of the membership, this motion is out of order (a motion is out of order when it violates the rules of the organization). It is out of order because it is putting a responsibility on the members that is not authorized in the bylaws.

Parliamentary Pearls

If you are considering joining an organization, my advice is to first read the bylaws. You can tell a lot about an organization by reading its bylaws. The areas that I find particularly insightful are the membership article, the meetings article, and the article on the board of directors. These articles give you a lot of information regarding membership rights and where the power of the organization is housed.

Construction of the Bylaws

Bylaws are usually divided into articles, and information within the articles is divided into sections. Some bylaws use headings within the sections. In organizations that have combined the constitution and bylaws into one document, the generally accepted articles of the bylaws are as follows:

- **Article I: Name.** The full name of the organization, properly punctuated, should be included here.

- **Article II: Object.** A concise statement of the objective of the organization.

- **Article III: Members.** The classes of members; qualifications of membership; method of becoming a member; and the duties, rights, and obligations of members.

- **Article IV: Officers.** The officer titles, terms, nomination and election process, duties that are different from those stated in *Robert's*, and the method of filling vacancies.

- **Article V: Meetings.** Information on regular, annual, and special meetings as well as how meetings are called; the quorum for a meeting and any information on changing the meeting in case of emergency.

- **Article VI: Executive Board.** The composition, powers, and rules of the board.

- **Article VII: Committees.** The names of the standing committees, their composition, manner of selection, and duties. Also, the requirements and composition for special committees.

- **Article VIII: Parliamentary Authority.** The parliamentary manual the organization will use as the basis for the rules for conducting business and the rights of the members.

- **Article IX: Amendments.** How the bylaws can be changed, who can change them, what kind of vote and notice is required, and so on.

Additional articles might include …

- Dues and fees.

- Finance.

- Nominations and elections.

- State, local, or regional bodies authorized to exist.

- Dissolution, if incorporated.

Format for Bylaws

Articles of the bylaws are usually organized using roman numerals. Sections are usually organized using numbers. Subsections are usually organized using letters of the alphabet, as illustrating in the following example.

Bylaws of the American Association of Fun Loving People

ARTICLE III

Members

Section 1. Eligibility. Any person with a degree in Fun Loving shall be eligible for membership, provided that such person shall be proposed by one member and seconded by another member of the Association. A proposal for membership, signed by the two endorsers, shall be sent to the association's head-quarters. A person shall be declared a member of the Association upon:

A. payment of the initiation fee;

B. payment of annual dues for the first year; and

C. proof of degree in Fun Loving.

Bylaw Advice

When writing or changing bylaws, keep the following tips in mind:

◆ **Avoid administrivia.** By *administrivia* I mean administrative details. The bylaws are not the place for bureaucratic minutiae. That's not to say that organizations don't have their fair share of administrivia, it's just that it belongs in the rules, which we'll get to later in the chapter.

◆ **Write in plain English.** Any member should be able to pick up a copy of the bylaws, read them, and, for the most part, understand what they say. Therefore, keep the language of the bylaws simple and straightforward. This is not the place to impress your friends with your use of big words and long sentences!

◆ **Keep them amendable.** You might as well provide for some way to amend your bylaws, because I guarantee that you're going to want to change them at some point in the future. In addition, if you include items in your bylaws that are required by a federal or state law, or by the parent organization, identify them as such so that members know what can and can't be amended—or at least not amended without first amending the governing document of the higher authority.

Parliamentary Pearls

A helpful way to identify what is governed by other laws is to add "in accordance with the requirements of the statute under which XXX is incorporated," or to simply include a statement similar to the following: "(as stated in the *Illinois Not For Profit Corporate Act*)."

- **Avoid dates.** Very seldom should you include dates in the bylaws. The bylaws become effective once they are adopted. If you don't want them to become effective upon adoption, all you have to do is add a *proviso* to them. If, for example, you amend your bylaws to eliminate the position of assistant treasurer and you currently have someone in that position whom you want to be able to finish out his or her term, you can use a proviso. The proviso might be as simple as stating that the bylaw amendment to eliminate the position of assistant treasurer shall not take effect until the end of the current term, and then indicate the end date of the current term.

Robert's Says

A **proviso** is a provision on when the new bylaws change will take effect. It is not a part of the bylaws. Provisos can be put on a separate sheet of paper or in a footnote and removed after they are no longer in effect.

- **Watch the little words.** Sometimes it is the littlest words that have the biggest impact. Don't write *may*—which means that it is optional—or *should*—which means ought to, but not necessarily will, when you mean *must, shall,* or *will.* Take the following example: "A local association shall provide for primary and affiliate members and may include provisional members ...." This statement *requires* the local association to have two classes of members: primary and affiliate. It also *allows* the local association to choose whether or not to have a third class of members, called provisional members.

- **Give freedom; avoid taking it away.** Bylaws shouldn't put unnecessary restrictions on the organization. Instead, the bylaws should be an empowering document. Only restrict those things that are necessary to restrict, such as duties of the members. Beyond that, allow for flexibility within the bylaws.

- **Specify a parliamentary authority.** Your bylaws should include an article that identifies the parliamentary authority for your organization, such as the current edition of *Robert's Rules of Order.* If a parliamentary authority is established in the bylaws, your bylaws don't need to include rules for every situation. Instead, if a particular situation isn't covered in the bylaws, the parliamentary authority will be your source for how to handle it.

Adopting the Bylaws

Once bylaws are written, they must be distributed to the membership, who must then vote on whether to accept them. The adoption of the original bylaws requires a majority vote.

Changing Bylaws

Once bylaws are adopted, there are basically two ways to change them: by amendment or by revision. Either change method usually requires previous notice and a two-thirds vote. The following table indicates what kind of vote is necessary for various changes.

Methods of Changing Bylaws

Change Method	Frequency	Vote Needed	Purpose
Adopt	Once	Majority	Create the org.
Amend	Most frequent	Usually two-thirds with notice	Fix a problem
Revise	Seldom	Same as amend	Complete rewrite

Amending Bylaws

If you only want to make one or a couple of changes, the proper way to change the bylaws is to amend them. This usually requires advance notice (so that they can't be changed at the whim of the attendees of a specific meeting) and a two-thirds vote. The bylaws should provide for changing them, so refer to the specific bylaws to find out how to amend them.

When notifying membership of plans to change a specific amendment, the following format comes in handy:

Proposed Bylaw Amendments

Proposed Amendment #1:

Amend Article V, Section 1 by striking "an Assistant Treasurer,"

Current Wording	Proposed Wording
The elected officers shall be a President, a Vice-President, a Secretary, a Treasurer, <u>an Assistant Treasurer</u>, and three Directors-at-Large.	The elected officers shall be a President, a Vice-President, a Secretary, a Treasurer, and three Directors-at-Large.

When your organization wants to make a
change that requires amendment of the
bylaws in several places, you might want to
tie them all together into a single amendment. If, for example, you are proposing to
change a name that occurs in six different
places in the bylaws, you could label the change
"Proposed Amendment #1" and then letter the
individual instances of the name change a, b, c,
and so on. You can then vote on the changes *in
gross* and have only one vote.

Robert's Says

When you are dealing
with several related amendments,
it is common practice to vote on
them all at one time, referred to
as **in gross**. It makes sense to
vote on them all at once since if
one was adopted and another
one was not adopted, then you
would have created an inconsis-
tency in the bylaws.

Scope of Notice

Scope of notice is a concept in parliamentary procedure that is designed to prevent
game-playing. Essentially, requiring that an amendment be limited to its scope of
notice prevents people from making changes beyond what was indicated in the notice
sent out in advance of the meeting.

Imagine that a member gives notice of an amendment to increase the dues of the
organization from $10 to $12. At the next meeting, a member moves to amend the
bylaws, and it is seconded, restated by the chair, and opened for discussion (the
motion-making process will be described in detail in Chapters 5 and 6). Sam thinks
that the organization should increase the dues even more. He looks around and notices
that most of the people who would object to a big dues increase are not in attendance
at the meeting. Sam believes that with the combination of members present, a higher
dues amount would pass. Sam moves to amend the amendment by striking $12 and
inserting $20.

Because changes to the bylaws require previous notice and because it would be unfair
to give notice of a specific change and then amend it to a higher amount, Sam's proposed amendment is out of order. It is out of order because it exceeds the scope of
notice. In this situation the scope of notice is $10 (the current amount) to $12 (the proposed amount). An amendment that is more than $12 or less than $10 is out of order.

Revising the Bylaws

Sometimes the proposed changes to the bylaws are so significant that amendments
would have to be made throughout the document. If this is the case, it is appropriate
to throw out the old bylaws and completely rewrite a new set of bylaws. That is called
a revision of the bylaws.

A bylaw revision is similar to a bylaw amendment in that it needs the same previous notice and the same two-thirds vote to pass. If the revised bylaws are adopted, the revision replaces the current bylaws. The revision is considered *seriatim*, which means it is considered section by section and voted on at the end of consideration of the entire document.

Robert's Says

Seriatim means considering a motion section-by-section or paragraph-by-paragraph, amending as you go, and voting on the entire document at the end.

Because notice is given that the entire document is to be substituted for the current bylaws, the concept of scope of notice does not apply to revision. You are starting with a clean slate and it is as if you were adopting the bylaws for the first time, so any changes are acceptable.

More Rules!

There are a few other rules that you should be familiar with. They include special rules of order, standing rules, and policies and procedures.

Special Rules of Order

The rules contained in the parliamentary authority are called the rules of order. Sometimes organizations feel a need to have additional rules of order, called *special rules of order*, that differ from the parliamentary authority. However, most organizations don't need to have special rules of order.

Standing Rules

Standing rules govern the administration of the organization as opposed to rules regarding parliamentary procedure. If you want to include some unusual duties of officers, this would be the place to do so.

When you attend a convention, rules are adopted at the beginning of the convention. These are usually called convention standing rules.

Policies and Procedures

Some organizations have additional detailed policies and procedures regarding the administration of the organization. Those organizations sometimes choose to combine all of their policies and procedures together in a single document. That document may be referred to as the organization's Policies and Procedures.

The Least You Need to Know

◆ Ignorance is not bliss—know the rules before you act.

◆ An organization's articles of incorporation and bylaws cannot violate federal and state statutes governing the organization.

◆ Bylaws should include all of the rules that the group considers to be so important that they cannot be changed at the whim of the members present at a single meeting and cannot be suspended.

◆ Amendments to bylaws require previous notice and a two-thirds vote to pass.

Part  Let's Get Moving: The Motion-Making Process

For a group to take an action, take a stand, spend money, or do almost anything else, it must first pass a motion. This part of the book is the how-to guide for taking your idea and turning it into group action. Follow the six simple steps to processing a motion that I describe in the next few chapters and you will be ready to get what you want done.

Getting Into the Motion

In This Chapter

- Processing motions in six simple steps
- Making and seconding a motion
- Putting the motion in writing
- Owning the motion and why it matters

Before a group can do anything or even take a stand on an issue, someone must make a motion. A motion states specifically what the maker of that motion wants the organization to do. Think of a motion as the ultimate action plan: In order to get anything done in the group, you need to start with a motion.

Kinds of Motions

There are two kinds of motions—main motions and secondary motions:

- **Main motions** bring business before the assembly. They can be further subdivided into two categories:

    a. **Original main motions:** Motions which bring before the assembly a new subject, sometimes in the form of a resolution, upon which action by the assembly is desired.

b. **Incidental main motions:** A main motion that is incidental to, or related to, the business of the assembly, or its past or future action.

♦ **Secondary motions** are any motions that are made while a main motion is pending. They can be further divided into three different classes:

a. **Privileged motions:** Motions that don't relate to the main motion or pending business but relate directly to the members and the organization. They are matters of such urgency that, without debate, they can interrupt the consideration of anything else.

b. **Subsidiary motions**: Motions that aid the assembly in treating or disposing of a main motion. They are in order only from the time the main motion has been stated by the chair until the chair begins to take a vote on that main motion.

c. **Incidental motions:** Motions that relate to matters that are incidental to the conduct of the meeting rather than directly to the main motion. They may be offered at any time when they are needed.

I'll discuss each kind of motion in detail in Part 3 of this book. For now, it's important to simply keep in mind that there are different kinds of motions and that they have different rules.

It's Time to Get in Motion!

To make any kind of motion, a person must be a voting member of the body that is meeting. That is, the person needs to be a member of the immediate group—not a larger constituency. For instance, even though I'm a citizen of the United States of America, I am not a member of the U.S. Senate. That means that I can't go to the Senate chambers, grab the microphone, and make a motion.

Point of Information

"The motion" is sometimes referred to as "the question." Both mean basically the same thing.

The motion process involves the following six steps:

1. A member makes a motion.

2. Another member seconds the motion.

3. The chair states the motion, formally placing it before the assembly.

4. The members debate the motion.

5. The chair puts the question (in this context, "question" means the same thing as "motion") to a vote.

6. The chair announces the results of the vote.

In this and the next chapter, I'll walk you through each of these steps.

Step 1: Making a Motion

To make a motion you need to seek recognition from the chair, which you typically do by raising your hand. After the chair recognizes you, you are free to make your motion. Although a lot of people say "I make a motion to ..." it's far simpler to use three short words: "I move that ...".

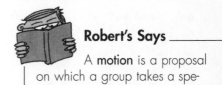

Robert's Says

A **motion** is a proposal on which a group takes a specific action or stand.

Be Precise

Make sure that the motion states exactly what you want the organization to believe or do. The following two motions might seem similar, but they aren't:

◆ "I move that we form a committee to investigate the purchase of a computer."

◆ "I move that we form a committee to purchase a computer."

Only three words are different, but it makes a big difference. The committee in the first motion is only authorized to investigate whether to purchase a computer. The committee in the second motion is authorized to purchase the computer.

Be specific in stating the motion. For example, let's say you make the following motion:

I move that we host a party Thursday night to celebrate Sam's birthday.

You're envisioning everyone going over to someone's house, someone else baking a cake, and everyone bringing their own beverages and snacks. After your motion has passes, Janice offers to set up the party, and everyone agrees. On Thursday night you go to Janice's house for the party and discover that she hired a caterer and ordered a fancy birthday cake from the local bakery. Whereas the party that you had in mind was simple and at no cost to the organization, the party that Janice had in mind cost the organization big bucks. Clearly, the wording of your motion wasn't clear enough. The confusion could have been avoided had you worded the motion as follows:

I move that we host a party Thursday night to celebrate Sam's birthday. The party should be at a member's house and everyone should bring food so there is no cost to the organization.

Only Make Motions That You Agree With

Although it's not a violation of *Robert's* to do so, members should try to phrase their motions in such a way that he or she agrees with them. This is particularly important since the member who makes the motion is restricted from speaking against his or her motion during debate (although that person can vote against the motion).

Gavel Gaffs

If, in order to make a motion, you have to be a voting member of the body that is meeting and you should agree with it, how can you get away with voting against it? The purpose of debate is to try to change members' minds, even the mind of the maker of the motion! It is unlikely, but possible, that during the debate the maker of the motion could see the light and now want to vote against his or her own motion. That's the democratic process in action!

The maker of the motion gets first right to speak on it. Again, logic and fairness come into play! The person who made the motion should get first chance to "sell" his or her idea to the other members.

~~Don't Make Negative Motions~~ Make Positive Motions

Use positive words to express a negative thought. Otherwise, members will need to vote "yes" on an issue that they disagree with, which can become very confusing. Consider the following two motions:

- ♦ I move that we not support the national dues increase.
- ♦ I move that we take a stand in opposition to the national dues increase.

Although they mean the same thing, the second motion is much easier to understand.

Put Your Motion in Writing

Even though the presiding officer has the right to ask for a motion in writing, most organizations don't require written motions. However, there are good reasons for you to put your motions in writing.

Most important, members are far less likely to forget or become confused about the meaning of a motion if it is written down. In other words, it ensures that what you say is what you get. Otherwise you get the secretary's interpretation of what you said, and that might not always be on target.

If you're in a more formal setting or in front of a large group, it's particularly important to write your motion down. It not only helps you to say exactly what you mean to say, it also can be passed on to the meeting chair and can even be included in the minutes. That way everyone is in agreement as to your motion and its intent.

Parliamentary Pearls

The longer your motion is, the more crucial it is that you present it in writing.

Putting the motion in writing can be remarkably simple. You almost always have pencil and paper with you in a meeting. If not, the person sitting next to you probably does. Write it down, and read it over to make sure it says exactly what you want to say. Then, when you are recognized by the chair, read the motion straight from your paper.

Your group could even put blank paper and pencils around the room so that members who don't bring pen and paper can write down their motions. For larger groups, I recommend that you get "no carbon required" (NCR) paper, which makes copies as you write on it. The person making the motion can keep the bottom copy and can pass the other copies to the presiding officer, the secretary for the minutes, and so on. That way, everyone who needs it will have a copy of the exact wording of the motion in front of them throughout the processing of the motion.

Avoid Saying "So Move"

A frequent faux pas in making a motion is saying, "so move." These two lovely words usually dance out of someone's mouth after there has been discussion on an issue at a meeting. It seems like shorthand. But, unless the statement made right before "so move" was called out is extremely clear, it can cause confusion. I once observed a meeting where an issue was discussed, a member stated a solution, another member said "so move." Everyone thought that the issue was settled until the secretary asked for the exact wording of the motion. It took the group over 20 minutes to agree on the wording! Had she not asked for the wording, different people would have left the meeting each with a different idea of what the motion that they had just agreed upon really said.

Although there are all kinds of situations where professionals can use it, a good rule is: Don't use "so move" unless it is a motion to approve the minutes, recess, or adjourn! The motion must be absolutely clear to everyone in the room before you use those two little words.

Step 2: Seconding the Motion

Once someone has made a motion, another voting member must second it. To second a motion is to publicly agree that the motion should be considered. The purpose of this step is to make sure that at least two members want to discuss this issue before the group spends time on it.

But I Don't Agree!

Unlike the maker of the motion, who should agree with the motion before making it, the person who seconds the motion doesn't have to agree with it—he or she must only believe that the issue should be discussed and decided upon. The person seconding the motion might even be against the motion, but in agreement that the organization should take a stand or make a decision on the issue.

An example might be helpful: Let's say that there has been a lot of discussion in your group about painting the headquarters' building green. You think it is a bad idea but you are tired of hearing about it. In a meeting, a member named Steve makes the motion to paint the building green. You may choose to second the motion, even though you are against it, simply so the group can finally decide on this issue and put it to bed!

Seconding a motion does not give you any special rights, like the right to speak before other members on the motion. It simply gives you the assurance that the members are going to make a decision on this motion.

No Second Needed

Particularly urgent or important motions, such as the motion to raise a question of privilege (which is explained in Chapter 11), don't need a second. Other motions that don't require a second are as follows:

- ◆ **Raise a question of privilege.** To bring an urgent request or a main motion relating to the rights of either the assembly or an individual up for immediate consideration. It may interrupt business (see Chapter 11).

- ◆ **Call for orders of the day.** By the use of this motion, a single member can require the assembly to follow the order of business or agenda, or to take up a special order that is scheduled to come up, unless two thirds of the assembly wish to do otherwise (see Chapter 11).

- ◆ **Point of order.** If a member feels that the rules are not being followed, he or she can use this motion to ask the chair to follow the rules. It requires the chair to make a ruling and enforce the rules (see Chapter 13).

- ◆ **Objection to consideration.** The purpose of this motion is to prevent the assembly from considering the question/motion because a member deems the question as irrelevant, unprofitable, or contentious (see Chapter 13).

- ◆ **Division of the assembly.** The effect of this motion is to require a standing vote (not a counted vote). A single member can demand this if he or she feels the vote is too close to declare or unrepresentative. This motion can only be used after the voice vote or hand vote is too close to declare (see Chapter 13).

- ◆ **Parliamentary inquiry.** A question directed to the presiding officer concerning parliamentary law or the organization's rules as they apply to the business at hand (see Chapter 13).

- ◆ **Point of information.** A nonparliamentary question about business at hand (see Chapter 13).

In addition, it's common practice today to not require a second on a motion when it comes from a committee. That's because the purpose of a second is to make sure that at least two people are interested in the issue before it is brought before the assembly, and in order for a committee to make a motion to a superior body, the committee must have voted on it. Therefore, at least two members are in favor of the motion, so a second is not needed.

Parliamentary Pearls

The practice of seconding a motion ensures that more than one person in the group is remotely interested in the issue. If no one seconds a motion, you go on to the next agenda item, having saved the time of the participants.

No Second, No Debate!

Since Step 2 of processing a motion is that a voting member seconds the motion, if no member is willing to second the motion, the process ends at that point. In other words, if there is no second, then the motion dies for a lack of a second. The group can then proceed to the next item on the agenda.

Step 3: The Chair States the Motion

Step 3 in the processing of a motion is that the presiding officer states the motion, formally placing it before the assembly. At first blush this step doesn't sound very important or even necessary, but it's an essential step. It ensures that everyone understands the motion that's before the assembly.

At this point in the process, the presiding officer will be very pleased if the maker of the motion has submitted the motion in writing. All the presiding officer has to do is to read the motion from his or her copy, thereby increasing the likelihood that it will be stated accurately. In situations where the presiding officer doesn't have a written copy of the motion, he or she can do one of the following things:

Gavel Gaffs

When the presiding officer doesn't restate the motion or have someone else restate it, the usual consequence is that the discussion wanders all over the place instead of staying focused on the particular motion under consideration.

- ◆ Read the motion from the notes made when the motion was made by the member.

- ◆ Ask the secretary to restate the motion.

- ◆ Ask the member who made the motion to restate it.

Proper restatement of the motion by the presiding officer helps make sure everyone has heard the motion exactly as it was proposed. Those who were daydreaming when the motion was first made will get a second chance to hear the motion. It also helps keep everyone on target as to the exact wording of the motion to be debated.

Robert's Says

Ownership of a motion is a concept that refers to whose property the motion is at a given time and therefore, who had a right to make any changes to it. In the six steps of the motion process, the maker of the motion owns the motion up until the completion of Step 3. After Step 3, the ownership of the motion is transferred to the assembly.

Ownership of the Motion

At the completion of Step 3 in the processing of a motion, the *ownership of the motion* is transferred from the individual who made the motion to the whole group. It might be helpful to envision that at the end of Step 3, the presiding officer goes over to the member who made the motion, takes the motion from that individual, and gives it to the entire group. Once the motion belongs to the group, it's the groups to do with as it pleases.

If you own something, you can change it. But if you don't own something, and you want to change it, you have to go to the owner and ask their permission to change it. And if you want to take it home with you, you have to ask their permission. This simple concept applies to motions as well. So if you understand who the owner of the motion is during each of the six steps of processing the motion, you then understand whose permission you must get to change it.

To fully understand the concept of ownership of the motion, let's return to Steve's motion to paint the building green. After Steve made the motion (Step 1), someone else seconded it (Step 2), and then the presiding officer repeated it (Step 3). As the members are discussing it (Step 4, which we'll cover in the next chapter), Tom speaks up and says that he wants to strike "green" from the motion and replace it with "blue." In other words, Tom wants to amend the motion.

Because the motion is owned by the group, Tom must get the permission of the members in attendance at the meeting to change the motion. He would do so by making the motion to amend by striking "green" and inserting "blue." After another member seconds Tom's amendment, the members would then talk about Tom's proposed change and decide, through a majority vote, whether they want the motion changed. Even if Steve disagrees with the amendment, there's nothing he can do about it except speak and vote against it. If the majority passes the amendment to the motion, Steve must accept the change—he cannot "take his ball and go home." He must live with the decision made by the current owners of the motion.

When could Steve by himself have made a change to the motion? After he made the motion and it was seconded, but before the presiding officer restated the motion—in other words, between Steps 2 and 3. Let's go back in time to the moment when Steve makes the motion to paint the building green and the presiding officer calls for a second. Right after someone seconds it, Tom informs Steve that the organization would have to buy green paint but that they currently have enough blue paint on hand to paint the building. Jill, the treasurer, also tells Steve that there is not enough money in the budget to pay for the green paint. At that time, Steve could change his motion from painting the building green to painting the building blue and he would not have to get anyone else's permission.

> **Point of Information**
>
> Before the completion of Step 3 in the processing of a motion, the motion is owned by the maker. After Step 3 it is owned by the assembly. Remember that, and you can answer many questions without memorizing rules.

Withdrawing a Motion

Continuing with our painting theme, let's say that Joan makes a motion to paint the building brown. The motion is seconded and restated by the chair. During debate of the motion, it is pointed out that there are too many other brown buildings, that brown is the color of an opponent organization, that brown paint costs too much, and that there isn't really enough money in the treasury to buy any paint. Joan wishes she had never made the motion in the first place.

Can Joan withdraw her motion at this time? The concept of ownership of a motion indicates that the motion no longer belongs to Joan. Therefore, Joan may not withdraw her motion without the permission of the owners of the motion. Since the motion is now owned by the members who are present, the presiding officer must ask them for permission to allow Joan to withdraw her motion. If any one member of the group objects, the presiding officer must put it to a vote on whether to allow Joan to withdraw her motion. They probably won't agree, since a majority wanted it painted pink.

Don't Memorize, Understand!

As you can see from these examples, understanding the concept of ownership of a motion makes it very easy to understand what can be done by whom. It beats memorizing rules! When you want to change a motion in some way, ask yourself "Who owns the motion at this specific time?" and you will know whose permission you must get.

This chapter covered the first three steps of making a motion. The next chapter picks up where this chapter leaves off, and covers the final three steps in processing a motion.

The Least You Need to Know

- You must be a member of the body that is meeting in order to make or second a motion.

- Whenever possible, state your motion in the affirmative.

- Putting your motion in writing and giving a copy to the chair ensures that the motion is restated exactly as you wanted it to be.

- After the presiding officer states the motion, the ownership of the motion is transferred from the member who made the motion to the people assembled.

Chapter 6

Getting Out of the Motion

In This Chapter

- ◆ What can happen during debate
- ◆ Amending the motion
- ◆ Taking a vote
- ◆ Announcing the results of the vote
- ◆ Making your vote count

Once the presiding officer puts a motion before the members (Step 3 in the motion making process), the members must process that motion, which essentially means that they must make a decision on the motion. At this point, it's up to the members to debate the issue and vote on it, and it's up to the presiding officer to ensure that the vote is properly counted and announced. If you have found yourself confused at meetings, it is probably at this point. Understanding all that can happen during the debate step will help you feel more comfortable during your next meeting.

Step 4: Members Debate the Motion

Step 4 is potentially the longest and most complicated of all of the steps in the motion process. It is at this point that the motion is considered *pending*, meaning that it has been stated by the presiding officer and hasn't

Robert's Says _____

A motion is considered **pending** when it has been stated by the presiding officer and has not yet been disposed of either permanently or temporarily (during Step 4).

yet been disposed of either permanently or temporarily. This is a critical time for a motion—many things can happen, and you must be prepared.

Not everyone in the group will see the problem and possible solutions the same way. (That is the beauty of the group process!) Therefore, in the group decision-making process, it's often the case that members spend a lot of time discussing, negotiating, and compromising before they are ready to take a vote. Step 4 is when all of this occurs.

Now's the Time to Fix It

While a motion is pending, members can amend it, postpone it, put it aside, send it to a committee, and so on. All of the actions that take place while the main motion is pending are secondary motions. (We will discuss secondary motions in detail in Chapters 11 through 13.)

If the group is dissatisfied with a motion before them and decides they want to change it, they must amend the motion before voting on it. To help you understand the amendment process, let's use the example of the motion to paint the building that we used in the previous chapter; this example will help you see why you must first amend the motion before you decide to vote on it.

Paint the Building Green Example ... Again

Let's return to our painting example from Chapter 5. Steve's motion to paint the building green has been seconded, restated by the presiding officer, and the group is debating it. You have done extensive research on the resale value of buildings as affected by the color of the building. Your research indicates that a green building loses 10 percent of its resale value over a building that is freshly painted another color. You also found that a building that is not freshly painted only loses 5 percent of its resale value. A fair bit of money hangs on what color you paint the building, so it only makes sense that you should debate the issue and, if necessary, amend it before voting on it. Let's look at the options:

◆ If you don't paint the building, it will lose 5 percent of its resale value, so your $100,000 building is now worth $95,000.

◆ If you paint it white, it would maintain its current resale value or even gain in value, making it worth $100,000 or more.

◆ If you paint the building green, it could lose 10 percent of its value, making it worth $90,000.

Based on this information, you decide that you will vote "no" on Steve's motion to paint the building green. However, if you could first amend the motion to strike "green" and insert "white," you would vote "yes" on the motion.

No matter how logical it may seem to do it the other way around, if there are amendments to be made to the motion, those amendments must be made while the motion is *on the floor*. If you wait until after the motion is voted on, it is too late to change it. (Okay, you can change it later [see Chapter 14], but not without jumping through a bunch of hoops! It is much easier to change it now.)

Robert's Says

When a motion is pending, it is also considered to be **on the floor**. These terms are interchangeable. Saying that the motion is on the floor is symbolic of having the motion before the members so that they can discuss and fix it.

Because debate is such an essential component of the parliamentary process, let's devote a few more pages to it before we move on to the vote, which is Step 5 in the motion making process.

Talk, Talk, Talk: Debate

One of the greatest time savers of parliamentary procedure is that debate is limited to the specific motion that is being considered. If this principle is followed, the debate portion of the motion process will not only stay focused, but it will also usually take far less time than it otherwise would. In addition, only the specific aspects covered in the motion are open to debate, and not the whole subject.

If the motion on the floor is that the organization paint the building green, the debate should be focused on discussing the advantages and disadvantages of painting the building green. The debate should not be allowed to wander off to other aspects of the building, such as whether or not the building needs a new roof or gutters. Nor should the debate be allowed to go into a general discussion of whether the building should be sold or kept for at least a few more years. Or that if someone

Robert's Says

A motion is considered **immediately pending** when several motions are pending and it is the motion that was last stated by the chair and will be first to be disposed of.

cut the grass on a regular basis fewer neighbors would complain about its appearance. As you've likely figured out by now, the examples could go on and on, as could the debate if it isn't focused.

As you'll discover in Chapter 7, more than one motion may be pending at any one time. However, the debate must be limited to the *immediately pending* motion, which is the last pending motion stated by the chair. You can't discuss other pending motions until they become the immediately pending motion. (Trust me: This will make a lot more sense after you read Chapter 7.)

Stay on Target

If a member gets off the subject, or starts talking about an aspect of the subject that isn't covered in the motion, it is important for the presiding officer to bring the focus back to the specific motion, even if that means interrupting the speaker. A kind way of doing this is to say "The motion before you is to paint the building green, please confine your remarks to a discussion of painting the building green." You might even add, "If you want to discuss the possibility of a new roof on the building, you could make a motion regarding the roof, after we have voted on the current motion to paint the building green. Is there any further discussion on the motion to paint the building green?"

> **Point of Information**
>
> If the members begin to stray from the subject matter, as frequently happens, a nice way for the chair to bring them back on task is to ask: "Is there any further discussion on the motion to ...?" This is a helpful way to remind the members of exactly what they are discussing.

> **Parliamentary Pearls**
>
> The most effective presiding officers are those who are willing to speak up, interrupt the unfocused speaker, and make sure the discussion is focused on the specific motion on the floor.

If the member continues to discuss an issue that isn't directly related to the specific motion that is pending, the presiding officer should interrupt the member and indicate that the comments are out of order. This is difficult to do because most people don't like interrupting someone and, in essence, asking them to stop talking. But an important part of the job of the presiding officer is to keep the discussion on track. And if the presiding officer doesn't keep the discussion focused, it might take far longer than it should to process the motion.

Don't Forget Your Manners

In addition, don't ...

♦ Discuss the personalities of the people involved.

♦ Question the motives of other members.

♦ Make any derogatory remarks, including name-calling, about other members.

By keeping the debate focused on the motion rather than on the people involved, the meeting will go much more quickly and everyone will be able to voice their opinion without fear of a personal verbal attack by other members.

Gavel Gaffs

During debate, avoid calling another member by his or her name, especially when there is a lot of controversy. This keeps the focus on the issue, not the person who said it.

Robert's suggests that you refer to another person by the office he or she holds, or when he or she spoke to the assembly. Some examples include the following:

- The previous speaker
- The bylaws committee chairman
- The treasurer
- The member who made the motion

What About Nonmembers?

In a meeting of members, all members are treated equally; therefore they all have the right to speak. But guests at the meeting do not have the same rights as members. A person who is not a member of the body that is meeting does not have the right to speak, unless the members give that nonmember permission to speak.

Point of Information

The following phrases can be of assistance to the presiding officer in concluding Step 4:

- Is there any further discussion?
- Are you ready for the question?
- Is there any further discussion on …?
- Are you ready to vote?
- Are there any other new points that need to be made before we vote on the motion?

Time to Wrap Up Debate

The presiding officer doesn't have the authority to put an end to debate when members still want to discuss the issue. (Only the members, by the use of the previous question motion, can stop debate when members want to speak. That motion is discussed in Chapter 12.) But, when it is clear that the members are finished discussing the motion, the presiding officer doesn't have to wait for a member to request that debate ends. The presiding officer can simply conclude the debate and move on to Step 5.

Step 5: Putting the Motion to a Vote

Once all members have had a chance to debate the issue, it's time for the fifth step in processing the motion: the vote. To begin, the presiding office should restate the motion to remind members of the exact issue they will be voting on. With our motion regarding painting the building, the presiding officer would say "We will now vote on the motion to paint the building green."

Don't Forget the "No" Vote

After telling the members what motion they are voting on, the presiding officer then gives direction on what method of voting will be used (see Chapter 9 for an explanation of the methods of voting). In addition to explaining the voting process, the presiding officer should tell members how to express the vote. For example, on a voice vote, the presiding officer might say "All those in favor say 'Aye.' All those opposed say 'No.'"

Even when it's obvious how the vote will turn out, the presiding officer should call for votes in favor of and votes against the motion. An exception to this is with courtesy resolutions. An example of a courtesy resolution is the resolution at the end of the convention that thanks everyone who worked on the convention.

The Declaration Is Up to the Chair

It is the responsibility of the presiding officer to determine whether the motion passed or failed and then to announce that determination to the members.

Vote Again, If Necessary

The presiding officer should never declare which side prevailed in a vote unless he or she is absolutely positive which side won. If there is the least bit of a doubt, the presiding officer has the right to have the vote taken in a different manner so that the results are clear before the decision is made. For example, if there is a voice vote and the presiding officer is unclear as to the outcome of the vote, he or she may simply say "The chair is unclear as to the outcome of the vote so we will have a standing vote." If the outcome still isn't clear, then the presiding officer might call for a counted vote (again, I cover voting methods in detail in Chapter 9).

Point of Information

The presiding officer can help to ensure that everyone is comfortable with the decision of the voting results by observing the members during the vote. Look for pockets of members who vote on the side that does not prevail. If, for example, there is a large group of people sitting together who vote in favor of the motion and the motion fails, it might appear to the people in that group that more members voted in favor of the motion than really did. Therefore, conducting the vote using a different method that will provide a clearer picture of the true outcome may be advisable. Redoing the vote in this situation is not done so that the presiding officer is sure of the results, but so that the members are comfortable with the announcement.

Step 6: Complete Announcement

The sixth and final step in processing a motion is the complete announcement of the results of the vote. This announcement should include the following four elements:

◆ **Which side has the vote.** The first part of the announcement indicates which side has the necessary votes, and is thus the prevailing side. It might be stated as "The affirmative has it" or "The negative has it." The exact wording of this portion would be adapted to the kind of vote that is taken. In a counted vote, the presiding officer should first give the count before announcing the prevailing side. Thus, it might sound like this "There are 10 votes in favor of the motion, and 7 votes against the motion; the affirmative has it."

◆ **Whether the motion passed or failed.** Simply state either "The motion is adopted" or "The motion is lost." If you question the necessity of this part imagine the lack of clarity where the vote was nine in favor and five opposed, and a two-thirds vote was required.

◆ **Effect of the vote.** If the motion was to purchase a computer and it passed, this part might sound like "And we will be purchasing a computer." If the motion was an amendment to the bylaws, this statement can be very simple. It might be "Our bylaws have been amended" or "Our bylaws have not been amended and will remain as they currently read."

◆ **The next step.** Where applicable, announce the next item of business. When one remembers that the role of the presiding officer is to facilitate the process, it is logical that when the group concludes one order of business, the facilitator tells the members where they are going next. The presiding officer might simply say "The next order of business will be the report of the finance committee." Or in a series of proposed amendments to the bylaws, "The next order of business is Proposed Bylaw Amendment 3."

Complete announcement of a vote has an additional effect that is difficult to quantify. In the case of highly controversial motions, a complete announcement of the results of the vote appears to have a very positive effect on the membership in attendance at the meeting. It is almost as if it helps bring closure to the issue, allowing members to put the issue behind them and move on to the next item of business.

The Least You Need to Know

- While a motion is pending, members should make sure that it is worded to their satisfaction, amending it as needed.

- When debating a motion, all members should focus their remarks on the issue and avoid personal attacks and straying off topic.

- The presiding officer should restate the motion before putting it to a vote.

- The four steps of the complete announcement of the vote lend closure to an issue and prepare the group to move on to the next item of business.

Chapter 7

The Ladder of Motions: a.k.a. the Precedence of Motions

In This Chapter

♦ Walking up and down the ladder of motions

♦ Timing of particular motions

♦ Why your motion might be out of order

♦ Knowing which motion is immediately pending

Suppose that you're sitting in on your first meeting in which parliamentary procedure is followed. After the chair calls the meeting to order and establishes the presence of a quorum, and the minutes are approved, a member makes a motion. The motion is quickly seconded, the chair states it, and it is being discussed. Makes sense so far.

Then another member makes another motion and that motion is allowed by the chair. That second motion is seconded, is restated by the chair, and is being discussed. Your head is beginning to spin when, suddenly, a third member makes a third motion. That motion is ruled out of order by the chair—much to your relief! But then another member makes a motion, and that motion is allowed by the chair. At this stage in the process you are probably wondering if there is a dartboard somewhere that the chair is using to decide on the rulings, because it makes about that much sense.

A concept in parliamentary procedure helps this scenario make sense. It is called the *precedence (pre SEED ens) of motions,* and if you understand the concept, you will know when motions are allowable (also called *in order*) and when they are out of order.

Concept of Precedence

Let's set the groundwork for explaining the concept of precedence of motions by reemphasizing three ideas that I covered in previous chapters.

- Only one main motion is allowed on the floor at a time. But many secondary motions can be on the floor at the same time.

Robert's Says

Precedence of motions is a list of specific motions that indicates the priority of motions. When a motion on the list is pending, any motion above it on the list is in order and any motion below it on the list is out of order.

- The term *pending* refers to Step 4 in the motion making process. It is the period after the motion has been restated by the presiding officer (Step 3) and the period before the presiding officer puts the motion to a vote (Step 5).

- As the term *immediately pending* suggests, many different motions can be pending at the same time. The immediately pending motion is, of the motions that are pending, the motion that was the last one made.

In *Robert's* the precedence of motions contains the following 13 motions:

- Fix the time to which to adjourn
- Adjourn
- Recess
- Raise a question of privilege
- Call for the orders of the day
- Lay on the table
- Previous question

- Limit or extend limits of debate

- Postpone to a certain time (sometimes called "postpone definitely")

- Commit or refer

- Amend

- Postpone indefinitely

- Main motion

The motion to amend, as will be further explained in Chapter 13, has two forms. A *primary amendment* is an amendment that changes the main motion and a *secondary amendment* is an amendment that changes the primary amendment. Therefore, when I list the motions included in the precedence of motions, I prefer to separate out *amendment* and make it a list of 14 motions, as follows:

1. Fix the time to which to adjourn

2. Adjourn

3. Recess

4. Raise a question of privilege

5. Call for the orders of the day

6. Lay on the table

7. Previous question

8. Limit or extend limits of debate

9. Postpone to a certain time (definitely)

10. Commit or refer to a committee

11. Secondary amendment—amend an amendment

12. Primary amendment—amend a motion or resolution

13. Postpone indefinitely

14. Main motion

Gavel Gaffs

The term *precedence* is usually pronounced *PRESS i dens*. However, in the world of parliamentary procedure it is pronounced *pre SEED ens*.

Robert's Says

There are two kinds of amendments. A **primary amendment** is an amendment to the main motion. A **secondary amendment** is an amendment to the primary amendment.

When any one of these motions on the list is the immediately pending motion, any motion above it on the list can be made at that time and any motion below it on this list cannot be made at that time. It is truly that simple. If you have this list in front of you at a meeting, you can easily check which motions can be made when.

The Vote and the Ladder

To understand how the votes are taken on the various motions in the precedence list, it would be helpful to walk through a scenario in which several motions are pending. In this sample situation, you need to assume that after each motion is made, it is seconded, is restated by the presiding officer, and is being discussed before another motion is made.

Higher on the List is Okay, Lower Is Out of Order

If a main motion is pending (that is, it's been made, seconded, and restated by the chair, and it's being discussed by the members) it is the immediately pending motion and is #14 on the precedence of motions list.

While discussing that main motion, a member moves to amend the main motion. That proposed amendment is in order because it is #12 on the list, and 12 is higher than 14 (I told you the concept was easy!).

While discussing the amendment, another member moves to make a secondary amendment—in other words, to amend the amendment. Secondary amendments are #11 on the list of precedence, and the motion is in order because 11 is higher on the list than 12.

While we are discussing the amendment to the amendment, another member moves to postpone the motion to the next meeting. The amendment to the amendment is the immediately pending question and is #11 on the precedence of motions list. The motion to postpone to the next meeting is #9, postpone to a certain time, and is above #11 on the list, therefore the motion is in order.

While we are discussing whether or not we should postpone this motion to the next meeting, another member moves that this motion be referred to a committee. That motion to refer (#10) is below the immediately pending motion (#9, postpone to a certain time) and is therefore out of order.

Needed: An Organized Method of Getting Out of This

Now stay with me, because things are about to get interesting! What you have now, besides potential confusion, are four different motions that are all pending, as follows:

#14: main motion

#12: primary amendment

#11: secondary amendment

#9: postpone to a certain time

What you need now is an organized method of getting out of this mess. That organized method does exist. Close your eyes, take a deep breath, and visualize a ladder.

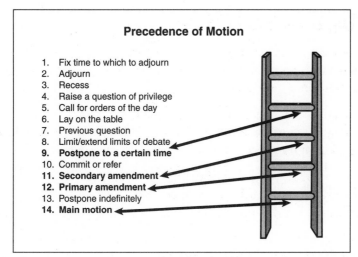

Precedence of Motion

1. Fix time to which to adjourn
2. Adjourn
3. Recess
4. Raise a question of privilege
5. Call for orders of the day
6. Lay on the table
7. Previous question
8. Limit/extend limits of debate
9. **Postpone to a certain time**
10. Commit or refer
11. **Secondary amendment**
12. **Primary amendment**
13. Postpone indefinitely
14. **Main motion**

The precedence of motions, with the pending motions in bold. You work your way out of the sequence of pending motions by stepping down the ladder, voting on each immediately pending motion as you go.

Every motion that is pending is a step up a rung of the ladder. When it is time to vote on the motion, you must come down the ladder, in reverse order of the steps you took up the ladder.

If we follow the ladder visually, the bottom rung of the ladder is #14, the main motion; the second rung is #12, the primary amendment; the third rung is #11, secondary amendment; and the top rung is #9, postpone to a certain time. We are up four rungs on the ladder and we are ready to come down. We must now vote on those four motions in reverse order of how they were made. In other words, the last motion made is the first one voted on and so on.

Vote in Reverse Order

Let's follow these steps in order:

1. **Vote on the motion to postpone to a certain time.** If this motion passes, the main motion and the amendments that are pending will be postponed with it until the next meeting. At the next meeting, you will have three motions still pending. If the motion to postpone to a certain time fails, you'll move on to the next motion down on the ladder, which is the secondary amendment.

2. **Vote on the secondary amendment.** If the secondary amendment passes, the primary amendment is now changed to reflect this change. If not, you move on to the primary amendment as it was originally stated.

3. **Vote on the primary amendment.** If the vote on the primary amendment passes, the main motion on the floor is the main motion as amended. If the primary amendment fails, the main motion on the floor is the original main motion.

4. **Vote on the main motion.**

If you skip any of those steps, you violate the rules and thus fall off the ladder!

There is, of course, an exception to the ladder voting rule. That exception is motion #13 on the precedence of motion, which is the motion to postpone indefinitely. As you will learn in Chapter 13, the purpose of the motion to postpone indefinitely is to kill the motion that is pending. Since the sole purpose of passing the motion to postpone indefinitely is to kill the motion, if it passes, the main motion is thus killed and there does not need to be a vote on the main motion. Thus, if there is an affirmative vote on the motion to postpone indefinitely, you do not come down the final rung of the ladder, and you do not vote on the main motion.

How to Apply It

A specific example may help in the application of the precedence of motions:

◆ Member A makes the motion: "I move that we purchase a computer."

The motion is seconded, is restated by the chair, and is being discussed by the members. This is a main motion (#14 on the ladder of precedence).

◆ Member B thinks that we better put a price limit on that computer or the person responsible for purchasing the computer will buy all kinds of extras that are not needed.

Member B says: "I move to amend the motion by adding the words 'not to exceed $2,000.'"

The motion made by Member B is a primary amendment—an amendment to the main motion (#12 on the ladder of precedence). It is in order. The presiding officer gets a second on Member B's amendment, restates the amendment, and opens the amendment to debate.

◆ Member C thinks that Member B is cheap or hasn't bought a decent computer in a while and doesn't realize the cost of a computer that meets the needs of the organization. Member C says: "I move to amend the amendment by striking '$2,000' and inserting '$4,000'"

The motion made by Member C is a secondary amendment (#11 on the ladder of precedence). It is in order. The presiding officer gets a second on Member C's amendment, restates the amendment, and opens the amendment to debate.

◆ Member D thinks that we need to know more than we currently do about the cost of a computer.

Member D says: "I move to postpone this motion until our meeting next month." The motion made by Member D is a motion to postpone to a certain time (#9 on the ladder of precedence). It is in order. The presiding officer gets a second on Member D's motion, restates the motion, and opens it for debate.

◆ Member E believes that the Finance Committee should decide what price range of computer to buy and have a recommendation for the group at the next meeting.

Member E says: "I move that we refer this to the Finance Committee and direct them to have a recommendation for us at next month's meeting."

The motion made by Member E is commit or refer (#10 on the ladder of precedence). Commit or refer is below postpone to a certain time on the precedence of motions and therefore must be ruled out of order.

We now have four motions on the floor and we still haven't decided whether to purchase the computer. The members appear to be ready to make a decision. We will now proceed down the ladder, voting on each of the motions in reverse order.

Motion from Member D

The immediately pending motion is the motion made by Member D, to postpone to a certain time. Therefore, discussion on that motion is concluded and the presiding officer calls for a vote on the motion. If the motion passes, all of the pending motions (the main motion, primary amendment, and secondary amendment) are postponed to the next meeting. The motion fails. What next?

Motion from Member C

Now the immediately pending motion is the motion made by Member C, the secondary amendment, to strike "$2,000" and insert "$4,000". The members discuss that motion and vote yes. The amendment is amended. What next?

If you guessed that the next step in the process is to vote on whether to purchase a computer, you just fell off the ladder!

Motion from Member B

The immediately pending motion is the motion made by Member B, the primary amendment. That amendment is now amended so the motion we will be voting on is "to amend the motion by adding 'not to exceed $4,000.'" The members discuss the motion and vote yes. The main motion is amended. What next?

Motion from Member A

Now the immediately pending motion is the motion made by Member A, the main motion. That motion now reads: "I move that we purchase a computer, not to exceed $4,000." The motion is discussed and the vote is yes. Finally we have decided to purchase a computer and we have also decided to put a price restriction on the computer that we are going to purchase.

If you keep the ladder in mind, and always ask "What is the immediately pending motion?" then it makes it much easier to make a decision.

Proceed with Caution

The concept of precedence of motions is critical in properly processing a motion.

It is easy to skip steps, so proceed with caution. For instance, when there is a primary amendment and a secondary amendment and the secondary amendment passes, it is very easy to forget to go back down the ladder and process the primary amendment as amended. Many times it appears that if the secondary amendment passed, the primary amendment becomes unnecessary. That is not the case.

To demonstrate this point, let's go back to the computer-purchase motion we just processed. The primary amendment and the secondary amendment were both dealing with money, but they had very different purposes. The purpose of the primary amendment was to add a price limit to the computer we were going to purchase. The purpose of the secondary amendment was solely to determine what that price limit would be.

Another way to demonstrate this is to point out that a member may have favored the secondary amendment and opposed the primary amendment. If you, as a member, believed that the person buying the computer was a real tightwad and incredibly knowledgeable about computers, you may not want to put a price limit on the computer. Therefore you would be against the primary amendment. But if the group was going to insist on putting a price limit on the purchase of the computer, you believe that it should be as high as possible. Therefore, you would be in favor of the secondary amendment.

You Can Go Back up the Ladder

The voting ladder in the precedence of motions is not a one-way ladder. You can move up and down it, and then up and down again before finally processing the main motion and getting off the ladder.

Let's go back to our example of the computer purchase. When the members voted down #9, the motion to postpone to a certain time, the motion that was immediately pending then was #11, the secondary amendment. If Member E still wanted to make the motion to commit or refer, #10, that motion would now be in order. It was out of order when #9 was immediately pending but it is now in order when #11 is immediately pending. So, although a motion may be out of order at one time, the same motion may be in order when a different motion is immediately pending.

The Least You Need to Know

- The immediately pending motion is the motion that was last stated by the chair.
- The precedence of motions indicates which motions precede other motions during debate.
- Motions that don't follow the precedence of motions should be called out of order.
- Don't skip steps on the ladder of motions!

Chapter 8

Let's Talk About It: Debate

In This Chapter

- ◆ The rules of debate
- ◆ What you can and can't debate
- ◆ Debate etiquette
- ◆ Making your debate effective

A critical part of the democratic process is for members to gather, discuss an issue, and make a decision. As a general rule, better decisions are made when the group has had an open discussion on the issue. Compromise and collaboration are more likely to occur in an environment of free and open discussion. Fortunately, *Robert's* provides you with the tools you need to create such an environment.

In this chapter, we will not only look at the rules you should follow to encourage free and open discussion, but how to debate politely and how to make your debate effective.

Rules of Debate

Robert's includes the following *debate* rules that can assist us in discussing motions in a very fair, well-mannered fashion:

◆ You need a motion before you can debate. An issue is not debatable until a motion has been made, seconded, and restated by the presiding officer.

◆ Only one person should speak at a time. The presiding officer calls on only one member at a time and therefore, only one member should be speaking at a time.

◆ Debate is limited to the motion immediately pending. See Chapter 7 for a discussion of the precedence of motions. (Note: Because the purpose of the motion to postpone indefinitely is to kill the main motion, that motion has relaxed debate rules and the debate can cover the merit of the motion it is trying to kill.)

Robert's Says

Debate is the discussion regarding a motion that occurs after the presiding officer has restated the motion and before putting it to a vote.

If a main motion is on the floor and so is an amendment to that motion, the discussion must be limited to the amendment. After the amendment is voted on, the discussion will then be limited only to the main motion, as amended, if amended.

◆ The maker of the motion, if he or she chooses to, has the right to be the first speaker on the motion.

◆ The maker of the motion is prohibited from speaking against the motion.

Limits on the Chair

The role of the presiding officer during the time of debate is critical. It is the presiding officer's responsibility to ensure that debate is conducted in a fair and appropriate manner. If debate rules are not being followed, the presiding officer should initiate corrective action. The effective presiding officer doesn't wait for a member to point out a problem.

Because the presiding officer is a member of the group, he or she should not have to give up the right to debate. However, the chair shouldn't be an active participant in the very debate that he or she is in charge of facilitating. So although the presiding officer has the right to debate, that right should be used very sparingly.

Leave the Chair!

When the presiding officer feels that it is important for him or her to speak on an issue, which should be very seldom, he or she must vacate the chair (sometimes called relinquish the chair) before speaking.

The presiding officer relinquishes the chair to the member who would normally take his or her place if he or she is not there. So if the bylaws indicate that the vice president would take over if the president were not there, the president should relinquish the chair to the vice president.

However, if the vice president has spoken on the motion, the chair should not be turned over to the vice president. If there are other vice presidents who have not spoken, they should assume the chair. If not, the presiding officer should get permission from the members to appoint another person who is judged to be objective on the issue.

Once the presiding officer has relinquished the chair, he or she should not resume presiding until that particular motion is disposed of.

> **Point of Information**
>
> The presiding officer may exercise his or her membership right and speak on a motion only after relinquishing the chair.

Exceptions

As with so many rules in parliamentary procedure, there are two exceptions to this rule. The presiding officer does not leave the chair when discussing the motion to appeal from the decision of the chair. Actually, as we will learn in a Chapter 13, the presiding officer has more debate rights with the motion to appeal from the decision of the chair than members of the assembly have. The second exception is when the presiding officer wishes to speak in a small committee or board. Of course, you remember that from the discussion of small committees and boards that we had in Chapter 2.

When the Chair Is Up for Election

Many people believe that if the presiding officer is up for election or reelection to a position, the presiding officer should relinquish the chair during that election. Not so! The presiding officer can preside over his or her own election. If, though, there is a motion that is specific to the presiding officer, such as a motion to censure the presiding officer, then the presiding officer should relinquish the chair, just as he or she would if he or she wished to speak on a motion.

Questions Through the Chair

While debating an issue, it is not unusual for members to have questions. The proper method of handling those questions is to address them to the presiding officer. If the presiding officer knows the answer and wishes to answer the question, he or she may do so. Otherwise the presiding officer may choose to direct the question to a member or a person in attendance who knows the answer.

Let's return to the motion to purchase a computer from an earlier chapter. When discussing what kind of computer to purchase, a member asks whether anyone knows which of the brands is rated highest on technical support. If the presiding officer knows the answer, he or she may simply answer the question. If the presiding officer knows that John knows the answer, the presiding officer could simply ask John whether he would answer the question. If the chair does not know whether anyone knows the answer, he or she may simply ask if anyone in the group knows the answer to the question.

> ### Parliamentary Pearls
>
> Whenever possible presiding officers should direct the question to someone else, rather than answer the question themselves. By directing another person to answer the questions, the presiding officer is sharing the limelight and giving members an opportunity to develop their leadership skills. In addition, if the issue is controversial, members may perceive any answer from the presiding officer as prejudicial. Thus, not answering questions increases the chances of being perceived as objective.

You Can't Debate Everything!

Although debate is a basic component of parliamentary procedure, there are times when the need to move on and make a decision outweighs the need to allow for debate to occur. Thus, the following motions are *undebatable:*

- ◆ Fix the time to which to adjourn
- ◆ Adjourn
- ◆ Recess
- ◆ Raise a question of privilege
- ◆ Call for the orders of the day
- ◆ Lay on the table
- ◆ Previous question
- ◆ Limit debate

> ### Robert's Says
>
> A motion is **undebatable** when there is no debate allowed on that motion. In essence, Step 4 in the processing of a motion is skipped.

Note, however, that all main motions are debatable. It is only when one of the preceding motions are secondary to the main motion that they are not debatable.

When a motion is undebatable, the presiding officer may recognize a member who wants to ask a question that, when answered, will aid the members in transacting business. However, the presiding officer should make sure that the question or brief suggestion is not debated, but simply helps clarify the motion on the floor.

Speaking Order

When a motion is pending, the general rule is that the first person to seek recognition of the presiding officer should be assigned the floor. Again, there are exceptions to this general rule. The times when the floor should be assigned to a person other than the first person seeking the floor are as follows:

◆ If the member who made the motion has not yet spoken on the motion, he or she can be recognized as the speaker even if he or she wasn't the first person to seek recognition.

◆ Anyone who has not spoken gets recognized before anyone who has.

◆ In cases where the chair knows the opinions of the persons seeking the floor, the assignment should alternate between those favoring and those opposing the motion. There are many ways the presiding officer can determine the side of the speaker. One easy method is to simply ask. After a member speaks against the motion, the presiding officer may simply say, "Are there any members who would like to speak in favor of the motion?"

Parliamentary Pearls

Alternating between members speaking in the affirmative on a motion and members speaking in the negative on the motion is sometimes a very effective way of controlling the length of debate on an issue. Let's say that the presiding officer asks whether anyone wants to speak in favor of the motion. Many hands go up, and the presiding officer calls on the first member to seek recognition. After that member speaks, the presiding officer asks whether anyone wants to speak against the motion, and no hands go up. When the presiding officer asks if anyone wants to speak in favor of the motion, most of the time fewer or no hands go up because it is obvious that the motion is going to pass even without further affirmative comments.

Speaking Time

To save time, no member may speak more than two times on any one motion on any one day, and each of those speeches are limited to 10 minutes. This rule may be the best-kept secret of parliamentary procedure! The basis of this rule is that in the democratic process everyone should be able to participate in the debate. If one member dominates the debate, that reduces the rights of the other members.

In conventions, because of the large number of people in attendance, the time limit is usually reduced to somewhere between two and five minutes. In small groups, there is no limit to the number of times a member may speak.

Debate Manners

Manners for debating a motion aren't much different than the manners that are appropriate in all aspects of our life.

In a group of people, it is considered mannerly to speak one at a time, not all at once. Therefore, in debate, if a member wants to speak, that member should seek recognition. How you seek recognition is usually set by the norms of the group. In most meetings seeking recognition is usually done as simple as raising your hand and waiting for the presiding officer to call on you. This is probably the most appropriate method for most situations.

Here are some other rules of parliamentary etiquette:

♦ **Only speak when called on.** Whatever method your group uses to seek the floor, a member should not speak until called on by the presiding officer.

Gavel Gaffs

Comments must be directed to the issue of the motion, not the personality of the members. Discussion should be refuting the facts, not making accusations against other members.

♦ **Direct all comments to the chair.** Avoid directing comments to another member.

♦ **Don't be disruptive.** Side conversations are not allowed. Neither is walking around the room in a manner that is disruptive to the meeting. That doesn't mean you cannot get up and go to the restroom during a meeting, just don't be disruptive about it. If the member is disruptive, the presiding officer should call the member to order.

♦ **You can make corrections.** If you hear information that you know is inaccurate, you have the right to call attention to the inaccuracy and to have the accurate information shared with the group. Of course, this must be done politely.

♦ **The chair can interrupt you.** While you shouldn't interrupt another speaker, if the presiding officer interrupts you while you are speaking, you should stop and listen to the presiding officer. There are situations in which the presiding officer has the right to interrupt a speaker, and you should assume that it is one of those situations and allow the interruption.

> ### Point of Information
>
> If you have already spoken on the motion, be aware of other members who have not spoken yet and attempt to help the presiding officer by inviting them speak before you. For example, if you are in line at a microphone to speak a second time on a particular motion, allow anyone who is behind you in line who has not yet spoken on the motion to step ahead of you in line. Since you do not have the right to speak before them, this action sets a cooperative tone among the members and is clearly seen as helpful to the presiding officer.

Debate Effectively!

We have all seen times when the right words spoken by the right person at the right time has swayed the whole group. Those times serve as a reminder of the power of debate. If you have strong feelings on the issue, put forth the extra effort to make your debate effective. I've including some tips to help you hone your debating skills.

Which Side?

It is a good idea to begin your debate by telling the members which side you are speaking on. You might say something like "Madam Chairman, I rise to speak in favor of the motion." Then, no matter how unclear the rest of your comments are, the members know which side of the motion you favor.

Organize Your Thoughts

The fact that the rules only allow you to speak two times on any motion on any one day should make it clear to you that you need to organize your thoughts. Also, remember that you cannot speak a second time until everyone who wants to speak has had the opportunity to speak the first time. You need to make sure that when you do speak that your thoughts are well planned and cover the major points you want to make.

In addition, pay close attention to your delivery. Speak clearly and slowly, project your voice, and say it like you mean it.

Organize your thoughts into two or three main points and communicate them during your debate time. Avoid going down a long list of reasons you favor or oppose the motion—the longer the list, the less likely people will remember it. Keep focused on the major reasons why you have taken your stand.

At the end of your debate speech, you should restate which side you favor and summarize the main reasons you have expressed during your debate. It might sound something like this: "I have spoken against this motion because, as I just explained, the cost of this program is too high and the potential harm of this program to our organization outweighs any possible advantage. Therefore, I urge you to vote against this motion."

As you can see from this example, the summary can reinforce the points you have made and leave the other members with a clear vision of where you stand on the issue and why you stand there.

The Least You Need to Know

♦ The presiding officer should appear neutral on the issues being debated at all times; when the chair feels that it is essential to speak up on an issue, she or he should first relinquish the chair.

♦ Use proper manners at all times when debating.

♦ The order of assignment of the floor is there to make sure every side gets its points heard.

♦ Think before you speak during a debate.

Chapter 9

Voting: The Democratic Way

In This Chapter

- ◆ Ways to conduct the vote
- ◆ The power of general consent
- ◆ What different votes mean
- ◆ Why you can't vote by proxy

One of the most valuable aspects of living in a democratic society is being able to vote. A vote is a formal expression of will, opinion, or choice by members of an assembly in regard to a matter submitted to it.

Methods of Voting

Parliamentary procedure allows for numerous methods of voting on a motion. Some are somewhat obscure and are used infrequently or only when specified in the bylaws, so we are going to leave those for the technical books. In this chapter, we'll focus on the six methods of voting that are commonly used and would be helpful for you to understand.

Robert's Says

Unanimous consent is interchangeable with **general consent** and is a method of voting without taking a formal vote. The presiding officer asks if there are any objections, and if none are expressed, the motion is considered passed.

Gavel Gaffs

Don't let the term *unanimous consent* mislead you. *Robert's Rules of Order, Revised* includes the following explanation of general consent: "It does not necessarily mean that every member is in favor of the motion, but, that knowing it is useless to oppose it, or even to discuss it, the opposition simply acquiesces in the informality."

Everybody Agrees—General Consent

General consent and *unanimous consent* are interchangeable terms. Voting by general consent involves the presiding officer saying "If there is no objection [states the issue under consideration]" Then, if there is no objection, you can skip all six steps of the motion-making process. This method should only be used when the motion is of little importance or when there appears to be no opposition to the motion.

General consent has some very valuable uses. Sometimes it is so obvious that the group is in agreement that it would be a waste of time to go through the six steps of processing a motion. For example, when there is no more business on the agenda and everybody is packing up their things, that would be a perfect time for the presiding officer to say "If there is no objection, the meeting is adjourned." [pause] "Hearing no objection, we are adjourned."

It takes only one member to object to force a more formal voting method. If a member objects, the chair has to state the motion and put it to a vote. Since it takes only one person to object, no membership rights are being violated by using unanimous consent.

Probably the best example of when to use general consent is in the approval of the minutes of the meeting. Assuming that the minutes have been printed and distributed to the members in advance of the meeting, the presiding officer might simply say "You have received the minutes. Are there any corrections to the minutes? [pause] "Hearing none, if there is no objection, the minutes are approved as printed."

Viva Voce—Voice Vote

The most commonly used method of voting is the voice vote. It is used effectively when there is little controversy and the outcome appears obvious. However, it should be avoided when a two-thirds vote is required because it is difficult to determine a two-thirds vote by voice.

For example, a call for a voice vote might sound like this: "Those in favor of the motion, say 'Aye'. Those opposed say 'No'."

After the presiding officer calls for a voice vote, the chair declares the motion to have passed (or lost). Members have the right to question the results of the vote and can request to have the vote clarified by having a uncounted rising vote. All that you have to do is call out "division of the assembly."

The division of the assembly motion requires the presiding officer to call for another vote, this time using an uncounted rising vote—sometimes called a standing vote (discussed later in this chapter). Unlike most other motions, a member can simply call out for a division of the assembly—it doesn't need a second and it is not a debatable motion. (Division of the assembly is discussed further in Chapter 13.)

> **Parliamentary Pearls**
>
> When serving as presiding officer it is advisable to use the words "If there is no objection, …" any time you are not putting an issue to a formal vote. These simple words can protect you from future criticism.

Show Me the Hand–Show of Hands Vote

The show of hands voting method is typically used in small groups because it usually only works when everyone can see everyone else. The wording of this method of voting could be as simple as "Those in favor of the motion, please raise your hand. [pause] Those opposed, please raise your hand." Make sure to pause between asking for those in favor and those against so that those voting in favor of the motion have a chance to put their hands down before those voting against it raise theirs.

> **CAUTION Gavel Gaffs**
>
> People sometimes mistakenly believe that the motion of a division of the assembly requires a counted vote. It only requires an uncounted rising vote because in very large groups a counted vote can take a very long time. If it required a counted vote, members in large groups could use it to delay business, or as we say in the parliamentary world, for dilatory purposes.

Stand and Maybe Count Off–Rising Vote

A rising vote sounds just like its name: Members cast their vote by standing up. The presiding officer might call for a rising vote by saying something like "Those in favor of the motion, please stand. [pause] Please be seated. Those opposed to the motion, please stand. [pause] Please be seated."

As noted previously, the rising vote should be used when a member makes a motion for the division of the assembly after a voice vote. This method is also effective when the vote requirement is greater than a majority because it's much easier to determine if the two thirds were obtained.

If a member isn't satisfied with the call on a rising vote, the member may move to have the vote counted. The motion to have a counted vote needs a majority to pass. But, if there is any doubt, it is smarter for the presiding officer to simply go immediately to a counted vote when requested. The time a counted vote takes is well worth the time spent counting if the members are at all in question of the results of the vote.

Gavel Gaffs

The Americans with Disabilities Act has influenced voting. It is not at all unusual for an organization to have replaced a rising vote with a vote using a voting card. Each voting member is given a voting card. Instead of rising, the presiding officer directs the members to raise their voting card. It has the same effect as a rising vote, but is easier on people who find standing up and sitting down difficult.

Write It Down—Ballot Vote

When secrecy is desired, groups can vote by ballot—usually paper ballots. Ballots are usually used for elections or any time the pressure of the group might keep people from voting what they really believe.

The usual wording for the ballot vote is "Please mark your ballot." That comment is usually followed by instructions on folding the ballots and where to deposit them.

Call the Roll—Roll Call Vote

The roll call vote is the exact opposite of a ballot vote. The purpose of the ballot vote is to conceal each member's vote. In a roll call vote, the purpose is to make official as part of the record how each member voted.

The roll call vote should only be used in situations in which the members are answerable to a constituency. For instance, the U.S. Senate and House of Representatives vote by roll call so that they remain accountable to the American people. Roll call voting is only appropriate for organizations whose members represent a constituency. You will most frequently see it used in governmental bodies.

The presiding officer states the motion and then calls for a vote by asking the secretary (or clerk) to call the roll. It is usual practice to call the roll in alphabetical order, except that the presiding officer's name is called last. However, some organizations have designed a method to get around that. Instead of always beginning with the first name in the alphabet, some groups rotate how they call roll. Each time there is a vote, they start with the next name on the list.

When a person's name is called that person answer yes, no, present (abstain), or pass. If a member calls out "pass" when his or her name is called, that person may vote before the results are announced. I bet you can already imagine how some people in politics use the pass to avoid revealing their vote too early in the game!

The roll should be entered in the minutes as a part of the record of that meeting.

Point of Information

Here are the words to use for each of the voting methods:

- **General or unanimous consent:** "If there is no objection …"
- **Voice vote:** "All those in favor, say Aye. [pause] All those opposed, say No."
  (If the chair is in doubt of the results of a voice vote, the chair should state "The chair is in doubt, and therefore a rising (or counted) vote will be taken." Then proceed with a rising or counted vote.)
- **Show of hands vote:** "All those in favor of the motion, please raise your hand. [pause] Please lower your hands. Those opposed to the motion, please raise your hand. [pause] Please lower your hands."
- **Rising vote:** "Those in favor of the motion, please stand. [pause] Please be seated. Those opposed to the motion, please stand. [pause] Please be seated."
- **Rising counted vote:** "Those in favor of the motion, please stand and remain standing until counted. [pause] Please be seated. Those opposed to the motion, please stand and remain standing until counted. [pause] Please be seated."
- **Ballot vote:** "Please mark your ballots clearly, fold them one time, and hand them directly to a teller."
- **Roll call vote:** "The secretary will now call the roll."

Absentee and Proxy Voting

It is a fundamental principle of parliamentary law that only the members physically present at a legally called meeting can vote. Therefore, the only way that an organization can allow for either absentee voting (voting prior to an election) or proxy voting (sending a representative to the election to vote for you) is if it is specifically permitted in the bylaws. However, it is recommended that neither absentee nor proxy voting be allowed because they violate the principles of parliamentary procedure. Because one member carries the votes of another member, in addition to his own, proxy voting is also in violation of the parliamentary principle of one member, one vote. With proxy voting, a member may have numerous votes.

Meaning of Vote

Although an organization is free to specify in its bylaws the number of votes necessary for adoption of a motion (two thirds, three fifths, three fourths, nine tenths, and so on) the majority vote and two-thirds vote are the most common. Let's look at each in turn.

Majority Vote

A majority vote is "more than half" of the votes cast. So if 20 votes are cast, you need at least 11 votes. If 19 votes are cast, you need at least 10 votes.

If a vote ends in a tie, a majority was not attained. That's because a majority means more than half, and a tie vote is not more than half. If the vote is tied and a majority vote is needed, the vote fails. We are well aware that a 13 to 14 vote fails. But a 13 to 13 vote also fails. It just doesn't fail by quite as much!

Two-Thirds Vote

A two-thirds vote simply means that there were at least twice as many votes in favor of the motion as there were against the motion.

Figuring out a two-thirds vote is much easier than most people think. Most of the time people take the votes in favor and add them to the votes against, divide that number by 3, and multiply that number by 2. Let's use an example to help understand that process. Twenty people voted yes and 10 people voted no. The yes votes plus the no votes is 30. Thirty divided by 3 is 10. Ten times 2 is 20. Therefore, a two-thirds vote of 30 votes is 20. I picked an easy number and it was still long and involved.

There is another very easy way to determine a two-thirds vote, and you don't need to be a math whiz to do it. You take the number of no votes, multiply that number by 2, and the result is the number of yes votes that are required for a two-thirds vote. Let's use an example here again. If the vote was 20 in favor and 10 against, and a two-thirds vote was needed, then the motion passed—10 times 2 is 20 and there were 20 votes, so the motion passed.

Gavel Gaffs _____

When calling for the vote, you will often hear the presiding officer ask for abstentions. It would sound like: "Those in favor, say Aye. Those opposed, say No. Abstentions?"

The presiding officer does not need to call for abstentions. An abstention is a member's way of not voting. When you don't vote yes or no, you have abstained.

In a ballot vote, a member abstains by not turning in a ballot or by turning in a blank ballot. The blank ballot is not counted as a vote.

Of What?

People sometimes try to figure out how many votes are needed for a majority or two-thirds vote before the actual vote is cast. However, in voting, if the rules don't say otherwise, *majority* is more than half of the votes cast and *two thirds* is two thirds of the votes cast. So you have no way of knowing in advance how many votes will be required to pass a motion. In an unrealistic, yet possible scenario, for instance, there may be 20 members present, yet 16 of those 20 members abstain from voting. In this case, only three votes would constitute a majority.

But there are many other basis for votes. They include majority or two thirds of the membership, and majority or two thirds of the members present. Let's look at how the various basis for voting play out in a situation in which there are 1,000 members, 100 members present at a meeting, and 90 members voting:

1,000 members in the organization

100 members present

90 members vote

Vote	Majority	Two Thirds
Of the members present	51	67
Of the entire membership	501	667
Of the members present and voting	46	60

Remember, in voting, the default basis is a majority of the votes cast or two thirds of the vote cast. If the bylaws only say "majority," it is a majority of the votes cast. If they only say "two thirds," it is two thirds of the votes cast.

Point of Information

Abstentions can have different effects depending on the basis of the vote:

◆ Of the members present and voting: no effect whatsoever

◆ Of the entire membership: same effect as a "no" vote since you are a member and you are not voting "yes"

◆ Of the members present: same effect as a "no" vote since you are present and you are not voting "yes"

You want to make sure that when you abstain, the vote requirement allows you to truly take a neutral stand on the issue—otherwise, your abstention is really a "no" vote.

Meaning and Use of Plurality Vote

A plurality vote requires that one candidate or proposition receive more votes than the others. A plurality vote is particularly nice when there are more than two candidates running for an office. When there are three or more candidates slated for the same office, it is difficult to get a majority vote. But most of the time one of those candidates will get more votes than the other two candidates. Thus, that candidate has a plurality.

Parliamentary Pearls

The advantage of the plurality vote over a majority vote is that it takes less time. Unless there is a tie vote, a plurality elects on the first ballot.

The advantage of the majority vote over a plurality vote is that more than half of the members support (voted for) the decision or the candidate elected.

Plurality vote can only be used for an election when it is specifically stated in the bylaws that the member shall be elected by plurality. Otherwise, the election is by majority vote. And with three or more candidates, it can take a lot of ballots to get to a majority vote.

The Chair's Vote

It's important that the chair maintain an appearance of objectivity. At the same time, the presiding officer should not lose his or her voting rights simply because he or she became the presiding officer. This is particularly important in bodies when the chair was elected by a constituency. Toward this end, the chair is allowed to vote when his or her vote will affect the results of the vote or if the vote is by (secret) ballot. People often mistakenly believe that this rule means that the chair can vote only to break a tie. Numerical examples would help here.

Vote Required	Yes Votes	No Votes	Presiding Officer Vote	
			Yes vote	No vote
Majority	13	13	Affects results	Doesn't affect results
Majority	14	13	Doesn't affect results	Affects results
Two thirds	9	5	Affects results	Doesn't affect results
Two thirds	10	5	Doesn't affect results	Affects results

The Least You Need to Know

♦ There are many ways to conduct a vote; be sure to use the one most appropriate for the situation.

♦ It only takes one member's objection during a vote by unanimous consent to force a formal vote.

♦ By default, a majority vote means a majority of voting members; however, the bylaws can also specify a majority of members or a majority of members present.

♦ The chair can only vote if the vote is by ballot or his or her vote will change the outcome of the vote.

Part

Motions for (Almost) Any Occasion

There's a motion for almost any situation imaginable. Want to take a bathroom break? Move to recess. Want to ask a question about parliamentary procedure? Make a point of parliamentary inquiry. Don't trust the presiding officer's vote count? Call out "division." Want to change a pending motion? Move to amend it.

I could go on and on … and I will!

In this part I explain approximately 25 motions that can help you move your ideas forward. In addition, I've provided a script for each of those motions so you can see them in action and know what to say when you have to use the motions.

Chapter 10

Main Motions

In This Chapter

◆ Understanding main motions

◆ How secondary motions perfect main motions

◆ How to say what you mean in a motion

◆ How to phrase a resolution

◆ Giving notice to minimize game playing

In Chapter 7, we learned that a main motion is the lowest motion on the precedence of motions ladder. It is the motion that all of the other motions in the precedence list can be applied to—they can be made while it is pending. In this chapter, we're going to explore main motions in more detail. While we're at it, we'll explore the difference between main motions and resolutions and secondary motions.

The Bottom Rung: Main Motions

Main motions are debatable, amendable, and can have all kinds of things happen to them. Not only can all of the other 13 motions on the motion ladder be applied to a main motion, but so can many other secondary motions (the variety of secondary motions are discussed in Chapters 11–13). As a general rule, a main motion needs a majority vote to pass. As usual, there are exceptions, but we'll deal with those later.

Because main motions serve as the bottom rung of the precedence of motions ladder, they take precedence over nothing, which means that a main motion cannot be made while any other motion is pending. That means that only one main motion is allowed on the floor at a time.

Point of Information

If a member made the motion that the association "purchase a copy of *The Complete Idiot's Guide to Robert's Rules* for each member of the board of directors," that motion would be a main motion. Another member could not now move to "purchase a computer for the association" while the first motion is pending, because the computer motion is also a main motion. It would be too confusing to decide on the book and the computer at the same time. But, while the motion to buy the book was on the floor, it would be in order to amend it by striking "of the board of directors" so that, if amended, the motion would now read "purchase a copy of *The Complete Idiot's Guide to Robert's Rules* for each member."

It's All About Relationships: Main and Secondary Motions

The content of the motion isn't what determines whether it's a main motion or a secondary motion. Rather, it is a motion's relationship to other motions that establishes the type of motion it is.

If a motion is made while another motion is pending and it is ruled to be in order, it is by its very nature a secondary motion. If a motion is made while no other motions are pending and it is ruled to be in order, it is a main motion. I know this is confusing, so stay with me.

On the motion ladder, you will find the motion to recess, which introduces an intermission, or break, during a meeting. Say we are in a meeting and have been debating a motion for more than an hour, and it looks like it still has a way to go. You notice that you aren't the only member squirming in your chair—almost everyone else is, too. During the debate, you get recognized by the chair and you say "I move that we take a 10 minute recess." Your motion passes, and you are the hit of the meeting! That was an example of a secondary motion, the motion to recess.

Go back to that same meeting. Discussion on the controversial motion ends after 1½ hours of nonstop debating, the vote is taken, and the motion passes. The next item of business is as controversial as the one that you just wrapped up. You get recognized by the chair and you say "I move that we take a 10 minute recess." This time, the motion to recess is not a secondary motion because no other motion is pending— remember we already voted on the controversial motion. The motion to recess can still be processed, but it is now processed as a main motion, not a secondary one. The secondary and main motions to recess are processed much the same except that since this motion is a main motion, when you come back from recess, there is no motion pending.

Parliamentary Pearls

When someone makes main motion that amends an existing document, like the bylaws, keep in mind that in a parliamentary sense it is a main motion, not an amendment. For example: "I move that we amend our bylaws, Article III, Section 2 by striking the words 'temporary member' and inserting 'affiliate member'."

Even though this motion is amending something that is already in existence, it is a main motion, not an amendment. If you keep in mind that it is a main motion then you will be able to follow the process better (or lead the process should you be chairing the meeting).

Resolution vs. Motion

Many people try to look for an elaborate difference between resolutions and motions. There isn't one. The difference is all about format. A resolution is essentially an elaborate, formally written motion. *Robert's* tells us that a resolution is used when the motion is of great importance or is very long.

A resolution includes the reasons for the motion as well as the actual action that the group is proposing. Resolutions have two parts, as follows:

◆ **Part 1: The preamble.** The preamble lists the reasons for adoption. Each reason is given its own paragraph and usually begins with the word "whereas."

◆ **Part 2: The resolving clauses.** This is the action part, where you identify the specific action or position you want the group to take. Each of these clauses, or paragraphs, begin with "Resolved, That."

The following is a sample resolution:

Whereas, the American Association of Fun Loving People (AAFLP) must choose a fun city for its 2010 convention;

Whereas, the city of Ain't-It-Fun, North Dakota was rated as the Funfest City of the Year; and

Whereas, the Fun-Fun-Fun Hotel is available during our convention dates and at a rate that should make it even more fun; therefore, be it

Resolved, That the 2010 Annual Convention of the American Association of Fun Loving People be held in Ain't-It-Fun, North Dakota, at the Fun-Fun-Fun Hotel, on April 1 and 2, 2010; and

Resolved, That the attendees at the 2010 Annual Convention have a fun time.

Some groups use the resolution format for all of their motions. Other groups never use the resolution format. I discourage the resolution format because I believe that it makes an easy process (writing a motion) unnecessarily difficult.

Point of Information

Points for processing a resolution:

♦ The words that a member uses in moving a resolution are "I move the adoption of the following resolution …."

♦ Since the resolving clauses are the important part of the resolution, they are opened first to discussion and amendments. After debate on the resolving clauses is concluded, the whereas clauses are open for debate and amendment.

Giving Notice of Motions

In Chapter 4, we introduced an example in which an organization wanted to change its dues from $10 to $12. Because that involved amending the organization's bylaws, we noted that it required previous notice, which is essentially informing the membership of the proposed change in advance of the meeting. Previous notice is usually required before a main motion can be made at a meeting when you are proposing to change something that has been adopted previously, such as amending the bylaws. The example you will see most often is a motion to amend the bylaws. Almost always, the bylaws indicate that in order to amend the bylaws the members must receive the proposed amendment at the previous meeting or in advance of the current meeting.

The notice requirement serves an important purpose by preventing people from taking advantage of certain situations. For example, let's say that at last month's meeting the bylaws were amended to increase the dues from $5 to $7, but it only passed by two votes. At this month's meeting, three of the people who voted in favor of the dues increase are not present and everyone who voted against it is present. Without the rule requiring previous notice, one of those members could move to amend the bylaws and reduce the dues back to the $5. You can see the potential problem with the bylaws being amended back and forth at each meeting, depending on who is in attendance.

Script of a Main Motion

Ever wonder how in the world presiding officers remember every step in the motion making process? While it's certainly the case that many presiding officers have a complete understanding of parliamentary procedure and know exactly what to say in almost every circumstance, a lot of presiding officers rely on what some might call "cheat sheets" but in the parliamentary world are called "scripts." That's right—they read from a prepared document which tells them exactly what they need to say and do for any particular motion. Beginning here, and throughout the book, you will find scripts of what you should say in processing the motion. They are meant to make you more comfortable in a meeting. Copy them and take them to meetings with you so you are prepared for whatever comes up.

Script: Main Motion

Member: I move that …

Chair: Is there a second to the motion? [This statement is eliminated if a member calls out "second" or if the motion is made on behalf of a committee.]

Second
member: I second the motion.

Chair: It is moved and seconded that [state the motion]. Is there any discussion? [Since the maker of the motion has first right to speak on the motion, the chair should call on the maker of the motion first.]

[It is during this time that a motion is considered pending and secondary motions may be applied to it.]

[After discussion] Is there any further discussion? Are you ready for the question? [Pause] The question is on the adoption of the motion to [clearly restate the motion].

Voice vote: All those in favor, say "Aye." [Pause for response]

All those opposed, say "No." [If the chair is in doubt of the results of a voice vote, the chair should state "The chair is in doubt, therefore a rising (or counted) vote will be taken." Then proceed with a rising or counted vote.]

continues

---

continues

Show of hands vote: All those in favor of the motion, please raise your hand. [Pause] Please lower your hand. Those opposed to the motion, please raise your hand. [Pause] Please lower your hand.

Rising vote: Those in favor of the motion, please stand. [Pause] Please be seated. Those opposed to the motion, please stand. [Pause] Please be seated.

Ballot vote: Please mark your ballots clearly, fold them one time, and hand them directly to a teller.

Roll call vote: The clerk will now call the roll.

Chair: [Announces the voting results]

Uncounted voice, rising, or show of hands vote: The affirmative has it, the motion is adopted, we will [state the effect of the vote] and the next business in order is …

or

The negative has it, the motion is lost and [state the effect of the vote]. and the next business in order is …

Counted majority vote: There are _____ votes in the affirmative and _____ votes in the negative. There is a majority in the affirmative and the motion is adopted. We will [state the effect of the vote] and the next business in order is …

or

There are _____ votes in the affirmative and _____ votes in the negative. There is less than a majority in the affirmative and the motion is lost [state the effect of the vote] and the next business in order is …

Counted two-thirds vote: There are _____ votes in the affirmative and _____ votes in the negative. There is a two-thirds vote in the affirmative and the motion is adopted. We will [state the effect of the vote] and the next business in order is …

or

There are _____ votes in the affirmative and _____ votes in the negative. There is less than a two-thirds vote in the affirmative and the motion is lost [state the effect of the vote]

Chair: The next business in order is …

Rules for a Main Motion:

◆ Needs a second.

◆ Is debatable.

◆ Is amendable.

◆ Needs a majority vote.

The Least You Need to Know

◆ There can only be one main motion on the floor at a time; many secondary motions can be on the floor.

◆ A resolution is essentially a very formal motion.

◆ Depending on the circumstances, the same motion, such as the motion to recess, can be either a main motion or a secondary motion.

◆ Scripts are great tools to use for introducing and processing motions.

Chapter 11

Privileged Motions

In This Chapter

- ◆ Understanding privileged motions
- ◆ How to make sure the meeting doesn't last forever
- ◆ How to work in bathroom breaks
- ◆ How to handle emergencies

Privileged motions are a class of motions that are important enough to warrant interrupting all other motions. Because they are by their very nature urgent issues, debate on them is not allowed. Their content does not relate to the main motion or pending business but to the members and the organization. Hence, the name *privileged*.

The privileged motions are usually secondary motions, meaning that they are made when a main motion is already on the floor. For instance, if your group is debating the main motion to purchase a computer and you have to go to the bathroom and can't wait until the debate on the computer is over, you can move for a 10-minute recess.

The Five Privileged Motions

The following five motions are in the class of privileged motions:

- ♦ **Fix the time to which to adjourn.** This sets the time for another meeting to continue business of the session. Adoption of this motion does not adjourn the present meeting or set the time for its adjournment.

- ♦ **Adjourn.** A motion to close the meeting.

- ♦ **Recess.** A short interruption which does not close the meeting. After the recess, business resumes at exactly the point where it was interrupted.

- ♦ **Questions of privilege.** To bring an urgent request or a main motion relating to the rights of either the assembly or an individual up for immediate consideration.

- ♦ **Call for the orders of the day.** By the use of this motion, a single member can require the assembly to follow the order of business or agenda, or to take up a special order that is scheduled to come up, unless two thirds of the assembly wish to do otherwise.

Privileged motions have special privileges only when they are offered as secondary motions. When they are main motions, they are treated like any other main motion and must follow the rules for a main motion.

Since this is not a rulebook (that's *Robert's* job), I will not include all of the specific rules for each of the privileged motions discussed. For the rules please refer to Appendix B, §16 through §20.

Point of Information

Privileged motions are unique in that they don't relate to the specific motion that is pending.

Explain, please!

If the main motion is to purchase a computer, and you move to amend that motion by adding "at a cost not to exceed $3,000" the amendment relates to that specific main motion. But if, while you were discussing the computer main motion, a member moved that you recess for 10 minutes, the recess motion is not related to the motion to purchase a computer. The recess motion could be made just as it was stated, no matter what the main motion was.

Fix the Time to Which to Adjourn

The motion to fix the time to which to adjourn does not adjourn the current meeting—it just sounds like it does! All this motion does is set up the time and sometimes the place for the continuation of the present meeting. This motion makes the next meeting a continuation of the present meeting, not a new meeting with a new agenda.

The time you fix for the next meeting must be before the next regularly scheduled meeting of the group. So if the group meets on the first Tuesday of the month and the motion to fix the time to which to adjourn is made at the February meeting, the continued meeting must be held before the first Tuesday in March.

You aren't going to use this motion a lot, but it's great to know that it's available if you do need it. Let's look at a couple of situations when it might be used:

♦ You are in the middle of discussion on a heated issue that must be decided before next week and you don't meet again until next month. Your time for meeting is up and you have to get out of the building you are meeting in because it is closing. With this motion you can continue this meeting tomorrow night or any time before the decision is needed next week.

♦ It is Tuesday. The decision on an important issue must be made by Friday. You need some more information to make the decision, but your rules require that to have a special meeting you must give four days notice. Because this motion calls for a continuation of the current meeting, you don't need the four days notice. So you could use this motion to continue the meeting on Wednesday or Thursday evening.

Script: Motion to Fix the Time to Which to Adjourn

"Motion A" is pending

Member:	I move that when this meeting adjourns, it adjourns to meet [give date and time] at [give location].
Chair:	Is there a second to the motion? [This statement is eliminated if a member calls out "second."]
Second member:	I second the motion.
Chair:	It is moved and seconded that when this meeting adjourns, it adjourns to meet [give date and time] at [give location]. This is not a debatable motion.

continues

continued

The question is on the adoption of the motion that when this meeting adjourns, it adjourns to meet [give date and time] at [give location]. This motion requires a majority vote.

All those in favor, say "Aye." [Pause for response.]

All those opposed, say "No."

The affirmative has it, and the motion is adopted; when this meeting adjourns, it adjourns to meet [give date and time] at [give location]. The motion before you is "Motion A". Is there any further discussion?

or

The negative has it, the motion is lost, and we have not set a time for a continuation of this meeting. The motion before you is "Motion A". Is there any further discussion?

Rules for Motion to Fix the Time to Which to Adjourn:

◆ Needs a second.

◆ Is *not* debatable.

◆ Is amendable but the amendment is not debatable.

◆ Needs a majority vote.

Adjourn

The motion to adjourn, which is used to close a meeting, is probably the most popular of all motions. At the end of this section, you will find a script for this motion, but it may be unnecessary. If the business on the agenda has been concluded, the presiding officer may ask if there is any other business to come before the group. If there is none, then the presiding officer may simply say "Since there is no other business, the meeting is adjourned."

The motion to adjourn is very high in the motion ladder. That's because if a majority of the attendees at a meeting want to conclude the meeting, the minority should not be able to keep them against their will.

Point of Information

Because the motion to adjourn is a privileged motion, it isn't debatable. However, a member may inform the assembly of an urgent matter that needs to be taken up before adjournment. For example, as the presiding officer begins to adjourn the meeting, a member raises his hand to be recognized. The presiding officer calls on him and the member says "the location of the meeting next week has been changed to the Woodward Technology Center, Room 141." The announcement in that example is appropriate because it is clearly business requiring attention before adjournment. Similar comments or even questions may be made during any privileged motion as long as such comments do not debate the motion itself.

In organizations that have regular meetings more than quarterly, the business on the agenda that is not covered before the adjournment is automatically placed on the agenda for the next meeting under Unfinished Business. So if we had three things on the agenda under New Business and we only completed items one and two, the third item would automatically go on the agenda for the next meeting under Unfinished Business.

Script: Motion to Adjourn

"Motion A" is pending

Member: I move that the meeting adjourn.

Chair: Is there a second to the motion? [This statement is eliminated if a member calls out "second."]

Second
member: I second the motion.

Chair: It is moved and seconded that the meeting adjourn. This is not a debatable motion.

     The question is on the adoption of the motion that we adjourn. This motion requires a majority vote.

     All those in favor, say "Aye." [Pause for response]

     All those opposed, say "No."

     The affirmative has it, the motion is adopted, and the meeting is adjourned. When we meet next week "Motion A" will be on the agenda under Unfinished Business.

continues

continued

> *or*
>
> The negative has it, the motion is defeated and we will not adjourn at this time. The motion before you is "Motion A". Is there any further discussion?

Rules for the Motion to Adjourn:

◆ Needs a second.

◆ Is *not* debatable.

◆ Is *not* amendable.

◆ Needs a majority vote.

Recess

A recess is a brief intermission taken by the assembly. It can be used for getting refreshments, using the restroom, getting a meal, or just giving people a chance to stand up, move around, and clear their heads. This is the second most popular motion, second only to adjourn!

Can Be Amended

The motion to recess is the third motion from the top of the ladder of motions. The motion to amend is the third motion from the bottom. According to the precedence of motions, the recess motion should not be able to be amended. But in this case, an amendment can be "applied" to the motion to recess, but it is limited to amending the length of time of the recess. This concept also applies to the previously discussed motion to fix the time to which to adjourn.

For example, a member moves that we recess for 10 minutes. The lines at the restroom will not allow for everyone to get back in 10 minutes, so you move to

Gavel Gaffs

If the recess is for a later time (such as at 3 this afternoon), it is not a privileged motion and can't be made when another motion is pending.

amend the motion to strike 10 minutes and insert 20 minutes. That amendment is allowed, but because the recess motion is not debatable, the amendment to it is not debatable.

Recess Without a Motion

If the agenda for the meeting has a recess scheduled, and the time for that recess arrives, the presiding officer can call for that recess without having to wait for a motion.

Recess vs. Adjourn at a Convention

Since a convention is a series of meetings that make up one session (as we learned in Chapter 5) people many times confuse the use of recess and adjourn at a convention.

Instead of giving a very detailed description of the difference, let's keep it simple. If the break is for a meal or for a few hours, the meeting should be recessed. If the break is overnight, or for a full day, then the meeting should be an adjourned. If it is the last meeting of the convention, then it should be adjourned *sine die*.

Parliamentary Pearls

Legislative bodies—such as the U.S. Congress or a state's House of Representatives—use the term "recess" differently than the term is commonly used in parliamentary procedure. They use it to indicate a time when they are not in session for days or weeks at a time.

Robert's Says

Adjournment sine die (pronounced *SIGN-ee DYE-ee*) means to "adjourn without day." You would most likely hear this term used at a convention. It is the adjournment at the end of the regular session of a convention. The last meeting of the convention is said to adjourn sine die.

Script: Motion to Recess

"Motion A" is pending

Member: I move to recess for 10 minutes.

Chair: Is there a second to the motion? [This statement is eliminated if a member calls out "second."]

Second
member: I second the motion.

Chair: It is moved and seconded that we recess for 10 minutes. Are you ready for the question? [Pause]

continues

continued

The question is on the adoption of the motion that we recess for 10 minutes. This motion requires a majority vote.

All those in favor, say "Aye." [Pause for response]

All those opposed, say "No."

The affirmative has it, the motion is adopted, we will recess for 10 minutes. When we return from recess the motion before you will be "Motion A". We are in recess.

or

The negative has it, the motion is defeated and we will not take a recess. The motion before you is "Motion A". Is there any further discussion?

Rules for the Motion to Recess:

◆ Needs a second.

◆ Is *not* debatable.

◆ Is amendable (only as to the length of the recess, and that amendment is not debatable).

◆ Needs a majority vote.

Questions of Privilege

Questions of privilege are used when there is a matter, either affecting the entire assembly or an individual in the assembly, that is so urgent that it must interrupt business and be taken care of right away. Sometimes it is simply a question that can be addressed by the presiding officer. Other times it must be made into a motion that is acted on by the group.

During a meeting in which a guest speaker is speaking, if a member raises a question of privilege indicating that the people in the back of the room cannot hear the speaker, the presiding officer could ask the speaker to speak louder or have the microphone system fixed and no motion would be needed. If though, the member asked that the group move the entire meeting to the room next door where the acoustics are better, and it's obvious that not everyone wants to move, then the presiding officer would want to turn that request into a motion and have it voted on.

The presiding officer must determine whether the question is of such urgency that it warrants interrupting the speaker. If a member is interrupted, as soon as the question of privilege is resolved, the presiding officer should go back to the member who was interrupted and allow them to pick up where they left off.

Questions of privilege fall into two general categories: questions of privilege affecting the assembly and questions of personal privilege, with priority given to those affecting the assembly. Let's look at each in turn.

Question of Privilege Affecting the Assembly

This version of the question is used when there is a problem affecting all or part of the assembly that needs immediate attention. It usually has to do with comfort issues (heating, lighting, ventilation, and so on). It can also refer to noise issues or other disturbances that prevent the members from hearing what is going on at the meeting.

Question of Personal Privilege

A question of personal privilege applies to a single member and is a rare occurrence in the parliamentary world. Keep in mind that it must be so urgent that it can interrupt a speaker or debate on the motion.

For example, during a meeting if a member receives notification that a child is sick at home and believes the child needs his or her immediate attention, that member may state: "Madam Chairman, I rise to a point of personal privilege." After recognition from the chair, the member would then request permission to be excused from the meeting.

Point of Information

Sometimes the issue before the assembly is so sensitive or private that it should be discussed only in front of members—for example, discipline of a member, or the review and pay of staff members.

While the motion is pending a member may rise to a question of privilege and move that we immediately go into executive session. If that motion passes, the nonmembers are asked to leave and the meeting proceeds.

It is important to remember that when meeting in executive session, everything that is discussed is confidential. Members may not share with anyone outside of the meeting what was discussed. If they do so, they may be subject to discipline.

Script: Question of Privilege

"Motion A" is pending

Member: I rise to a question of privilege.

Chair: State your question of privilege.

Member: [States Question of Privilege, e.g. noise preventing from hearing, temperature of room, etc.]

Chair: [Chair resolves the question, e.g. decreases the noise level, has room temperature changed, etc.]

     or

     [If not urgent] The chair rules that the question is not of such an urgent nature that it is one of privilege to be entertained immediately. [It might be helpful to add:] When there is no other business before us, you could raise that question again.

Chair: [After handling the question] The motion before you is "Motion A". Is there any further discussion?

Rules for a Question of Privilege:

- ◆ Can interrupt the speaker, if deemed appropriate to do so.
- ◆ Ruled by the chair.

Script: Question of Privilege Motion

"Motion A" is pending

Member: I rise to a question of privilege.

Chair: State your question of privilege.

Member: [States Question of Privilege]

Chair: [If the question is raised in the form of a motion and is urgent] The chair rules that the question is one of privilege and is to be entertained immediately.

Is there a second?

It is moved and seconded that _____

The question is on the adoption of the motion that _____
_____. This motion requires a majority vote.

All those in favor, say "Aye." [Pause for response]

All those opposed, say "No."

The affirmative has it, the motion is adopted, and _____
_____ (effect of the motion). [After processing the motion, the chair states: The motion before you is "Motion A". Is there any further discussion?]

or

The negative has it, the motion is lost and _____
_____ (effect of the motion). The motion before you is "Motion A". Is there any further discussion?

Rules for a Question of Privilege Motion:

♦ Can interrupt the speaker, if deemed appropriate to do so.

♦ Needs a second.

♦ Is not debatable on whether or not to admit the question. But once the motion has been made and is pending, it is debatable.

♦ Is amendable.

♦ Needs a majority vote.

Call for the Orders of the Day

The call for the orders of the day is used when the agenda or program is not being followed or if an item was set to be taken up at a certain time and that time has passed. This motion requires the presiding officer to follow the established agenda.

One Is Enough

It only takes one member to call for the orders of the day. It does not need a second and is not voted on. It is really more like a demand than a call.

When you think about the circumstances behind this motion, you understand why only one person is needed for the call. The agenda has been set and the presiding officer does not have the right to deviate from the agenda without permission of the membership. If the presiding officer is deviating from the agenda, it should not take a majority vote to get him or her back on the established track.

Must We?

Sometimes when a group is not following the established agenda, it isn't because the presiding officer is failing to keep them on track. Sometimes, it is because the group willingly went off track and wants to stay there. So what if that is the case and a member calls for the orders of the day? Well, the group can decide whether they want to go back to the agenda. Because that is a change from what the group had decided earlier in the agenda, it requires a two-thirds vote. After the call for the orders of the day a member may make a motion to extend the time for the issue that is on the floor. Or the presiding officer may sense the group does not want to move on and may put it to a vote. In either case, it will take a two-thirds vote.

What's Next?

What happens to the issue on the floor at the time that a member called for the orders of the day if the assembly decides to follow the set agenda? After the assembly has completed the orders of the day that were called up, the business that was interrupted by the call for the orders of the day is taken up right where it was interrupted.

If a member called for the orders of the day and the assembly voted to continue with the issue they were dealing with, that same member or any other member can not call for the orders of the day again until the current issue has been dealt with. Otherwise, it would be a delay tactic.

Script: Call for the Orders of the Day

"Motion A" is pending

Member: I call for the orders of the day. [May add what was scheduled to come before the assembly at this time.]

Chair: The orders of the day are called for.

[Proceed to what was scheduled for this time.]

or

Chair: It appears that the members wish to continue discussing the current issue and not call up the orders of the day. We will take a vote. The question before you is "Will the assembly proceed to the orders of the day?" This motion needs a two-thirds vote in the negative for us to continue with the current issue and not follow the agenda.

Those in favor of proceeding to the orders of the day will please stand. Be seated.

Those opposed to proceeding to the orders of the day will please stand. Be seated.

There are fewer than two thirds in the negative, the meeting will proceed to the orders of the day

or

There are two thirds in the negative and the motion to proceed to the orders of the day is lost. The motion before you is "Motion A".

Rules for a Call for the Orders of the Day:

◆ Can interrupt the speaker.

◆ If the orders are going to be followed, it takes only one member to make this motion and no vote is needed.

◆ If the group is going to deviate from the established agenda, a vote is needed. It takes two thirds in the negative to deviate from the established agenda.

The Least You Need to Know

- Privileged motions can be main or secondary motions depending on what's on the floor.

- Urgent matters can be processed urgently if done correctly.

- One person can get the meeting back on track!

Chapter 12

Subsidiary Motions

In This Chapter

- ◆ Setting aside a motion temporarily and permanently
- ◆ Limiting and extending limits on debate
- ◆ Referring issues to committees
- ◆ Amending amendments

Subsidiary motions aid the assembly in treating or disposing of a main motion. They are in order only from the time the main motion has been stated by the chair until the chair begins to take a vote on that main motion. These motions help you get the main motion into its best form before you have to vote on it.

You may want to change the main motion (amend it); or send it back to a committee to do more research on it (commit or refer); or put off the decision on it to the next meeting (postpone to a certain time); or you may just want to kill it (postpone indefinitely).

The Seven Subsidiary Motions

The seven following motions are in the class called subsidiary motions:

- **Lay on the table.** This motion places in the care of the secretary the pending question and everything adhering to it. If a group meets quarterly or more frequently, the question laid on the table remains there until taken off or until the end of the next regular session. This motion should not be used to kill a motion.

- **Previous question.** The effect of this motion is to immediately stop debate and any amendments and to move immediately to a vote on the motion. It must be seconded, no debate is allowed, and a two-thirds vote is needed to close debate.

- **Limit or extend limits of debate.** This motion can reduce or increase the number and length of speeches permitted or limit the length of debate on a specific question.

- **Postpone to a certain time** (also called the motion to postpone definitely). If the body needs more time to make a decision or if there is a time for consideration of this question that would be more convenient, this motion may be the answer. If a group meets quarterly or more frequently, the postponement cannot be beyond the next session.

- **Commit or refer.** This motion sends the main motion to a smaller group (a committee) for further examination and refinement before the body votes on it.

- **Amend.** This motion is used to modify the pending motion before it is voted on.

- **Postpone indefinitely.** This motion, in effect, kills the main motion for the duration of the session without the group having to take a vote on the motion.

Since this is not a rulebook (that's *Robert's* job), I will not be including all of the specific rules for each of the motions discussed. For the rules please refer to Appendix B §28 through §34.

Lay on the Table

The object of this motion is to allow the group to set aside the pending motion in order to attend to more urgent business. The pending motion is laid aside in such a way that the members can bring it back up at will, which is easier than introducing a new motion.

How long it stays on the table (set aside) depends on how often the group meets. If you meet at least one time a quarter (four times a year), the motion laid on the table remains there until taken off or until the end of the next regular session.

Abused and Confused

This motion clearly wins the award for the most overused and abused of all of the motions. All too often it is improperly used to kill a motion. It is also improperly used to postpone a motion to the next meeting.

It is frequently confused with and used in place of two other motions: postpone indefinitely and postpone to a certain time (definitely). The following table of the three motions should help clarify the proper use of the motions:

Motion	Debatable	Position on Ladder	Purpose
Lay on the table	No	6	Temporarily set aside
Postpone indefinitely	Yes	13	Kill
Postpone to a certain time	Yes	9	Put off to specific time

With this table in mind, let's look at why it matters when you confuse the motions.

Whereas the motion to lay on the table is frequently used to kill a motion, that is not its proper use—it is intended to be used to temporarily set aside a motion. If you want to kill a main motion, you should use the motion to postpone indefinitely. Why? Lay on the table is not debatable and is very high on the motion ladder. Therefore, you can't talk about it or amend it before you vote on it. Those are two things you would want to do before you killed an idea; if you don't, you run the risk of violating the rights of the members.

The motion to lay on the table is also frequently improperly used to put a motion off to the next meeting. If you want to table something to a time specified, the proper motion is to postpone to a certain time. The difference? Lay on the table is not debatable, is not amendable (so you can't set a time and date for when to address it again), it is high on the motion ladder, and when you do bring it back up, it needs a motion (the motion to take from the table) to accomplish that. Postpone to a certain time is debatable, is not as high on the motion ladder, and automatically comes up at the next meeting as an item of unfinished business.

So you see, using the appropriate motion protects the rights of the members, who should at least be allowed to discuss a motion before it is killed (postponed indefinitely).

Proper Use

Now that you have seen the improper use of the motion to lay on the table, what is its proper use? This motion is designed for unexpected urgent situations. It is also designed for setting something aside when you do not know when it will be time to bring it back again.

Point of Information

When a motion is laid on the table, all motions that are currently adhering to it go with it to the table and come back with it off the table. For example, the motion to purchase a computer was made, someone moved to amend that motion, and the amendment was being discussed at the time of the emergency. If the motion is tabled at that time, when it comes back from the table you have the motion to purchase a computer plus the amendment to deal with.

An Example Would Be Very Helpful About Now!

Your group is meeting at 6 tonight and has invited a guest to speak at 7. That gives you an hour to attend to your other business before the guest is scheduled to arrive. However, at 6:30, while the group is in the midst of debating a controversial motion, the guest speaker shows up—she's a half-hour early, and you haven't finished your business! Now what do you do? If you continue the discussion, you will have a heated debate in front of her, which isn't appropriate. But this is an issue that really needs to be addressed, and you don't know when the guest will leave so you are not sure whether you can continue the debate tonight or at the next meeting. This is a perfect time to use the motion to lay on the table. If, after her presentation, she leaves and you have time to complete the debate and vote, a member can move to take it from the table. If not, you can wait until the next meeting and take it from the table at that time.

Gavel Gaffs

The scripts in this chapter are only applicable when the subsidiary motion is a secondary motion. When it is a main motion (no other motion is on the floor) then you should use the script in Chapter 10, the script for a main motion.

How Do You Control This?

After the member moves to lay the motion on the table, the presiding officer should ask the member who made the motion "For what purpose does the member seek to lay the motion on the table?" If it is a proper use of the motion, the chair should then proceed to process it. If it is an improper use of the motion, the chair should rule the motion out of order. In addition, the chair should tell the member what motion to use to achieve the desired end. For example, if the member wants to kill the motion without actually taking a vote on it, the chair should guide him or her to make the motion to postpone indefinitely.

Script: Motion to Lay on the Table

"Motion A" is pending

Member: I move to lay the motion on the table.

Chair: For what purpose does the member seek to lay the motion on the table? [If it is a legitimate request, proceed. If not, the motion should be called out of order. If you call it out of order, try to tell the member how to do what they want to do.]

Chair: Is there a second to the motion? [This statement is eliminated if a member calls out "second."]

Second member: I second the motion.

Chair: It is moved and seconded to lay the question on the table. This is not a debatable motion.

    The question is on the adoption of the motion to lay "Motion A" on the table. This motion requires a majority vote.

    All those in favor, say "Aye." [Pause for response]

    All those opposed, say "No."

    The affirmative has it, the motion is adopted, "Motion A" is laid on the table.

    or

    The negative has it, the motion is lost and we will continue discussing "Motion A". Is there any further discussion?

Rules for the Motion to Lay on the Table:

◆ Needs a second.

◆ Is *not* debatable.

◆ Is *not* amendable.

◆ Needs a majority vote.

Previous Question

The previous question motion is used to stop debate on a motion and any subsidiary motions except the higher ranking motion to lay on the table. The motion must be seconded, no debate is allowed, and a two-thirds vote is needed. If the motion passes, it requires an immediate vote on the pending motion. The proper statement of this motion is "I move the previous question."

This is the second most overused and abused of all of the motions. It is abused by people who don't understand that it is a motion that needs a two-thirds vote. They try to call it out, as a command, and intimidate the presiding officer into stopping debate without a vote. It is also frequently called by other names, such as "close debate," "call for the question," "call the question," or "question." Whatever name it is called by it should be treated as a previous question motion.

> **CAUTION**
>
> **Gavel Gaffs** _____
>
> Usually someone with a Godlike voice, calls out from the back of the room "Question." Then, as if God came down and whispered "They can't talk about this anymore," in the presiding officer's ear, he or she jumps up and says, "The question has been called, we will now vote."
>
> It doesn't make sense that one person can tell the rest of us that we have to stop discussing an issue and move to the vote. That should be your cue that calling it out without a vote is not proper parliamentary procedure.

On This or All Pending Questions?

If there are multiple motions on the floor (pending), the previous question motion must be qualified. You must indicate when making this motion whether it is referring only to the motion that is immediately pending or to all of the pending motions. However, the previous question motion must always include the immediately pending motion. Let's say that there are four motions on the floor as follows:

1. Main motion: I move we purchase a computer.

2. Primary amendment: I move that we amend the motion by adding "not to exceed $2,000."

3. Secondary amendment: I move to amend the amendment by striking "$2,000" and inserting "$4,000."

4. Refer to committee: I move to refer this motion to the finance committee.

While the group is discussing the motion to refer to a committee (#4) someone could "move the previous question" (which would only apply to #4) or he or she could "move the previous question on this and all pending questions" (which would apply to all four pending motions). If the previous question motion applies to all four motions and passes, the presiding officer would first call for a vote on #4, refer to a committee. If that motion fails, then, immediately, with no further discussion, the vote would be taken on #3, then #2, then #1. If the vote on #4, refer to a committee, passes, the discussion stops and the motion, along with the two amendments, is referred to the committee. After the committee has considered it, it comes back to the meeting, with the primary and secondary amendment still in place, waiting to be voted on.

In this example, the previous question motion could have been made to apply to the motion to refer to a committee and the two amendments without having included the main motion. If that had happened, the vote would be taken on #4. If that motion failed, then, immediately, with no further discussion, the vote would be taken on #3, and #2. Because the previous question motion didn't apply to the main motion, discussion would be allowed before a vote is taken on it.

Script: Previous Question

"Motion A" is pending

Member: I move the previous question [or "I move that we close debate," or simply "Question."

Chair: Is there a second?

Second member: I second the motion.

Chair: The previous question is moved and seconded on "Motion A". This is not a debatable motion. It takes a two-thirds vote. The effect of the passage of this motion is that we would immediately stop debate and vote on the motion. If you want to close debate, vote in favor of the motion; if you want debate to continue, vote against the motion.

    All those in favor of the previous question (closing debate), please raise your hand. [Pause] Please lower your hand. Those opposed to the motion, please raise your hand. [Pause] Please lower your hand.

    If two-thirds vote in favor of the motion:

    The affirmative has it, the motion is carried, and the previous question has been ordered. We will now move to the vote on "Motion A".

continues

continued

or

The negative has it, the motion is lost, and the previous question has not been ordered. We will continue to discuss the motion "Motion A".

Rules for the Previous Question Motion:

◆ Needs a second.

◆ Is *not* debatable.

◆ Is *not* amendable.

◆ Needs a two-thirds vote.

Unique form: I move the previous question on this and all pending motions.

Effect: Go immediately to the vote on this motion, and then immediately to the vote on the each of the pending motions.

Limit or Extend Limits of Debate

This motion can reduce or increase the number and length of speeches permitted or limit the length of debate on a specific motion. *Robert's* gives each member the right to speak twice on any one motion on any one day and each of those speeches can be 10 minutes long. Sometimes, however, it is determined that members need more or less time to debate an issue, and that's when the motion to limit or extend limits of debate comes in handy.

This motion can apply to the total amount of time that the group spends on any one motion, to the amount of time of each speech on the motion, or to both.

Parliamentary Pearls _____

Some possible forms of this motion:

◆ I move that the debate on the pending motion be limited to 20 minutes.

◆ I move that debate on the pending motion be closed and we proceed to the vote at 8 P.M.

◆ I move that each speaker on this motion be limited to five minutes per speech.

The Limit on the Limit

This motion is only applied to the limit on debate of the pending motions and subsequent subsidiary motions, unless it is specified otherwise. It also is only applicable to the session in which it was adopted.

Script: Motion to Limit or Extend the Limit of Debate

"Motion A" is pending

Member: I move to [specifically state how to limit or extend the limit of debate. For example, limit debate to a total of 30 minutes on this main motion. Limit debate to two minutes per speaker. Extend the limit on debate by 20 minutes.]

Chair: Is there a second to the motion? [This statement is eliminated if a member calls out "second."]

Second member: I second the motion.

Chair: It is moved and seconded that we [specifically state how the motion was stated to limit or extend the limit on debate.] This is not a debatable motion. Are you ready for the question? [Pause]

The question is on the adoption of the motion that we [state specifically]. This motion requires a two-thirds vote.

Chair: All those in favor of the motion, please raise your hand. [Pause] Please lower your hand. Those opposed to the motion, please raise your hand. [Pause] Please lower your hand.

The affirmative has it, the motion is adopted, we will have the following limits on debate: _____ The motion before you is "Motion A". Is there any further discussion?

or

The negative has it, the motion is lost and we will not have additional limits on debate. The motion before you is "Motion A". Is there any further discussion?

---

continues

continued

Rules for the Motion to Limit or Extend the Limit of Debate:

♦ Needs a second.

♦ Is *not* debatable.

♦ Is amendable, but the amendment is not debatable.

♦ Needs a two-thirds vote.

Postpone to a Certain Time (Postpone Definitely)

Sometimes you just don't have the information you need to make a decision, you are not ready to make that decision for other reasons, or the right people are not present for this decision to be made. Under any of those circumstances, this motion, to postpone to a certain time, is for you.

Postponed to When?

For groups that meet at least quarterly, the postponement is limited to the remainder of the current session and up until the close of the next regularly scheduled session. That would include a special meeting called before the next regular meeting. If there is more than a quarterly time interval between your meetings (e.g. annual convention), you can only postpone it until sometime before the end of the current session.

> **Point of Information**
>
> When a motion has been postponed to the next meeting, it automatically comes up under Unfinished Business at the next meeting.

Once you have postponed something to a certain time, you cannot take it up before that time unless you reconsider the motion to postpone it or suspend the rules to allow for it to be taken up earlier.

Don't Try to Make It Something It Isn't!

Just as with the motion to lay on the table, you cannot move to postpone something to a time that would in effect kill it, thus really making the motion to postpone in definitely.

For example, your organization has been asked to send a representative to a special function on March 15. The current meeting is on March 3, and your next meeting isn't until March 17. At the current meeting it would be out of order to postpone the motion to the next meeting. The motion would be out of order because the next meeting is after the function, and so by postponing it until that time it would have the effect of killing it. If you really want to kill it, then you need to make the motion to postpone indefinitely.

Postpone Ahead of Time?

If a matter is prescribed in the bylaws to occur at a certain meeting (e.g. election of officers at the November meeting) you cannot, in advance, postpone it to a later time. But when the time arrives, you can then move to postpone it. To meet the bylaws requirement you would have to set up a meeting that would continue the current meeting and then postpone it to that meeting.

Script: Motion to Postpone to a Certain Time

"Motion A" is pending

Member: I move to postpone this motion to [state another time, such as "our next regular meeting"].

Chair: Is there a second to the motion? [This statement is eliminated if a member calls out "second."]

Second member: I second the motion.

Chair: It is moved and seconded that we postpone this motion to [state when]. Is there any discussion?

[After discussion]

Are you ready for the question? [Pause]

The question is on the adoption of the motion that we postpone this motion to [state when]. This motion requires a majority vote.

All those in favor, say "Aye." [Pause for response]

All those opposed, say "No." The affirmative has it, the motion is adopted, we will postpone this motion to [state when]. At that meeting it will come back automatically under Unfinished Business. The next business in order is …

continues

---

continued

> *or*
>
> The negative has it, the motion is lost, and we will not postpone Motion A. The motion before you is "Motion A". Is there any further discussion?

Rules for the Motion to Postpone to a Certain Time:

- ◆ Needs a second.
- ◆ Is debatable.
- ◆ Is amendable.
- ◆ Needs a majority vote.

Commit or Refer

This motion sends the main motion to a smaller group (a committee) for further examination and refinement before the body votes on it. Be sure to be specific, i.e. what committee, the size of the committee, and so on.

This motion can have as much or as little detail as you choose. You can simply refer the motion to a committee. Or the motion can tell what committee, when they will report, and what their authority is. Whenever any these details are added, that part of the motion is amendable.

Parliamentary Pearls

A special committee automatically ceases to exist when the committee gives its final report. If the group wants to have the committee cease to exist before that or take back something they have referred to a committee, it is done by a motion to discharge a committee. The committee is discharged from further consideration of the issue referred to it.

Check the Bylaws

You can't just put any detail you want into the motion to refer. You should first check out the bylaws to see if you can do what you want to do. For instance, you can't refer something to a special committee if a standing committee is already authorized to take care of issues in that class. If you have a bylaws committee and there is a bylaws amendment on the floor, it is out of order to move to refer the motion to a special committee formed for this purpose. The referral must be to the bylaws committee. Another example: In the motion you name who should be on the committee. If the bylaws indicate that the president appoints all committees, you can't appoint the committee in the motion to refer, because that would be a violation of the bylaws.

I highly recommend the inclusion of a report due date in the motion to refer. In a longer project, it might even be a date for an initial report. Most of us work better when we have a deadline date, and committees are no different.

Script: Motion to Commit or Refer

"Motion A" is pending

Member:	I move to refer "Motion A" to the _____ committee. [Can specify details like date the committee is to report back. If it is to be referred to a special committee, you can tell size of committee and give direction as to makeup of committee.]
Chair:	Is there a second to the motion? [This statement is eliminated if a member calls out "second."]
Second member:	I second the motion.
Chair:	It is moved and seconded to refer "Motion A" to the _____ committee. [Pause]
	Is there any discussion?
	[After discussion] The question is on the adoption of the motion that we refer "Motion A" to the _____ committee. Are you ready for the question? This motion requires a majority vote.
	All those in favor, say "Aye." [Pause for response]
adopted,	All those opposed, say "No." The affirmative has it, the motion is "Motion A" is referred to the _____ committee.
	or
	The negative has it, the motion is lost and "Motion A" is not referred to the _____ committee. The motion before you is "Motion A". Is there any further discussion?

continues

continued

Rules for the Motion to Commit or Refer:

◆ Needs a second.

◆ Is debatable.

◆ Is amendable.

◆ Needs a majority vote.

Amend

This motion is the embodiment of the democratic process. If a motion is made and it is not acceptable as is, the amendment process gives the group the opportunity to fix it in a way that at least a majority can live with it. True democracy! The intent of this motion is to modify the pending motion before it is voted on. In other words, amendment is the continuous improvement process at work.

There are many rules applicable to amendment. I am not going to try to duplicate them here, so if you need the specifics go to Appendix B §33.

Be Specific

An amendment to a motion can take three forms, as follows:

◆ **Insert or add.** This involves inserting or adding words or paragraphs.

◆ **Strike out.** This involves cutting words or paragraphs.

◆ **Strike and insert.** This involves substituting a word, paragraph, or the entire text with new text.

The maker of the motion should specify in the amendment the format it should take (insert, strike out, strike and insert) and the location of the amendment, such as "I move to insert the words 'PC compatible' before the word 'computer'."

Germane

We have all heard examples of bills that passed in Congress where something totally unrelated (and sometimes very stupid) was added to the bill as an amendment. When the bill passed, so did the amendment. The good news is that this cannot happen when you are following *Robert's* because *Robert's* says that an amendment must be *germane*, which means that it must relate to the subject of the motion it is amending. You cannot introduce a new, independent issue as an amendment. Makes sense to me!

Germane, But It Doesn't Have to Agree

Although the amendment must be germane, it does not have to maintain the intent of the motion it is amending. It can even contradict the motion it is amending. The classic example used by *Robert's* himself helps to clarify this:

> The motion on the floor: "I move that we censure our president."

> Amendment: I move to amend the motion by striking the word "censure" and inserting the word "thank" so that the motion will read "I move that we thank our president."

That motion to amend is germane and is also allowed because it is the members who own this motion, and it is totally within their rights to change the intent of the original motion. (See Chapter 5 for more on ownership of a motion.)

Robert's Says

Germane means related to the subject. An amendment must be germane to the motion it is amending. A secondary amendment must be germane to the primary amendment it is amending.

Limited Number

To avoid confusion, there is a limit on the number of amendments that can be pending. There can be only one main motion, one primary amendment, and one secondary amendment pending at a time. The primary amendment amends the pending motion. The secondary amendment can only amend the primary amendment.

Some people refer to the primary amendment as an amendment to the first degree and the secondary amendment as an amendment to the second degree.

Remember that after a primary amendment has been voted on, if it passed, it becomes a part of the motion it was amending. At that point a new primary amendment could be offered. The same is true for a secondary amendment.

Vote Needed

To amend a motion you must have a majority vote. This is true even if the motion it is amending takes a two-thirds vote. For example, the main motion on the floor is to amend the

Gavel Gaffs

Not all motions can be amended. For a list of motions that cannot be amended refer to Appendix B, §33.

bylaws by changing the dues from $10 to $15. If you amended the motion by striking $15 and inserting $12, the amendment to change the proposed dues increase from $15 to $12 would only take a majority vote. If your amendment passed, the bylaw amendment to raise the dues from $10 to $12 would take a two-thirds vote.

Script: Motion to Amend

"Motion A" is pending

Member:	I move to amend "Motion A" by [inserting; striking out; striking out and inserting; or substituting] as follows _____
Chair:	Is there a second to the motion? [This statement is eliminated if a member calls out "second."]
Second member:	I second the motion.
Chair:	It is moved and seconded that we amend "Motion A" by [inserting; striking out; striking out and inserting] as follows _____. If the amendment is adopted the main motion would then read _____ _____

Is there any discussion?

[After discussion] Are you ready for the question? [Pause]

The question is on the adoption of the motion that we amend "Motion A" by [inserting; striking out; striking out and inserting; or substituting] as follows _____. If the amendment is adopted, the main motion would then read _____

All those in favor, say "Aye." [Pause for response]

All those opposed, say "No."

The affirmative has it, the "Motion A" is amended and now reads _____. Is there any discussion on "Motion A" as amended?

or

The negative has it, the motion is lost and "Motion A" is not amended. The motion before you is "Motion A". Is there any further discussion?

Rules for the Motion to Amend:

◆ Needs a second.

◆ Is debatable.

◆ Is amendable.

◆ Needs a majority vote.

Postpone Indefinitely

A motion is made, and you don't think it is a good idea for this particular group. If the group votes it down, however, it will make the organization look bad. You just wish you could make it go away without having to vote on it …

Your wish is *Robert's* command! The motion you want is the motion to postpone indefinitely. As noted earlier in this chapter, this motion, in effect, kills the main motion for the duration of the session without having to take a vote on it. It helps you reject an ill-advised motion without risking the embarrassment of passing it or failing it.

Debate Rules

The rules of debate on this motion are very lenient. The rules allow you to debate the motion to postpone indefinitely as well as the main motion it applies to.

Using the Motion to Postpone Indefinitely as a Straw Vote

In addition to using the motion to postpone indefinitely to kill an ill-advised motion, members opposed to the main motion can use it as a straw vote to find out whether they have a majority. If the motion to postpone indefinitely passes, they have succeeded at killing the

Parliamentary Pearls

The liberal debate rules for the motion to postpone indefinitely can be used to the advantage of a member who has already spoken his or her two times on the main motion but wants to speak again. He or she can make the motion to postpone indefinitely and, while speaking on the motion to postpone indefinitely, speak on the main motion as well. Pretty clever!

motion. If it fails, the opponents to the motion still have the vote on the main motion and they can rethink their strategy.

Exception to Ladder

In Chapter 7, we learned about the motion ladder. At that time, I mentioned that there is one exception to the motion ladder. This motion is it. If the motion to postpone indefinitely passes, you do not take the final step down the ladder. You do not vote on the main motion.

Script: Motion to Postpone Indefinitely

"Motion A" is pending

Member: I move to postpone "Motion A" indefinitely.

Chair: Is there a second? [This statement is eliminated if a member calls out "second."]

Second member: I second the motion.

Chair: It is moved and seconded to postpone indefinitely "Motion A". The effect of the motion to postpone indefinitely is to kill the motion. Postpone indefinitely is used to allow the assembly to not take a position on a motion, without having to vote down the motion.

Chair: The question is: Shall "Motion A" be postponed indefinitely? Is there any discussion?

[After discussion] Are you ready for the question? [Pause] The question is: Shall "Motion A" be postponed indefinitely?

All those in favor, say "Aye." [Pause for response]

All those opposed, say "No."

The affirmative has it, and the motion has been postponed indefinitely. The next business in order is _____.

or

The negative has it, and the motion has not been postponed indefinitely, and we will continue discussion of "Motion A".

Rules for the Motion to Postpone Indefinitely:

◆ Needs a second.

◆ Is debatable.

◆ Is *not* amendable.

◆ Needs a majority vote.

The Least You Need to Know

◆ Subsidiary motions are made when a main motion is already on the floor.

◆ The motion to lay on the table is like 911—use it only for emergencies!

◆ Be sure to check your bylaws before you refer a motion to a committee.

◆ You can use the motion to postpone indefinitely to kill a motion without voting on it.

Chapter 13

Incidental Motions

In This Chapter

- ◆ Keeping all members in line
- ◆ Asking questions about procedure and the issues
- ◆ Appealing the chair's decisions
- ◆ Making sure the vote count is accurate

The class of motions called incidental motions usually relate to matters of the business meeting rather than directly to the main motion. They may be offered at any time when they are needed.

All incidental motions are secondary motions, meaning that they are made when a main motion is already on the floor. Some of these motions, such as suspend the rules or point of order, can be made while nothing is pending; in those situations they are called incidental main motions.

Six Incidental Motions

The following motions are in the class called incidental motions:

- ◆ **Point of order.** If a member feels the rules are not being followed, he or she can use this motion. It requires the chair to make a ruling and enforce the rules.

- **Appeal from the decision of the chair (appeal).** A motion to take a decision regarding parliamentary procedure out of the hands of the presiding officer and place the final decision in the hands of the assembly.

- **Object to the consideration of a question.** The purpose of this motion is to prevent the assembly from considering the question/motion because a member deems the question as irrelevant, unprofitable, or contentious.

- **Suspend the rules.** This motion is used when the assembly wants to do something that violates its own rules. This motion does not apply to the organization's bylaws; local, state, or national law; or fundamental principles of parliamentary law.

- **Division of the assembly.** The effect of this motion is to require a standing vote (not a counted vote). A single member can demand this if he or she feels the vote is too close to declare or unrepresentative. This motion can only be used after a voice vote or hand vote.

- **Division of the question.** This motion is used to separate a main motion or amendment into parts to be voted on individually. It can only be used if each part can stand as a separate question.

Parliamentary Pearls

Because leadership should be shared by all members in attendance at a meeting, it is every member's right and responsibility to call a point of order if the presiding officer fails to do so.

This is not an exhaustive list, and other incidental motions exist that relate to methods of voting and to nominations, but we will only cover these more commonly used motions in this chapter.

Since this is not a rulebook (that's *Robert's* job), I will not be including all of the specific rules for each of the motions discussed. For the rules please refer to Appendix B, §21 through §27.

Point of Order

If something inappropriate happens in a meeting, such as a member stooping to name-calling during a heated debate, it's the presiding officer's responsibility to call the member to order. Or if a motion is worded in a way that makes it a violation of your bylaws, the presiding officer should call the motion out of order. However, if the presiding officer fails to call the member to order or fails to call an action out of order, any other member may call a point of order. Because it might be too late if you wait until the person is finished speaking, if the point needs to be made right away, it can even interrupt the speaker.

Use Point of Order to Disagree with the Chair

Point of order isn't just used when members are not following proper decorum. Members can also use it when they disagree with the presiding officer's decision. For example, let's say that the motion on the floor is to purchase a computer. A member moves to amend the motion to add "and carpet the office." The chair allows the amendment, but you believe that it is out of order because the carpet for the office and the computer are really two different issues and therefore, the amendment is not germane to the computer motion (for more on amendments and the requirement that they be germane, see Chapter 12). You could then call a point of order and state your point; if the chair agrees with you, the amendment would be ruled out of order. If the chair does not agree with you, the amendment would be allowed.

> **Parliamentary Pearls**
>
> Point of order and the next motion I'll discuss, appeal, are closely related. If members do not agree with the ruling of the chair on a point of order, the members can appeal from the decision of the chair. An appeal is the democratic method of having the decision of the chair overturned. But we are getting ahead of ourselves here. Appeal is the next motion we will discuss. Back to point of order!

What Does Point of Order Require?

So a member calls out "point of order" if they disagree with something or believe that another member is acting improperly. What next? First, the presiding officer asks the person to state his or her point. Then, after the member makes the point, the presiding officer must rule on it. If the group agrees with the ruling, it is carried out and the issue is over.

Turning the Ruling Over to the Assembly

But what if the presiding officer isn't sure how to rule? Let's say that it's a tough call, and the chair isn't sure what to do. Instead of making a decision and then having it appealed, the presiding officer can turn the decision over to the members—now there's a democratic process in action!

Here's how it would work: Let's return to the motion to purchase a computer— "I move that we purchase a computer"—which now has been amended by adding "and a printer." A member calls "point of order." The chair asks the member to state his or her point, and the member says that "the amendment to add 'and a printer' is not germane to the motion 'I move that we purchase a computer.'" The chair can't decide whether it is germane or not. Instead of ruling one way or the other (and probably having an appeal no matter which way the chair rules) the chair decides to put the question to the members for a decision.

Here is how it might sound. The presiding officer: "A member has raised a point of order that the amendment to add 'and a printer' is not germane to the motion. The chair is in doubt, and submits the question to the assembly. The question before you is 'Is the amendment germane?'"

Parliamentary Pearls

When ruling on a point of order …

- ◆ Use a soft voice.
- ◆ Make your concern for fairness apparent.
- ◆ Take the time to think about how to handle issues.
- ◆ Call for a consultation with parliamentarian, if there is one.

This is debatable, since if an appeal was filed it would be debatable. Therefore, debate occurs, and at the end of the debate the presiding officer puts the question to a vote. "Those who are of the opinion that the amendment is germane and should be allowed, say 'aye,' those who believe the amendment is not germane and should be ruled out of order, say 'no.'"

No matter which way the vote goes, no appeal is allowed when the decision has been made by the assembly. That's because the appeal from the decision of the chair applies only when the chair makes the decision and, in this instance, the chair turned the decision over to the membership.

Do It Now, Because Later Is Too Late!

If something is so inappropriate that it is out of order, it should be clear that it is out of order when it occurs or immediately after it occurs. Therefore, you must call a point of order at the time the violation occurs, not later. In other words, you don't get a chance to think about it and mull it over.

The only exception to the rule that the point of order must be called immediately is if the breach is of an ongoing nature, such as a breach of the governing documents. In such cases, a point of order can be raised at a later time. For example, if your bylaws indicate that the finance committee will have three members and the current finance committee has five people, that is an ongoing breach and can be brought up at any time.

Script: Point of Order

Member: Point of order!

Chair: The chair recognizes _____. State your point of order.

Member: [States point of order]

Chair: If the chair agrees with the point of order:

The chair rules that the point is well taken. The reason for the chair's ruling is that ... [state here your reason for the ruling and the effect of the ruling.]

or, if the chair disagrees with the point of order:

The chair rules that the point is not well taken. The reason for the chair's ruling is that ... [state here your reason for the ruling and the effect of the ruling.]

[If you choose, you can end your ruling with a reminder that if the member does not agree with the ruling of the chair that member is free to make the motion to appeal from the decision of the chair.]

Rules for Point of Order:

◆ Does not need a second.

◆ May interrupt the speaker.

◆ Is *not* debatable.

◆ Is *not* amendable.

◆ Ruled by the chair.

Appeal from the Decision of the Chair (Appeal)

This is one of my favorite motions because it serves as a reminder to everyone that parliamentary procedure is all about a democracy. If the presiding officer ever gets big-headed and thinks he or she decides it all, this motion quickly puts that person in his or her place!

Earlier I mentioned that the motion to appeal from the decision of the chair—or the appeal, as it's frequently called—is closely related to point of order. That's because

Gavel Gaffs

When you use the motion to appeal, remember it is not the presiding officer that you are appealing, it is the *decision* of the presiding officer that you are disagreeing with. Keep the focus of parliamentary procedure on the issue, not the person!

after the member makes a point of order, the presiding officer is required to rule on that point of order. If a member disagrees with that ruling, he or she can appeal the decision of the chair.

Do It Now, Because Later Is Too Late!

Just as with the point of order, the appeal must be made immediately. If you disagree with the decision of the chair, you must appeal it at the time of the occurrence.

Doing It

The appeal may interrupt the speaker, and it may be made on any decision made by the chair. The only exception (you knew there had to be one) is when another appeal is pending. Only decisions may be appealed—if the presiding officer gives information, that is not a decision, and the information cannot be appealed.

Script: Motion to Appeal from the Decision of the Chair

Member: I appeal from the decision of the chair.

Chair: Is there a second to the motion? [This statement is eliminated if a member calls out "second."]

Second
member: I second the motion.

Chair: It is moved and seconded to appeal the decision of the chair that …

The question is: Shall the decision of the chair be sustained? The debate rules on this motion are a little different, let the chair explain. First, the chair has the opportunity to explain the decision of the chair that is being appealed. Then members may speak, but each member is limited to one chance to speak on this motion, not two. Then, at the end of discussion, the chair is again allowed to explain. Then the motion will be put to a vote.

The reason for the chair's decision is that …

Is there any discussion? [Pause]

We will now vote on the motion to appeal from the decision of the chair. This motion needs a majority vote.

Chair: All those in favor of sustaining the chair's decision, please say "Aye." [Pause] All those opposed to sustaining this decision, say "No." [Tie vote sustains the decision of the chair.]

The affirmative has it. The motion to sustain the decision of the chair passes. You have agreed with the decision of the chair and that decision will now go into effect.

or

The negative has it. The motion to sustain the decision of the chair fails. You have not agreed with the decision of the chair and that decision has been overturned. We will now continue with …

Rules for the Motion to Appeal from the Decision of the Chair:

◆ Needs a second.

◆ Is debatable unless it is made when the immediately pending question (motion) is undebatable. In debate, no member is allowed to speak more than one time, except the presiding officer who may speak two times and does not need to vacate the chair when speaking.

◆ Is amendable.

◆ Needs a majority vote in the negative to reverse the decision of the chair. Therefore, a tie vote sustains the decision of the chair.

Objection to the Consideration of a Question

The motion to object to the consideration of a question is rarely used. Okay, I'll confess: The only time I have ever seen it properly used was at a convention of parliamentarians! Part of the reason is that it has so many stringent requirements on it.

The purpose of this motion is to prevent the assembly from considering the question/motion because a member deems the question as irrelevant, unprofitable, or contentious. It is appropriate to use this motion if the member judges the motion to be outside of the object of the organization and the presiding officer has not ruled the motion out of order.

This is one of the few places where the distinction between original and incidental main motions (see Chapter 5) matters. An objection to the consideration of the question can only be made on an original main motion, it can not be made on an incidental main motion, such as an amendment to the bylaws or a motion to ratify a previous action.

No Daydreaming Here

Not only do you have to be awake enough to know whether the motion is an original main motion or an incidental main motion, but you have to be quick enough to realize that you object to it before anyone discusses it. This motion must be made before there is any debate on the motion and before any subsidiary motion on it is stated by the chair. I wasn't kidding when I said you couldn't daydream! The objection must be made right away because if the question is so objectionable, it should be obvious that it is objectionable when it is made, and the members should not need time to think it over.

Vote Needed

If at least two thirds of the group does not judge the motion to be objectionable, the assembly can consider the motion. Therefore, the chair should put the motion to object to consideration of the question to a vote with the question "Shall the question be considered?" It takes two thirds in the negative to have the objection to consideration pass.

Script: Objection to the Consideration of a Question

"Motion A" is pending

Member: I object to the consideration of the question. [Note: this motion must be made before there has been any debate on the motion, and before the chair has restated any secondary motions applying to the motion.]

Chair: The consideration of the question is objected to. Should the question be considered?

    This motion is not debatable or amendable and needs a two-thirds vote in the negative. The effect of this motion is to prevent the consideration of this motion during this session.

All those in favor of considering the question, please raise your hand. [Pause] Please lower your hand. Those opposed to considering the question, please raise your hand. [Pause] Please lower your hand.

[Two-thirds vote in the negative is needed to object to consideration of the question.]

There are two thirds in the negative and the question will not be considered. The next item of business is …

or

There are fewer than two thirds in the negative and the objection is not sustained. The motion before you is "Motion A." Is there any discussion?

Rules for Objection to the Consideration of a Question:

♦ This motion must be made before there has been any debate on the motion, and before the chair has restated any secondary motions applying to the motion.

♦ Does not need a second.

♦ Is *not* debatable.

♦ Is *not* amendable.

♦ Needs a two-thirds vote in the negative to prevent consideration.

Suspend the Rules

The motion to suspend the rules is used when the group wishes to do something that cannot be done without violating its own rules. But even with this motion, the group cannot violate its constitution, bylaws, or fundamental principles of parliamentary law.

When you make this motion, you should include the object of the suspension. For example, some of your friends have to leave the meeting and you want "Motion Q" voted on before they go. But, "Motion Q" is not on the agenda until much later in the meeting. You might say "I move that we suspend the rules so that we can consider 'Motion Q' at this time." If the motion passes, the group will take "Motion Q" up now instead of later in the agenda.

Gavel Gaffs _____

When you make the motion to suspend the rules, you don't necessarily have to tell the exact rule you are suspending, but you do have to tell the object of the suspension. You can't simply say "I move to suspend the rules" and then ignore all of the rules and do whatever you want, having a free for all.

Rules That Cannot Be Suspended

Robert's makes some very specific requirements regarding what can be suspended and what cannot be suspended. Remember that the constitution and bylaws of the organization are meant to be the rules that cannot be changed at the whim of the group attending one meeting. As a result, the constitution and bylaws cannot be suspended. The only exception to that rule is if the constitution or bylaws include a rule allowing for their own suspension.

Other rules that cannot be suspended are the fundamental principles of parliamentary law—in other words, rules that protect the basic rights of the individual member, deal with voting rights, and so on. For example, rules that protect absentee members are not suspendable. If the rules require previous notice, the members in attendance at the meeting cannot suspend that rule and consider the motion without previous notice.

Rules That Can Be Suspended

Rules that relate to business procedures and to priority of business can be suspended. In addition, rules that are in your standing rules or policies and procedures can be suspended.

Vote Needed

Here is where this motion gets a little confusing. I would like to tell you the vote is always a majority or always two thirds, but I can't. The kind of vote you need depends on the kind of rule that you are suspending.

If the rule is in the nature of a parliamentary rule of order, a two-thirds vote is required. So a motion to suspend the rules and not allow debate on the motion would require a two-thirds vote.

If the rule is in the nature of guidelines relating to the way your organization carries out its business, a majority vote is all that is required. These include things like the hour the meeting begins, the order of business, and so on. Most of the rules that are contained in the organization's standing rules (see Chapter 4) need a majority vote to suspend.

Parliamentary Pearls _____

Instead of treating the suspend the rules motion as a formal motion that needs to be voted on, consider handling it by general consent. In most cases, there is no objection to suspend the rules. When that is the case, instead of processing it, the presiding officer should say "Is there any objection to suspending the rules and taking up 'Motion Q' at this time?" Pause. "Hearing no objection, we will now proceed to 'Motion Q.'"

Script: Motion to Suspend the Rules

Member: I move to suspend the rules [Indicate which rule you want to suspend or what you want to do that the rules interfere with]

Chair: Is there a second to the motion? [This statement is eliminated if a member calls out "second" or if the motion is made on behalf of a committee.]

Second
member: I second the motion.

Chair: It is moved and seconded to suspend the rules for the purpose of ...

Chair: This is not a debatable motion. The question is on the adoption of the motion to suspend the rules for the purpose of ...

[Needs a two-thirds vote or majority vote, according to the rule suspended]

Chair: All those in favor of the motion, please raise your hand. [Pause] Please lower your hand. Those opposed to the motion, please raise your hand. [Pause] Please lower your hand.

The affirmative has it, the motion is adopted, we will suspend the rules for the purpose of ...

or

continues

continued

The negative has it, the motion is lost and we will not suspend the rules for the purpose of …

Rules for the Motion to Suspend the Rules:

- Needs a second.

- Is *not* debatable.

- Is *not* amendable.

- May be made while another motion is pending, as long as it applies to that motion.

- Vote needed: If the rule is in the nature of a parliamentary rule of order, a two-thirds vote is required. If the rule is in the nature of guidelines relating to the way the organization carries out its business, a majority vote is required.

Division

There are two division motions. One is division of the assembly and the other is division of the question. Just as the two names indicate, the division of the assembly "divides" the members who are voting (by having members voting one way stand and members voting the other way remain seated) and the division of the question divides the motion. We will examine them separately.

Division of the Assembly

Imagine that you are sitting in a meeting and a vote is conducted. The presiding officer says "All those in favor, say 'aye'; all those opposed, say 'no'. The 'ayes' have it and the motion passes." You are sitting there thinking, "No way do the 'ayes' have it, they just have bigger mouths and louder voices!" In that situation, this is the motion for you! All you have to do is call out "division" and your problem is solved.

This motion requires the presiding officer to conduct the vote again, and this time by a standing vote. It does not have to be a counted standing vote because in large conventions/meetings, a vote can take hours to count and that would possibly be only a delay tactic.

This motion has a lot of unusual rules: It can only be called on a voice vote or a show of hands, and no other kind of vote. It only takes one person to call it out, it does not require a second, it cannot be debated, it is not amendable, and it can have no other subsidiary motions applied to it. It does not require a vote, because one person calling out "division" is enough to require a standing vote. It's based on the idea that if one person is unclear on the outcome of the vote, that is enough!

Like most of the other motions in this chapter, the window of opportunity for using this motion is very small. It can only be called after the vote is taken and before another motion has been stated. Also, it is applicable only to a voice vote or a show of hands. It is not applicable to any other kind of vote, even though people try to use it that way.

Robert's Says

Division of the assembly—The effect of this motion is to require a standing vote (not a counted vote). A single member can demand this if he or she feels the vote is too close to declare or unrepresentative. This motion can only be used after the voice vote or hand vote is too close to declare.

Division of the question—This motion is used to separate a main motion or amendment into parts to be voted on individually. It can only be used if each part can stand as a separate question.

Division of the Question

Sometimes, for the sake of speed, one motion includes multiple ideas. For example a committee recommends that we buy the outgoing president a gavel and the outgoing treasurer a calculator. If you agree with both, it works beautifully to offer them both in one motion. However, if you only like the idea of a gavel for the president and think it is a stupid idea to buy a calculator for the treasurer, you can use the division of the question motion to split them up.

The question under consideration must be dividable, so be sure to give it some thought before moving to have it divided. For example if the motion under consideration is that we "purchase a computer and a printer" and we currently own neither, the motion is not dividable. Even though a computer without a printer is useful, a printer without a computer would be of absolutely no use. If you want the computer without the printer, then you should use the motion to amend and move to strike "and a printer".

To divide the motion a member should say "I move to divide the question" and then state exactly how he or she wants it divided. This motion takes a majority vote, but is usually handled by general consent. Once the question is divided, each part is treated as separate motions, with discussion on each followed by the vote on each.

Script: Division of the Assembly

Right after a voice vote or a vote by show of hands

Member: Division.

Chair: A division is called for; a standing vote will now be taken. The question is on the adoption of the motion to _____

Those in favor of the motion, please stand. [Pause] Please be seated. Those opposed to the motion, please stand. [Pause] Please be seated.

The affirmative has it, the motion is adopted, we will [state the effect of the vote] and the next business in order is …

or

The negative has it, the motion is lost and [state the effect of the motion].

Rules for the Division of the Assembly:

◆ Does not need a second.

◆ Is *not* debatable.

◆ Is *not* amendable.

◆ Required on the demand of one member.

Script: Division of the Question

While a motion is pending that has three separate recommendations.

Member: I move that the motion be divided and we consider each of the three recommendations separately.

Chair: It is moved that we divide the question and consider each of the three recommendations separately. Is there any objection to dividing the question? [pause] Hearing no objection, we will divide the question. The motion before you at this time is Recommendation 1. Is there any discussion on Recommendation 1?

Rules for the Division of the Question:

♦ If there is an objection, it must be processed as a motion.

♦ Needs a second.

♦ Is *not* debatable.

♦ Only amendable as to how the motion is divided.

♦ Needs a majority vote.

♦ If the question is divided, each section is treated as a separate motion that has already been made. So you discuss one, vote on it, and then go to the next one.

Requests and Inquiries

Many motions fit into the category of "requests and inquiries." However, you are likely to come across only three of them, so I will only cover those three:

♦ **Parliamentary inquiry.** A question directed to the presiding officer concerning parliamentary law or the organization's rules as they apply to the business at hand.

♦ **Point of information.** A nonparliamentary question about the business at hand.

♦ **Withdrawal of a motion.** A request by the maker of a motion to remove the motion from consideration. After the motion has been stated by the presiding officer, it belongs to the assembly and the assembly's permission (majority vote) is needed to withdraw the motion.

For details on other requests and inquires, please refer to Appendix B, §26 and §27.

Parliamentary Inquiry

You are in a meeting. You want to do something, but you don't know how to do it. This is the motion for you! All you have to do is rise and say "Mr. Chairman, I rise to a parliamentary inquiry." The presiding officer should then say "Please state your inquiry." You state your inquiry and the presiding officer answers the inquiry. It is at that exact moment that the presiding officer is glad he or she got this book, which will help in answering the inquiry!

Point of Information

When making a parliamentary inquiry or point of information you can interrupt the speaker, but only if doing so is absolutely necessary. Neither motion requires a second, and they are not debatable or amendable. There is no vote taken since the inquiries are responded to by the chair or by someone the chair appoints.

Point of Information

You are in a meeting. This time you are listening to the debate and believe that it would be helpful to have additional information on this motion that surely someone knows, but you don't know. To find out if anyone else has this information, you simply rise and say "Mr. Chairman, I rise to a point of information." The presiding officer should then say "Please state your point." You state your question and the presiding officer answers the question or calls upon someone else to answer it.

Withdrawal of a Motion

You made a motion. Now that you have heard the debate, you think that making that motion wasn't the wisest move you've ever made. You're in luck—all you have to do is request permission to withdraw your motion.

Does this motion need a vote? That depends! I am not trying to be a smart aleck; it really depends upon when you want to withdraw it. Let's briefly review the six steps of a motion:

1. A member makes a motion.

2. Another member seconds the motion.

3. The chair states the motion, formally placing it before the assembly.

4. The members debate the motion.

5. The chair puts the question to a vote.

6. The chair announces the results of the vote.

If you remember that at the completion of Step #3 the ownership of the motion is turned over from the individual who made the motion to the assembly, you probably already know when the motion needs a vote and when it doesn't. If the member wants to withdraw the motion during steps 1, 2, or 3, the member can withdraw the motion without anyone else agreeing. Of course, someone else could turn around and make the same motion.

If the member wants to withdraw the motion during Step 4, it now belongs to the assembly and the mover must get permission from the assembly. This is usually handled by general consent, but if anyone objects, the member then makes the motion to withdraw the motion and it takes a majority vote for it to pass.

Parliamentary Pearls

If Tom requested to withdraw his motion during Step 4, the presiding officer would say: "Is there any objection to allowing the maker of the motion to withdraw his motion?" [Pause] "Hearing no objection, the motion is withdrawn. The next business in order is …"

The Least You Need to Know

♦ It's up to the chair to call a member to order, but if he or she fails to do so, any member can make a point of order.

♦ The motion to appeal from the decision of the chair ensures that the chair doesn't abuse his or her power.

♦ Even parliamentarians find the objection to the consideration of a question motion confusing.

♦ Use parliamentary inquiry when you just don't know the best way to do something using parliamentary procedure.

♦ Withdrawing a motion is allowed, but you may have to vote on it.

The "Bring Back" Motions

In This Chapter

- How to take back a motion
- How to clear off the table
- Ways to update motions
- What to do if you change your mind

The "bring back" motions are a group of motions that are used to bring back a motion that has already been before the assembly for reconsideration, just in case once wasn't enough!

These motions are methods of properly getting around two of the basic principles of parliamentary procedure. The first is that an assembly cannot be asked to decide the same, or substantially the same, question twice during one session, unless a special motion is made to allow that. The second is that a motion that conflicts with a motion adopted at the same session or one previously adopted that is still in effect is not in order.

Four "Bring Back" Motions

The following motions are classified as "bring back" motions:

♦ Rescind

♦ Amend something previously adopted

♦ Take from the table

♦ Reconsider

Since this is not a rulebook (that's *Robert's* job), I will not be including all of the specific rules for each of the motions in this chapter. For the rules please refer to Appendix B, §35 through §37.

Rescind

This motion is used to cancel something that the voting body did at a previous meeting. Life changes, we change our minds, circumstances change, and this is the motion that allows you to respond to that change.

> ### Point of Information
>
> An example of the vote needed for rescind:
>
> An organization has 45 members. At the April meeting, the members in attendance approved the motion to hold a road race in August as a fundraiser for the organization. At the May meeting, members realize that absolutely nothing has been done to start the fundraiser and, besides that, another local organization is also having a road race fundraiser the same weekend in August. A member moves to rescind the motion adopted at the April meeting to have an August fundraiser. At that May meeting 30 members are present and all 30 vote either yes or no. What is the vote needed at the May meeting to pass the motion to rescind?
>
> ♦ A two-thirds vote: 20 in favor, 10 against.
>
> ♦ A majority vote if previous notice is given. Previous notice was not given, but if it had been given, only 16 votes would be needed.
>
> ♦ A majority of the entire membership: 23 votes.

Vote Needed

A member should not be able to wait until just the right number of people who voted in favor of the motion are absent, and then move to rescind that motion. That would be a violation of the right of the absent members. To protect those rights a higher than normal vote is needed.

For the motion to rescind, any of the following votes are needed:

- A two-thirds vote

- A majority vote if previous notice is given

- A majority of the entire membership

What Can't Be Rescinded

Here are some of the things that you cannot rescind:

- A vote after something has been done as a result of that vote and it is too late to undo it. If, for example, the motion was made at the March meeting to buy ice cream treats for the next three monthly meetings and you are at the April meeting and the ice cream treats have been served and eaten, it is not possible to undo the buying and serving of ice cream treats for the April meeting.

- An action in the nature of a contract, once the other party in the contract has been informed. If, for example, a contract is signed or verbally committed to.

- A resignation that has been acted upon. For example, if the treasurer submits his resignation and that resignation is formally accepted by the assembly.

- An election to or expulsion from membership, if the person was present or has already been notified.

- A motion that could still be reconsidered. (See Appendix B, §36 for a list of these motions)

Script: Motion to Rescind

Member:	I move to rescind the motion adopted at the _____ [state the month] meeting to [state the motion].
Chair:	Is there a second to the motion? [This statement is eliminated if a member calls out "second" or if the motion is made on behalf of a committee.]
Second member:	I second the motion.

continues

continued

Chair: It is moved and seconded that we rescind the motion adopted at the _____ [state the month] meeting to _____ [state the motion].

Is there any discussion?

[After discussion] Is there any further discussion? Are you ready for the question? [Pause] The question is on the adoption of the motion that we rescind the motion adopted at the _____ [state the month] meeting to _____ [state the motion].

All those in favor of the motion to rescind, please raise your hand. [Pause] Please lower your hand. Those opposed to the motion, please raise your hand. [Pause] Please lower your hand.

The affirmative has it, the motion is adopted, and we have rescinded the action adopted at the _____ [state the month] meeting to _____ [state the motion].

or

The negative has it, the motion is lost, and we will not rescind the action adopted at the [state the month] meeting. We will _____ _____ [state the motion].

The next business in order is …

Rules for the Motion to Rescind:

♦ Needs a second.

♦ Is debatable.

♦ Is amendable.

♦ Vote needed: a two-thirds vote; a majority vote if previous notice is given; or a majority of the entire membership.

Amend Something Previously Adopted

Ditto is the word here. Everything that applied to the motion to rescind applies to the motion to amend something previously adopted. If you understand one, you understand the other.

There are only two differences. First, instead of canceling a previously adopted motion, this motion changes it. Second, you must include how you propose to change the previously adopted motion in the motion to amend something previously adopted, just like you would in any other motion to amend.

Gavel Gaffs _____

It is very easy to get the motion to amend something previously adopted mixed up with the motion to amend. The main difference is that the motion to amend is a secondary motion and the motion to amend something previously adopted is a main motion. Because the motion to amend is a secondary motion, it can only be applied to a main motion. So if the motion on the floor is to purchase a computer, a secondary motion to amend might be to insert the words "PC compatible" before the word "computer." No other motions can be pending when the main motion to amend something previously adopted is made.

Script: Motion to Amend Something Previously Adopted

Member:	I move to amend the motion adopted at the _____ [state the month] meeting to _____ [state the motion], by striking _____ and inserting _____.
Chair:	Is there a second to the motion? [This statement is eliminated if a member calls out "second" or if the motion is made on behalf of a committee.]
Second member:	I second the motion.
Chair:	It is moved and seconded that we amend the motion adopted at the _____ [state the month] meeting to _____ [state the motion], by striking _____ and inserting _____. Is there any discussion?
	[After discussion] Is there any further discussion? Are you ready for the question? [Pause] The question is on the adoption of the motion that we amend the motion adopted at the _____ [state the month] meeting to _____ [state the motion], by striking _____ and inserting _____.

continues

continued

All those in favor of the motion to amend something previously adopted, please raise your hand. [Pause] Please lower your hand. Those opposed to the motion, please raise your hand. [Pause] Please lower your hand.

The affirmative has it, the motion is adopted, we have amended the motion adopted at the _____ meeting, and we will _____ [state the motion as amended].

or

The negative has it, the motion is lost, and we will not be amending the action adopted at the _____ meeting. We will _____ [restate the original motion].

The next business in order is …

Rules for the Motion to Amend Something Previously Adopted:

◆ Needs a second.

◆ Is debatable.

◆ Is amendable.

◆ Vote needed: a two-thirds vote; a majority vote if previous notice is given; or a majority of the entire membership.

Take from the Table

You'll recall from Chapter 12 that the motion to lay on the table allows a group to set aside a pending motion in order to attend to more urgent business. To bring the tabled motion back before the group, a member must make the motion to take it from the table by the end of the next regularly scheduled meeting.

Time Restrictions

A motion that was laid on the table can only be taken from the table during the remainder of the meeting at which it was laid on the table or before the conclusion of the next regularly scheduled meeting. For example, let's say that your group meets on the first Thursday of each month. In February, a motion was laid on the table early in the meeting. That motion can be taken from the table during the remainder of the February meeting and up until the end of the meeting held on the first Thursday in March. The "next regular meeting" must be within a quarterly time interval. Therefore, if you have an annual convention, you can't put it on the table at one convention and take it off the table at the next convention.

What happens to it after the March regular meeting? It falls off the table! If you want to bring it up again at the April or May meeting, it is as though it was never moved in the first place and must come up as new business.

Point of Information
Have you ever wondered what table you are laying a motion on or taking it from? The table is the secretary's table. In essence, the motion is placed in the care of the secretary (symbolically on his or her table) until it is needed again.

Other Restrictions

The motion to take from the table can be made by any member, and it requires a majority vote to pass.

If the motion is taken from the table at the same meeting, individual debate restrictions apply. So, if you already spoke on it two times before it was laid on the table, you cannot debate it again after it is brought from the table. But if it is brought from the table on a later day, the restrictions do not carry over. So even if you spoke on it two times on the first day, at a later day you can debate it two more times.

As noted in Chapter 12, when you lay a motion on the table, all pending motions go with it. Take the motion to purchase a computer as an example. Let's say that a motion is made to amend by inserting "PC compatible" before the word "computer." It is then moved to refer the motion to a committee. Then, it is moved to lay it on the table, and that motion passes. When the motion is taken from the table, all those subsidiary motions still apply to it, and you must first deal with the motion to refer to a committee, then the amendment, and finally the main motion to purchase a computer (as amended, if the motion to amend passed).

Script: Motion to Take from the Table

Member: I move that we take from the table the motion relating to

_____.

Chair: Is there a second to the motion? [This statement is eliminated if a member calls out "second" or if the motion is made on behalf of a committee.]

Second
member: I second the motion.

Chair: It is moved and seconded that we take from the table the motion relating to _____. This is not a debatable motion. The question is on the adoption of the motion to take from the table the motion relating to _____.

All those in favor, say "Aye." [Pause for response.]

All those opposed, say "No."

The affirmative has it and the motion is adopted; _____ is taken from the table and before you for your consideration at this time. Is there any further discussion on the motion _____?

or

The negative has it, the motion is lost, and we will not take from the table the motion relating to _____. The next business in order is ....

Rules for the Motion to Take from the Table:

◆ Needs a second.

◆ Is *not* debatable.

◆ Is *not* amendable.

◆ Needs a majority vote.

◆ May be made during the Unfinished Business or New Business portion of the agenda.

Reconsider

This motion clearly wins the award for the most challenging of all of the motions. If you want to understand all of the intricacies of this motion (and there are plenty of them) you need to check out *Robert's*. With that disclaimer, let's proceed.

Effect

The effect of the adoption of this motion is to erase the original vote on the motion and put the assembly in exactly the place it was in right before that vote occurred. If the motion to reconsider passes, the motion is put back on the floor, as if the original vote had not occurred, and discussion continues.

Parliamentary Pearls

The motion to reconsider is recognized as a uniquely American motion. Actually, it is the only motion of American origin. It is universally accepted by all of the major American parliamentary authorities. But, when you realize how complicated it is, it may be something we don't want to put the "Made in USA" brand on!

Who and When

The motion to reconsider can be made only by a member who voted on the prevailing side. So if the motion passed, you had to have voted "yes" on it to move to reconsider it; if the motion failed, you had to have voted "no" to move to reconsider it. The whole idea is that at least one person in the group has changed his or her mind before the entire group should have to go back and consider this motion again.

The motion to reconsider can be made only on the day that the original motion was made. Exception: During a convention or when you are meeting for multiple days in a row, can be made on the next day as well.

Two Parts: Make It, Call It Up

Here's the part that's really unusual. This motion can be made at one time and processed (or called up) at another time. So even if you can't process the motion for whatever reason, such as time constraints, you can still make the motion and then call it up to discuss at a later time. This is covered in detail in Appendix B, §36.

Can't Be Reconsidered

The motion to reconsider is not a free-for-all, and a lot of motions can't be reconsidered. You will find them listed in Appendix B, §36 as well.

Script: Motion to Reconsider

Member: I move to reconsider the vote on _____.

Chair: The motion to reconsider can be made only by a member who voted on the prevailing side. That motion [passed/failed]. Therefore, you needed to have voted [in favor/against] the motion. Is that how you voted?

Is there a second to the motion?

Second
member: I second the motion.

Chair: It is moved and seconded to reconsider the vote on _____ _____.

The question is: Shall the motion be reconsidered? Is there any discussion?

[After discussion] Are you ready for the question? [Pause]

We will now go to the vote. The question is: Shall the motion to _____ be reconsidered?

All those in favor, say "Aye." [Pause for response]

All those opposed, say "No."

The affirmative has it, the motion is adopted, the motion is reconsidered. The motion on the floor and open for discussion at this time is _____.

[Proceed with discussion and the vote on the motion that is reconsidered.]

or

The negative has it, the motion is lost, and we will not reconsider the motion. Therefore, the original decision made by the members on this motion stands. [Repeat the original motion and the original vote.]

The next business in order is …

Rules for the Motion to Reconsider:

◆ Is debatable only if the motion being reconsidered was debatable.

◆ Is *not* amendable.

◆ Needs a majority vote.

◆ Can only be made by a person who voted on the prevailing side.

◆ Can be moved only on the same or the next succeeding day after the original vote was taken.

The Least You Need to Know

◆ You cannot rescind a motion that the group has taken action on that can't be undone.

◆ If you don't move to take a motion from the table by the end of the next regularly scheduled meeting after it was laid on the table, the motion falls from the table. If you want to consider the motion, it must be brought up as a new item of business.

◆ The rules for the motion to rescind are almost identical to the rules to amend something previously adopted.

◆ To move to reconsider a motion that has already been voted upon, you must have voted in favor of it if it passed or against it if it failed.

Part 4

Let's Get to Order

There is more to displaying leadership in a meeting than knowing the motions. Leadership is about preparing for the meeting, conducting it in an orderly fashion, and handling those difficult situations in a manner that's perceived to be fair.

This part covers some of the fine details of a meeting. If you are already a leader or if you would like to be a leader, this section is crucial for you. It will give you the guidance you need to prepare for and run your meeting, no matter what kind of meeting you are leading.

On the Agenda

In This Chapter

- ◆ The correct order for agenda items
- ◆ Moving right along on the minutes
- ◆ Receiving reports
- ◆ Where special orders come from
- ◆ Distinguishing between new and unfinished business

The *agenda* is a predetermined sequence of items of business to be covered at a specific meeting. An agenda, which is sometimes referred to as an order of business, can be a huge time-saving tool, but only if it is prepared and used correctly. All too often the chair creates an agenda but fails to stick to it. It takes discipline to follow an agenda, but that discipline will pay off in time saved.

The idea behind the agenda is to look at all the elements of business that need to come before a group and then put them in order of importance. Items should be ordered from most to least important so that if a meeting is cut short, the most important things would have (hopefully) already been resolved. Let's take a closer look at that order.

The Order of Business

If your group meets at least quarterly (four times a year), has *Robert's* as its parliamentary authority, and has not adopted a special order of business, the following is your order of business for your meetings:

Robert's Says _____

An **agenda** is a pre-determined sequence of items of business to be covered at a specific meeting. Also called an order of business.

1. Reading and approval of minutes

2. Reports of officers, boards, and standing committees

3. Reports of special (select or ad hoc) committees

4. Special orders

5. Unfinished business and general orders

6. New business

Let's look at each of these business items in turn.

Approval of Minutes

If this agenda item is done correctly, it can and should take only a minute or two.

Ideally, the secretary prepared the minutes from the previous meeting immediately after the meeting and sent them out to the members—either by e-mail or regular mail—before the next meeting. When the minutes are printed and distributed in advance of the meeting, there is no need to have the minutes read during the meeting and the members can quickly move to approve them.

Approval Verbiage

Approval of the minutes could be this simple: The presiding officer says "You have received the minutes of the last meeting. Are there any corrections to the minutes? [Pause] Hearing none, if there is no objection, the minutes are approved as printed and distributed to the members." (By the way, this is an example of voting by general consent, which you learned about in Chapter 9.)

Changes to the Minutes

Notice that the verbiage suggested is "Are there any corrections to the minutes as printed?"

If a member suggests a correction to the minutes, it is usually best to handle it by general consent. After a member offers a change, the presiding officer would say "Is there any objection to making that change? [Pause] Hearing no objection, the change will be made."

If there is an objection, the change is handled by following the amendment process: The motion to approve the minutes is on the floor and a member states exactly how the minutes should be amended; the amendment is seconded, restated by the presiding officer, discussed, voted on, and announced. The approval of the minutes, as amended, requires a majority vote. It is unusual to have to vote on a change in the minutes. If your group's minutes are changed on a regular basis, you're probably including too much information in the minutes. Refer to Chapter 18 for help.

> **Gavel Gaffs**
>
> You might have heard presiding officers ask "Are there any additions or corrections to the minutes as printed?" It is not necessary to ask for additions as well as corrections because an addition *is* a correction.

Reports

Not every officer and committee will have a report at each meeting unless it is an annual meeting, at which all officers and committees might be required by the bylaws to present a report.

Reports are divided into four different groups and are given in the following order:

1. Officers
2. Boards
3. Standing committees
4. Special committees

The order of these reports within the four groups should be given in the order in which they are listed in the bylaws, or in the case of special committees, in the order they were created.

Printed Reports

If everyone gets in the habit of putting all of the reports in writing and distributing them before the meeting, this part of the agenda could move along very quickly. Just as with the minutes, if all the members have received the printed report in advance of the meeting, all the presiding officer has to do when he or she gets to a specific officer is to ask, "Do you have any additions to the report as printed and distributed to the members?" Most of the time the answer is no, and then the meeting can move right along.

Point of Information

A motion arising from an officer, board, or committee report must be taken up immediately.

Motions to adopt or implement any recommendations made by an officer should be made from the floor by a member other than the reporting officer.

Motions to implement any recommendations made by a committee should be made by the committee chairman or other reporting member.

Saying "Thank You" Is Enough

After a member gives a report, the presiding officer should simply acknowledge receipt of the report by thanking the member who presented the report and moving on to the next agenda item.

When you adopt, accept, or approve a report, you are making it a permanent official document of the organization. Very seldom should a report become an official document of the organization. Therefore, very seldom should there be a motion to adopt, approve, or accept a report.

Gavel Gaffs

You should never approve the treasurer's report because it should always be audited after the treasurer presents it. If you feel a need to approve, accept, or adopt a financial report, it should be the auditor's report that is approved.

When a report is said to be received, it simply means that it was heard. So if, after a report has been given and a member makes the following motion "I move to receive the report of the finance committee," that member is a day late and a dollar short. The report has already been heard and therefore received. Again, it is usually best simply to thank the person giving the report and announce the next item of business.

For complete information on the content of the officers' reports, and guidance on what to include in committee reports, refer to Chapter 20.

Special Orders

The *special orders* category of the agenda allows a group to specify a certain time for considering a specific subject, and gives it an absolute priority for that time.

A two-thirds vote is required to make something a special order. Such a high vote is necessary because the special order takes away from the members the right to follow the typical agenda and, when the time of the special order arrives, it forces them to stop what they are doing and take up the special order. When the time for the special order arrives, it has the effect of suspending the current business so that the members can take up the special order.

Robert's Says

Special orders—This category of the agenda has the effect of setting a certain time when a specified subject will be considered, and of giving it an absolute priority for that time.

Bylaws Give Special Orders

In most organizations the only time you will see special orders on the agenda is when the bylaws require that a particular item be handled at a specific meeting. A good example is the election of officers—it's common for the bylaws to indicate at which meeting the election of officers is to be conducted. When that is the case, the election of officers comes on the agenda under special orders.

Convention Special Orders

You might also see the special orders item of business used at a convention or a meeting that will take place over several days. People frequently travel to conventions and might need to know which day and time a specific issue will be brought up so they can be in attendance at that time.

Order of the Special Orders

When there are multiple special orders for the same time, the special order that was made first is considered first. For specific information on how to handle multiple special orders, refer to Appendix B, §20.

That Business Is Unfinished, Not Old

The most misunderstood and abused section on the agenda is unfinished business. Not familiar with that term? Probably because you have heard it referred to as Old Business, which is incorrect. There is no category called "Old Business." The category is actually called unfinished business and general orders. Let's look at each of those subsections separately.

Unfinished Business

Unfinished business is just that—business that was started but that hasn't been finished.

Gavel Gaffs _____

The term *old business* gives no indication whether we finished that business or not. Referring to it as *unfinished business* makes it clear that the business was started but not yet finished. "So what?," you ask. Remember that the agenda is in order of priority. If a group started business at the previous meeting and didn't finish it, that business should have a higher priority than something completely new or a new spin on an old subject.

In order for something to be included in the unfinished business section of the agenda, it must be something that the group started at a previous meeting but didn't complete. For example, in a group that meets monthly, if an item was on the agenda at the March meeting and the group did not get to it before time to adjourn, it would come up automatically at the April meeting under unfinished business.

Point of Information

The only business that comes up under unfinished business and general orders is ...

- ◆ A motion that was pending when the previous meeting was adjourned.
- ◆ Items that were on the agenda at the previous meeting but didn't get taken up before that meeting was adjourned.
- ◆ Items that, at the previous meeting, were postponed to this meeting.
- ◆ An item that was laid on the table at the current or the previous meeting. When a motion is taken from the table it does not automatically come up under unfinished business, but the motion to take from the table could be made during unfinished business portion of the meeting.

However, just because a group discussed a topic at last month's meeting, doesn't give it higher priority at this month's meeting. For example, let's say that at the March meeting a motion was made and passed to have a fundraiser in August. After the March meeting you got the idea to have a raffle and have the drawing at the August fundraiser. At the April meeting you move that the group have a raffle and have the drawing at the August fundraiser. That motion would come up under new business. The decision at the March meeting was to have an August fundraiser and that decision was voted on and passed at the March meeting. The motion at the April meeting was a subject the group had discussed before (the August fundraiser) but the raffle had not been discussed before, so in April it is new business.

General Orders

If at the March meeting a motion was postponed to the next meeting, it would be included in the general orders section of the agenda at the April meeting. General orders is a category of the agenda that includes any motion which, usually by postponement, has been made an order of the day (item of business) without being made a special order. Translated, that means that if an item is postponed until a certain day or after a certain event, it fits in this category. Unlike special orders, general orders do not suspend any rules and therefore cannot interrupt business. To make an item a general order requires a majority vote.

When it gets to the point in the agenda for unfinished business and general orders, the presiding officer should not announce this category unless there is business in this category. Unlike the next category, new business, there is no possibility for surprise here. If nothing was postponed or not completed at the last meeting, and nothing was laid on the table at the last meeting or the current meeting, there is no possibility for unfinished business.

If there is no unfinished business or general orders, when that time comes on the agenda the presiding officer should say, "Since there is no unfinished business or general orders for this meeting, we will now proceed to new business." If there is unfinished business or general orders, then when it comes that time in the agenda, the presiding officer should simply announce the first item of unfinished business. Business in this category is taken up in the order of the time to which it was postponed, regardless of when the general order was made.

New Business

It's easy to determine what fits in this category. Basically, anything that the group can properly take up and that doesn't fit anywhere else fits in new business. This is where you present to the members for their consideration any new items of business.

If a motion was laid on the table at this meeting or the previous meeting, it can be taken from the table under new business. It does not

> ### Point of Information
>
> During a convention, the agenda is approved early in the first meeting of the convention. During regular meetings of a group that meet weekly or monthly, the agenda does not have to be approved, unless it has specific times for specific items.

automatically come up under new business, but the motion to take from the table can be made during new business.

The presiding officer cannot refuse to allow business to come up under new business as long as the business is within the purpose of the group.

Taking Business Out of Order

There are four ways that business can be considered out of the order given in the printed agenda:

- **General consent.** Sometimes it is clear that it is the will of the group to change the order. It might be because of the arrival of a special guest, or the lateness of the hour. The presiding officer might simply say: "If there is no objection, we will change the agenda and have our guest speak now. Immediately after his or her presentation we will continue with this item of business and the remainder of the agenda. Is there any objection to changing the order of business? [Pause] Hearing none, the order will be changed."

- **Suspend the rules.** When some of the members want to change the order and it is obvious that others do not, it will take a motion to change the order. That motion would be to suspend the rules (see Chapter 13). It should state exactly how the order should change. This motion takes a two-thirds vote.

- **Lay on the table.** When a motion is pending and an urgent matter comes up, a member may move to lay on the table the pending motion (see Chapter 12). This motion is undebatable and takes a majority to pass. If there are many items on the agenda between where you are and where you want to be, you can repeat this motion for each item.

  Once a motion is laid on the table and you have finished the next item of business, if someone wants to discuss the tabled item, it requires a motion to take it from the table (see Chapter 14).

- **Reconsider the making of an item a general or special order.** If an item has been made a general or special order and you want to bring it up before the time specified, you can either suspend the rules, which takes a two-thirds vote, or you can reconsider the motion that made it a special or general order. All the rules of the motion to reconsider must be followed (see Chapter 14).

Consent Agenda

Some organizations that have routine business find that an efficient way of handling that business is to include it on a *consent agenda*, which is also called a *consent calendar*. This is an agenda category that includes a list of routine, uncontroversial items that can be approved with a single motion, no discussion, and one vote.

The consent agenda is most frequently used by governmental bodies that have routine business that must approved. If you are going to follow this process, you may want to have a section in your rules explaining the procedure.

When you get to this part of the agenda, the presiding officer first asks whether any member wants to remove any item from the consent agenda. The items are usually numbered or lettered, and the member simply states which number he or she would like removed. No explanation is necessary. A member would ask to remove an item if that member wanted to discuss it, ask questions on it, or have a separate vote on it.

Robert's Says

A **consent agenda**, or **consent calendar**, is an agenda category that includes a list of routine, uncontroversial items that are approved with one motion, no discussion, and one vote.

After members have had plenty of opportunity to remove any item from the consent agenda, a member moves to approve all of the remaining items on the consent agenda or the chair assumes this motion. There can be no discussion or amendment of this motion. The vote is taken and all items that were on the consent agenda are approved by the one vote.

Tips on Agenda Preparation

Presiding officers over the years have developed many ways to make preparing the agenda easier. Some of those tips are based on electronic tools, others on good old common sense. Let's take a look at a few of them.

Use Past Minutes

Agenda preparation can be made easier by referring to two sets of past minutes: the minutes of the previous meeting and the minutes of the meeting held one year ago.

The minutes of the previous meeting are very helpful in reminding you of any business that was begun at the last meeting but not yet concluded and should be included on the agenda for the next meeting.

The minutes of the meeting one year ago will shed light on what annual items should be put on the agenda for this meeting, such as the annual audit.

Create a Template

Many people who use a computer to prepare the agenda open the file of the agenda from the previous meeting and then make changes on that file. The problem is that sometimes you miss the obvious (like changing the date of the meeting). Instead, create a template. All major word processing programs allow users to create templates, which they can then store and pull up each time they are ready to create a new version of that document. Simply go to the "Help" section of your word processing program and put in "Create a Template." It will instruct you how to create the template, and you'll find that you not only save a lot of time, but produce more accurate agendas!

Warning Flags

Members can prepare more easily for a meeting if they can determine with a quick glance at the agenda which items will require action and which items have material included in the agenda packet. If members know that they are going to have to vote on an issue, they will probably give it more attention before the meeting, particularly if they only have limited time to prepare.

You can simply place a symbol—in this case I'm using an asterisk—in front of each item that requires action and another symbol—in this case I'm using the pound sign—in front of each item that has material on it in the premeeting packet. An example of the first three items on an agenda, using these symbols, follows.

#1. Approval of minutes

*2. President's report

 3. Vice president's report

The Least You Need to Know

- ◆ *Robert's* specifies the order in which items of business should be taken up.

- ◆ Only business that the group has previously discussed should be included as unfinished business.

- ◆ Your group can change the order of the agenda, but it requires a vote to do so.

- ◆ Create and use a computer template to prepare the agenda for every meeting.

Chapter 16

Presiding Secrets

In This Chapter

- How to facilitate instead of dictate
- Observing nonverbal cues
- Watching the clock
- How 10 minutes of prep can save hours of meeting time
- Preparing and using scripts

Unfortunately, all too many presiding officer take what I like to call the "dictator approach" to presiding. In other words, they like to be in complete control of the meeting, to the point that it inhibits the parliamentary process. Let me qualify that. When a person has the dictator approach and you ask them about it, they quickly deny it. But if you pursue the topic further, you will hear them say things like, "The chair can close debate" or "The chair doesn't have to call on someone if he doesn't want to." These are examples of the dictator philosophy.

However, as I noted previously, the role of the presiding officer is to facilitate the meeting, not to dictate what happens in the meeting. To facilitate means to "make easier," and that is clearly the role of the presiding officer. In this chapter, we'll consider the skills that a presiding officer needs to be an effective, but fair, leader.

Presiding Qualities

Every effective presiding officer should have the following qualities: credibility, neutrality, judgment, and fairness.

Credibility

Members won't give someone a fair hearing if they don't judge that person as knowledgeable, honest, and fair. Presiding officers must establish their credibility early and reinforce that credibility often by taking actions that are perceived as fair and honest.

Neutrality

Members will put up with a lot of faults in a presiding officer, but one thing that they won't forgive is showing obvious partiality in a controversial issue. Presiding officers must stay neutral and should go out of their way to demonstrate neutrality to the members.

One way of displaying neutrality is never to enter into the debate. If presiding officers can't stay neutral, they are obligated to have someone who can stay neutral preside.

While presidents can't make motions, they can suggest motions. For example, if an issue is being discussed and someone suggests a possible solution and the nonverbal reaction is very positive, the presiding officer might at that time ask "Would you like to put that in the form of a motion?"

Judgment

Being an effective presiding officer is all about making the correct judgment calls, particularly during a vote. For instance, presiding officers shouldn't indicate whether the vote passed or failed unless they are absolutely positive of the outcome. If there is any doubt, the vote should be retaken.

Presiding officers should also recognize when it is time to let group members have a moment to clear their heads. In the latest edition of *Robert's*, this is referred to as a "Stand at Ease." If things are very sensitive or difficult, a presiding officer shouldn't hesitate to give the members time to take a deep breath by asking them to stay in their place and "stand at ease."

Gavel Gaffs

Don't hesitate to admit when you have made a mistake, but then make sure that you take steps to correct it! People don't expect perfection from their presiding officer—honesty, yes; perfection, no.

Fairness

Fairness is a lot like beauty—it's in the eyes of the beholder. Therefore, presiding officers should do all that they can to make sure that their actions are perceived as fair by others.

Consistency in how presiding officers address the members can dramatically impact the appearance of fairness. Presiding officers should pay attention to their tone of voice and facial expressions when they recognize a member to speak. Even if that person is very irritating, it's important to not display that irritation. In addition, presiding officers should avoid calling on some people by first name and not others.

Parliamentary Pearls

The words "If there is no objection …" are very helpful. If you do something that isn't exactly according to parliamentary procedure and you preface it with these five words, and no one objects, then you have gotten general consent to proceed. Of course, if there is one objection, then you have to proceed to process it as a motion.

Presiding Skills

In addition to personal characteristics, presiding officers must have certain skills to be effective at their job. The good news is that skills can be developed. If you want to be a good presiding officer, here are the skills you should develop.

Communication

Presiding is one of those times when it is good to remember that we were given two ears and one mouth for a reason. The verbal part of communication is helpful to the presiding officer, but the part that is most crucial is the listening, observing, and sensing the mood of the group. If you can do this, you can overcome almost any other fault you might have as a presiding officer. When a member is speaking, give that member your full attention. Make sure that you are not distracted by all the other things happening around you.

Parliamentary Pearls

Make sure the members know that they are being listened to! One of the most interesting things I have learned about communication is that people who are upset usually calm down when they feel that they are being heard. Notice, I did not say when they feel they are being agreed with. Most people only ask that they receive a fair hearing, not agreement. Once the member feels heard, he or she is more likely to calm down and listen to others.

If you are listening to what the members are saying and how they are saying it, you will be able to summarize their ideas and help them focus on what they want to do. And they are usually very impressed when they observe you display this skill.

More than half of what we communicate is communicated nonverbally. Therefore, when presiding you must be tuned into the nonverbal communication that is occurring throughout the meeting. To do that, you must listen not only with your ears, but also with your eyes. Look at the participants. Emotions are communicated, but only if you are watching for them.

When you have seen, heard, or sensed something, check it out by asking. "I'm sensing that you feel uncomfortable with moving ahead with the vote. Is that correct?"

Facilitation

Facilitating is a difficult but important skill. It entails figuring out what group members want to do and then assisting them in doing what they (not you) want to do. The skill of facilitating a meeting includes focusing on procedure and keeping the meeting moving.

Organization

Remaining organized during the meeting will make your meetings more efficient.

Presiding Techniques

The techniques in this section can help you improve your presiding skills.

Parliamentary Pearls

Confidence is the name of the game! Even though you may not always feel confident when you are presiding at a meeting, you should always display confidence. However, remember that there is a fine line between confidence and arrogance, and few things are more annoying than an arrogant chair.

Share the Ownership

The presiding officer who approaches the meeting with the mindset that it is his or her meeting is approaching it very differently from the presiding officer who approaches the meeting with the mindset that it is the members' meeting.

If you and the members see the meeting as belonging to the members and not to the presiding officer, the members are much more likely to own the meeting. When they feel ownership in the meeting, they share the responsibility with the presiding officer for running it. For instance, if the members feel as if the meeting belongs to them, they will be more likely to use peer pressure to help maintain decorum in the meeting. But if the members feel the meeting belongs to the presiding officer, they will wait for the presiding officer to call the members to order.

Set the Tone

When the presiding officer sets a tone of fairness and respect for the members, the members usually follow suit. If the minority point of view is treated with the same level of decency that the majority point of view is treated, the atmosphere of the meeting will remain very positive.

Reduce Confusion

One way to keep the meeting moving is to keep confusion out of the meeting. Earlier in the book we discussed the six steps of a motion.

Three of those steps, if done correctly, will help keep the meeting moving and keep the confusion out:

♦ **Step 3: The presiding officer states the motion.** You will be amazed at how much confusion restating the motion will eliminate. When members know exactly what the motion is before the discussion begins on that motion, they will be much more likely to stay focused.

♦ **Step 5: The presiding officer restates the motion and puts it to a vote.** Being reminded of exactly what the group is voting on right before the vote makes the whole voting process less confusing, especially for the members who were daydreaming. (And believe me, some members *will* be daydreaming.)

♦ **Step 6: The presiding officer announces the result of the vote.** When the members know which side prevailed, the implication of the vote, and what the next item of business is, there will be far less confusion. For information on the content of a complete announcement of the results of a vote, refer to Chapter 6.

Reduce Extraneous Debate

When the debate is dragging on, and on, and on, it's up to the presiding office to help move it along. Let's say that the motion on the floor is to purchase a computer and the issue has been debated for 45 minutes. In addition, members are beginning to stray off topic just a bit. The presiding officer can move things along by making any of the following statements:

- "Is there any further discussion on the motion to purchase a computer?"

- "Please limit your discussion to the specific motion, which is to purchase a computer."

- "We've heard many good points of view but are beginning to repeat some of the same ideas. Are there any new opinions on the motion to purchase a computer?" or "Please limit your comments to new opinions."

Another way of reducing extraneous debate is to recognize alternate sides when speaking. After someone has spoken in favor of the motion, before calling on the next person, simply ask, "Is there anyone who would like to speak against the motion?" Alternating between an affirmative speaker and a negative speaker sometimes helps reduce the debate, especially when the debate has been rather one-sided.

Call Members Out of Order as Politely as Possible

There's an old saying that goes something like *It isn't what you say, but how you say it.* That has never been truer than in ruling comments of a member out of order. Calling a member to order is one of those times when your communication skills will be tested. Don't just rule the comments of the member out of order; instead, explain why the comments are out of order and how the member can do what he or she wants to do and still be in order.

Gavel Gaffs

Humor is a wonderful quality for a presiding officer to possess. It can be used positively to release tension during a difficult meeting. But use humor wisely! Never use humor at the expense of any member, even the member who has been a thorn in your side throughout the meeting.

Focus on Procedure

Knowing and displaying knowledge of parliamentary procedure can go a long way in helping the members see you as a skillful presiding officer. They will have more confidence in your presiding skills when they see you smoothly handle the processing of a motion. When they watch you help the group through a difficult procedural issue, they will trust you to appropriately handle any situation.

Expediting the Meeting

People don't want to be in a meeting any longer than is judged absolutely necessary. So if you can be seen as expediting the meeting, that is a good thing.

But a word of caution! Remember that it is important to establish credibility early in the meeting. One of the best ways to do that is to start the meeting slowly. You don't want to look like you are trampling on the members' rights to get the group out on time.

So early on in the meeting, go slowly, be deliberate, and do things that help members see that you are fair. Make sure everyone has had a chance to speak before going to the vote. Take the first few votes slowly and deliberately. Once you have established credibility, you can pick up the pace. How do you know when that time has come? The members will tell you, if only through nonverbal cues.

Share the Agenda Preparation

Get other members involved in agenda preparation and you will soon find that the members are taking ownership of the agenda and the meeting. Have in place and known to all members a system for them to contact you with an agenda item. If the members know the day on which they must have items to you in order to get them placed on the agenda, they are more likely to participate in the agenda preparation.

Parliamentary Pearls

E-mail can be a very effective tool in agenda preparation. For example, if you are going to prepare the agenda next weekend, e-mail the members during the early part of the week and ask them to e-mail agenda items to you by Friday.

Prepare in Advance

I know this is going to sound like typical parliamentarian advice, but it is a good idea to review the bylaws and rules of the organization before the meeting. I can't tell you how many times I have seen a presiding officer become embarrassed when a member called to the attention of the chair a rule that the chair was obviously not aware of.

Advance preparation by the presiding officer should also include going through the agenda and trying to second-guess what might come up during the meeting. Then, if you think that a motion might come up that you are not comfortable with, you could take with you a copy of the script on how to handle that motion. I have included scripts throughout this book to aid you in preparing for the meeting.

Follow the Rules

My favorite *Robert's* quote is "Where there is no law, but every man does what is right in his own eyes, there is the least of real liberty." I like that quote because it reminds us why rules are so necessary and why relying on everyone's good judgment just doesn't work. Therefore, it is important to follow the established rules of the group (probably *Robert's*) instead of following "rules according to the current chair."

Starting the meeting on time is an excellent way to display your respect for the rules. When you wait to begin the meeting because certain people are running late, you have rewarded those who did not follow the rules and have punished those who did follow the rules.

Parliamentary Pearls

You should always have an agenda for the meeting. The agenda should be shared with all of the members, ideally before the meeting. Follow the agenda religiously. If you don't follow it, you can't expect the members to follow it. And, if the group decides not to follow the agenda, do it in an orderly fashion—suspend the rules.

If you are presiding over the meeting of a group that has never followed any rules, be careful not to shock them by a sudden, strict application of the rules. Be proactive by first explaining that you are going to apply the rules. Determine in advance the most important rules to have the group follow and explain them and how you intend to follow them. Then begin with those. For example, you might state "The chair wants to be sure that all members who wish to speak are heard. Therefore, before a member will be recognized to speak a second time on a motion, the chair will recognize other members who have not yet spoken on that motion."

Preparing and Using Scripts

I've already told you that successfully presiding at a meeting of any size requires preparation and practice. Like many sports and professional activities, those who do it well make it look much easier than it really is. Because presiding officers are the focus of attention, sometimes even a simple question can throw them off—it's as if you can't remember your own mother's name, much less what you are supposed to say next.

There is a solution to this problem! No, not the one about your mother's name, but what to say next. And you've already encountered several of them in this book: Use a script. A script is a document that states what is to be said, when it is to be said, and by whom it is to be said. The amount of detail in the script varies with the person writing the script and the person using the script.

Scripts vary from parliamentarian to parliamentarian and organization to organization, but here are the three most common kinds of scripts:

◆ **Gavel to Gavel:** The gavel to gavel script includes words that will be said from the beginning of the meeting to the end. This kind is most frequently used in conventions but is also used in meetings where controversy is expected. This script includes all that will be said, not only by the presiding officer but by reporting officers and presenters as well. Obviously it does not include the discussion of the motions, but other than that, much of what will happen can be prepared for and included in the script.

- **Difficult situation scripts.** Sometimes a presiding officer will only want a script to cover parts of the meeting where difficulty is anticipated. Sometimes those problems are parliamentary in nature, such as how to handle the opening of the convention and the necessary parliamentary business needed for that opening. Other times the script is nonparliamentary in nature, such as the list of dignitaries, along with their titles, that will be used for introducing those people.

- **Motion Scripts.** These provide the presiding officer with the words to say when handling a specific motion.

Why Script?

Even if you don't usually need a script, it might be reassuring just to know you have it in case a difficult situation comes up. In addition, relying on scripts can save an organization a lot of time by helping the presiding officer avoid mistakes that could be timely to fix.

Point of Information

Imagine that you are facing a difficult election in your organization. There are many people running for office and getting a majority vote on the first ballot for some of the positions is unlikely. The election is for president, vice president, secretary, treasurer, and two directors-at-large positions. You are concerned about getting confused, so you want to prepare a script for any possible situation. You might prepare scripts for the following potential scenarios:

- If there is a tie for any officer position
- If more than two candidates are running and no one candidate receives a majority vote
- If only one candidate for the position of director-at-large receives a majority vote
- If no candidate for the position of director-at-large receives a majority vote
- If no candidate for the position of director-at-large receives a majority vote on the second (or any other number) ballot

How to Script

You have seen many examples of scripts in this book. They are designed for you to copy and use. Although they cover many scenarios and motions, you might decide you want to create scripts for other situation.

Parliamentary Pearls

Your script should be adapted to the situation and the group. When writing a script, keep the following in mind:

- The size of the group
- The level of formality you wish to use
- The personality of the presiding officer
- The typical language of the presiding officer

When you are building that first script for your organization, consider using the following documents for guidance:

- The minutes of previous meetings.

- The agenda of the current meeting.

- Some conventions hire a court reporter to record every word said at the convention. That document from last year would be helpful in producing the first script.

- Scripts used by other organizations.

Preparing to Use the Script

One of the most useful parts of the script is in the preparation for its use. For conventions or important meetings, I encourage the president, vice president, president-elect, executive director, secretary, parliamentarian, AV technicians, and any committee chairmen who will be reporting to get together and read through the script and make any changes that are needed.

When they get to any part of the script that might be controversial, they can stop and discuss all that might happen during that part and how to handle any of the issues that might surface.

The script review meeting not only helps the presiding officer determine what to expect, but it usually also increases his or her confidence!

The Least You Need to Know

- Presiding officers should be facilitators, not dictators.

- As a presiding officer, don't be afraid to make mistakes—members will respect you more for admitting you're not perfect.

- A good presiding officer listens to what a member is saying while also observing the member's nonverbal communication for clues.

- While it may seem simple, starting the meeting on time sets the tone for the meeting—you show that you follow the rules and expect others to as well.

- Don't be afraid to use scripts to keep the meeting running smoothly.

Cast Your Ballot! Nominations and Elections

In This Chapter

- ◆ Documents governing nominations and elections
- ◆ Common nominating methods
- ◆ The nominating committee in action
- ◆ Who counts the ballots?

In parliamentary procedure, selecting leaders of an organization is a two-step process: Members first nominate candidates for positions, and then members hold an election for the offices. Since the choice of leaders frequently determines the future direction of the organization, these two steps are of utmost importance.

Don't Jump In Without Reading Your Organization's Rules!

Before you begin the nomination and election processes, you should first check your organization's bylaws, as they usually contain important information about these activities. If rules regulating your elections and nominations are in the bylaws, you *must* follow them.

In addition to the bylaws, you should review the following information:

◆ **Other printed rules.** These include standing or special rules of the organization. If it is in the other rules and those rules don't conflict with the bylaws, you must follow those rules.

◆ **Custom.** If your organization has handled the nominations and elections process a certain way for a while and that process doesn't conflict with the bylaws or other rules, then that is the way you should do it, unless directed otherwise by the members.

If a way of proceeding isn't in the bylaws or other rules and you don't have a custom established, or if you don't like the custom and want to change it, a member must make motion to establish how the nomination or election process will work.

Parliamentary Pearls _____

The timing of the nomination and election process is frequently indicated in the bylaws. For example, if the bylaws provide that the election shall occur at the November meeting or at the annual meeting, at that meeting, the election comes up under the agenda heading of special orders. It comes after the reports and before unfinished business. Think of it as a special order from the bylaws.

Who Nominates and How Do You Do It?

Nominating candidates for office is the process of narrowing down the field and focusing the election on those members who were nominated. However, it's important to note that a person who was not nominated for a position can be elected.

There are many different methods of nominating candidates for office. They include ...

◆ Nominations by a committee

◆ Nominations from the floor

◆ Nominations by the chair

◆ Nominations by ballot

- Nominations by mail or e-mail

- Nominations by petition

Nominations by committee and from the floor are by far the most frequently used methods. They are usually done in connection with each other. The nominating committee first gives its report and then the presiding officer asks for nominations from the floor.

Since the first two are most frequently used, I will cover them here. To get additional information on the other methods of nomination, I refer you to Appendix B, §66.

Nominating Committee

The nominating committee is the most important committee in an organization because it is responsible for choosing the future leaders of the organization. What an awe-inspiring job!

Gavel Gaffs _____

If you can't keep your mouth shut, don't become a member of a nominating committee! Confidentiality is a necessary part of the nominating committee process. The process works best when members come together, openly discuss the strengths and weaknesses of each of the candidates for each of the offices, and then determine which candidate to slate for each office. If committee members cannot talk open and freely in the candidate discussion, the whole purpose of the nominating committee has been defeated.

I strongly recommend that your organization prepare a procedures manual for the nominating committee. It should include all the rules applicable to the nominating committee, the roles of each member of the nominating committee, and what forms the committee should use. I guarantee that members of the nominating committee will find such a manual to be invaluable.

In addition, many nominating committees are given a candidate qualities checklist, in which they can rate each candidate for particular qualities that an organization seeks for each office. Here's a sample checklist—if you want to create one of your own, simply use this format, but include only the qualities that you are seeking:

Candidate Qualities Form

Instructions: Rate each candidate from 1 through 5 on each quality. (5 is highest score possible)

Candidates for (office): _____

Rating of Qualities of Candidates for Office

Candidate Qualities	Candidate's Name and Rating			
	Name A	Name B	Name C	Name D
Meets all of the requirements of the bylaws and standing rules				
Demonstrated commitment to the organization				
Demonstrated leadership skills				
Commitment to the leadership team				
Ability to professionally represent the organization				
Ability to distinguish between major and minor issues and focus on the major issues				
Ability to serve as a role model within and outside of the organization				
Ability to work with staff				
Compatibility with officers team				
Past history of work for this organization				
Timeliness of output of expected work				
Ability and willingness to work as a team player				
Interpersonal communication skills				
Public communication skills				

Who Can Be Nominated?

In order to be properly nominated for an office, a member must meet the qualifications for office as they are described in the bylaws. For instance, the bylaws might require that someone be a member for a minimum length of time before he or she can hold office, or that a candidate must have been on the board of directors for a specified amount of time before holding the office of president or vice president. If the qualifications are stated in the bylaws, they cannot be suspended.

Parliamentary Pearls _____

The bylaws are meant to ensure members' rights. If a member is given a right in the bylaws, it cannot be taken away without changing the bylaws. Running for an office is a membership right. If there are no qualifications for a specific office stated in the bylaws, an organization can't require that a candidate have any particular qualifications to hold an office. Otherwise, you would be adding a qualification to the membership right that is not stated in the bylaws. The only exception is if the laws of the state include qualifications, which is highly unlikely.

Can Nominating Committee Members Be Nominated?

If your organization uses a nominating committee, the members of that committee are not barred from being nominated for an office. Being a member of the committee should not prevent someone from being nominated for a position.

Nominations from the Floor

Unless the rules of the organization say otherwise, the presiding officer must call for nominations from the floor. If there is a nominating committee, this part of the process would come after the committee report. Organizations usually allow for nominations from the floor to give each member a chance to exercise his or her right to fully participate in the selection of the nominees.

After the presiding officer calls for nominations from the floor, any member may make a nomination. The nomination does not require a second, although in some organizations there is a tradition of allowing for one or two seconding speeches.

It's Election Time!

When the nominations process is completed, it is time for the election—which means that it's time to check the bylaws again to see whether there are any rules applicable to the election. There usually are. Some of the election rules frequently found in bylaws include the following:

- **Requirement for ballot election.** If the rules indicate that the election must be by ballot, it must be by ballot. You cannot waive having a ballot vote—even if there is only one candidate for an office—unless the bylaws allow you to do so.

- **Requirement for a majority vote.** Unless the bylaws indicate otherwise, it takes a majority vote (more than half of the votes cast) to elect a person to office. Sometimes the bylaws specify a plurality vote. In that case, the candidate who receives the highest number of votes is said to have a plurality. The advantage of a plurality vote is that you usually can complete an election on the first ballot. The disadvantage is that it means a person might be elected to office without the vote of a majority of the members.

- **You can't drop the lowest vote-getter.** Sometimes the election doesn't happen on the first ballot. For example, if there are a lot of candidates running for one office and no one candidate gets a majority vote on the first ballot. Or if there are three board positions open and only two candidates get a majority vote on the first ballot. Then a second ballot is needed. The second ballot must have the same names (minus those elected) on the ballot unless someone withdraws. You can't drop the name of the person(s) who received the fewest votes unless the rules authorize doing this.

  The reason for this rule? Since elections are so important, we need to preserve all options. One option is that the person farthest behind could be elected as a compromise candidate.

- **No mail ballot without a rule.** You can only conduct an election by mail ballot if the bylaws authorize a mail ballot.

- **One ballot or multiple ballots.** There are two ways to conduct a ballot vote when multiple offices are up for election. The first involves a single ballot with all the offices to be elected appearing on that ballot. The second is to conduct a ballot vote for each office, one at a time. The bylaws may specify which system to use. To illustrate the difference between these two processes, consider an election in which the offices for president, vice president, secretary, and treasurer are to be filled. The first method would have a single ballot with each office and the candidates for each office listed. The members would vote on all four offices on a single piece of paper.

Parliamentary Pearls

There are many different methods of conducting an election. In this chapter we have focused on the most common method, the ballot election. Other methods are listed and explained in *Robert's*—See Appendix B, §46 and §66.

The second system would first call for the election of the president and issue ballots for that office. When that election was completed, ballots would be issued for the office of vice president, and so on. These elections should occur in the order that they are listed in the bylaws.

The advantage of the one ballot system is efficiency—you can usually have the election of all four officers done on one ballot, all at one time. However, the single ballot method allows a person to run for more than one position if they aren't elected for one office. For instance, someone who was not elected president may choose to run for vice president, secretary, or treasurer.

1-2-3—Count Those Ballots!

The group of people responsible for counting ballots is usually referred to as the tellers. They are usually appointed to the committee before or at the beginning of the election meeting. Only members whom the membership considers to be honest, accurate, and dependable should be appointed. In addition, ballot counters should not be personally involved in the election. Tellers should be familiar with the bylaws, standing and special rules, as well as the parliamentary rules regarding election process.

During an election, tellers distribute, collect, and count the ballots and then report that count. They also frequently assists in counting a standing vote as well.

Point of Information

When counting ballots follow these rules:

◆ Blank ballots don't count; they can be thrown away.

◆ Illegal ballots cast by legal voters are listed as illegal votes. They count in determining the number of votes cast. An example of an illegal vote is a vote for someone who is ineligible.

◆ In determining whether or not a ballot should be counted, you should use common sense. If it is clear for whom the person intended to vote, but for example, the voter misspelled the candidate's name, the ballot counts.

◆ When the ballot has places for elections for multiple offices or multiple votes allowed for a particular position, blank spaces do not affect the rest of the ballot. In other words, your vote will count if you vote for too few candidates, but it will not count if you vote for too many.

◆ It is okay to have fewer ballots than the number of eligible voters; it is *not* okay to have more ballots than the number of eligible voters.

The tellers make sure that only members eligible to vote receive ballots and that no extra ballots are floating around. After the ballots are marked, at the instruction of the chair, tellers collect the ballots, go to a secluded place, and count the ballots. *Robert's* includes very specific instructions on the process of counting ballots, see Appendix B, §46.

Tellers' Report

The tellers prepare and sign a report that is read to the assembly and is used by the presiding officer to declare who is elected. That report is entered in full in the minutes. The tellers' report should include the following information:

- ◆ The number of votes cast

- ◆ The number of votes needed for election or for the proposal to pass

- ◆ The number of votes each candidate or side received, each listed separately

- ◆ Any illegal votes cast, including the reason they were illegal and the number of illegal votes

Chair Declares

The chairman of the tellers reads the tellers' report, but the presiding officer declares who is elected for each office. Here's how the process works: After the tellers' chairman reads the tellers' report, he or she hands it to the presiding officer who reads it again and then declares who was elected to each position.

Chair Presides

We learned earlier that if the presiding officer is going to debate a motion, he or she should relinquish the chair to the vice president who presides in his or her absence. But, if the presiding officer is a candidate for an office, he or she stays in the chair for the election. No need to relinquish the chair!

When the Election Is Final

The election for each office is considered final when the candidate who won the election is notified and accepts the position. The only exception to this rule is if the candidate is not present but has, in advance, consented to the candidacy, in which case the election is final at the completion of the election. If the candidate is not present, has not consented in advance, and declines the election, an election to fill the vacancy can take place immediately, unless the bylaws give other instructions.

What happens if a person is elected to two offices but can only hold one office? If the member is present, the member can decide which office he or she wants, and then another election should be held to fill the other office. If the member is not present, the members who are present will select, by majority vote, which office the person will take. Makes you want to be in attendance if you are up for a couple of offices!

The bylaws should specify when newly elected members take office. In organizations that meet monthly, it's not unusual for a member to be elected at one meeting but not take office until the next.

The Least You Need to Know

♦ If you can't keep a secret, don't be on the nominating committee—it requires strict confidences.

♦ Check your bylaws for your organization's voting processes.

♦ Although there are several acceptable methods for nominating members to office, the two most common are nominations by committee and nominations from the floor.

♦ The chairman of the tellers reads the results of the vote, but the chair declares the vote.

Part 5

Officers, Committees, and Meetings

This part covers a lot of material that will be helpful to you as you prepare for meetings. If you are an officer or a committee chairman you will find help in preparing your report or the meeting minutes. If you serve on a committee, you'll find a chapter that will help you understand the committee process and how to make the most of it.

Maybe you picked up this book because you have a responsibility in an upcoming convention. If so, you're in luck, because I've included a chapter on conventions and their unique demands. And if your group is thinking about holding electronic meetings, the final chapter is for you.

Chapter 18

Just a Minutes

In This Chapter

◆ What the minutes should include

◆ What the minutes shouldn't include

◆ Making minutes easier to prepare

◆ Reviewing and approving the minutes

People make preparing *minutes* out to be a lot worse than it really is. They often think of the minutes as a daunting document to create because they believe that they must note everything everyone said at the meeting. Since it's hard to keep track of everything, they frequently don't keep track of *anything*. But minutes aren't that bad. They are simply the written record of the proceedings of a deliberative assembly. They serve to record the actions taken at a meeting, not what was *said* at that meeting.

Minutes serve as the institutional memory for the organization. Because you have them to refer back to, they prevent a group from doing the same thing over and over.

In addition, minutes serve as a record of what was decided at the meeting. If the organization gets involved in a lawsuit, the minutes are one of the first documents that all parties will request. And when ruling, a judge or jury will give much more weight to the official minutes of the meeting than to what any particular individual recalls happening.

What to Put in the Minutes (and What to Leave Out)

Robert's recommends that minutes contain the following items:

- Kind of meeting (regular, special, and so on).

- Name of the organization.

Robert's Says

Minutes are the written record of the proceedings of a deliberative assembly. They are a record of what was done at the meeting, not what was said at the meeting.

Parliamentary Pearls

Although it's not necessary to include the full report of the treasurer in the text of the minutes, many groups find it helpful to include the previous balance, income totals, disbursement totals, and current balance in the minutes.

- Date, time, and place of the meeting.

- Names of the presiding officer and secretary, or in their absence, the names of their substitutes.

- The approximate number of members present (optional).

- The establishment of a quorum (optional).

- Record of the action taken on the minutes of the previous meeting.

- The exact wording of each main motion as it was voted on, and whether it passed or failed, along with the name of the maker. In addition, if the vote was counted, the count should be included, as well as the tellers' reports, if any; in roll call votes, the record of each person's vote is included.

- Any notice given at the meeting. Previous notice is sometimes required, such as with amendments to the bylaws; if any such notice was given at the meeting, it should be included in the minutes.

- Points of order and appeals.

- For committee reports, the name of the committee, and the reporting member. If the committee provides a printed report, attach it to the minutes and note that it is attached.

- The hour of adjournment.

Robert's is equally clear about what should *not* be included in the minutes. The following should not be included:

- The opinion or interpretation of the secretary.

- Judgmental phrases such as "heated debate" or "valuable comment".

- Discussion. Minutes are a record of what was *done* at the meeting, not what was *said* at the meeting.

- Motions that were withdrawn.

- Name of person who seconded a motion.

- Flowery language.

- Reports in detail.

- Transcripts of the meeting. While some groups choose to have a transcript of the meeting, it should never substitute as the minutes of the meeting.

Getting the Minutes Approved

The minutes are made official only after they are approved, which usually takes place at the next meeting.

If your organization frequently makes changes to the minutes, you might want to send out the initial, unapproved set with the word "draft" clearly printed on them. Then, when the minutes have been changed and approved, the official minutes can be sent out.

If your organization seldom has changes to the minutes, two sets, one draft and one approved, will probably be unnecessary.

Sign 'em

After the minutes have been corrected and approved by the membership, they should be signed by the secretary (the president's signature isn't required). The word "approved" and the date of the approval should also be included.

> **CAUTION**
>
> **Gavel Gaffs**
>
> Although including the words "Respectfully submitted" right before the secretary's signature used to be common practice, it is considered outdated to do so today. Instead, simply sign your name.

Book 'em

The official copy of the minutes are the property of the organization. They should be entered in the *minutes book* and kept by the secretary if the organization doesn't have a headquarters office. If there is an office, the official copy of the minutes should be kept there.

> **Robert's Says**
>
> The **minutes book** is usually a three ring binder, that contains a complete copy of all of the minutes.

The official copy of the minutes should have attached to it the original signed copies of each of the following:

- ♦ Committee reports
- ♦ Officers' reports
- ♦ Written motions
- ♦ Tellers' reports
- ♦ Correspondence

If the secretary distributes copies of the minutes to the members, it isn't necessary to include all of the attachments with them. Instead, you can include a brief summary of the attachments or at least a reference to them. Members can get a copy of them from the secretary if they wish to review them.

Parliamentary Pearls _____

Just because the minutes are an official document doesn't mean that the they have to be hard to read. Some simple formatting can make the minutes easier to read. Here are a few suggestions:

- ♦ Set off each section with a boldfaced heading
- ♦ After each motion, bold the words that indicate if it passed or failed
- ♦ Turn on the line numbering feature so that each line of the minutes is numbered.

Make a Minutes Template

In Chapter 15, I suggested creating a template for the agenda. Creating and using a template for the minutes also saves a tremendous amount of time. The following document is a sample of a minutes template.

Sample Minutes Template

MINUTES of [Organization name]

Meeting date: _____

Call to order: A _____ [kind of meeting] meeting of the _____ [organization name], was held in _____ [place, city, state] on _____ [date], 20__. The meeting convened at _____ [time], President _____ [name] presiding, and _____ [name], secretary.

[Some small organizations choose to list attendees. This works well for boards of directors.]

Members in attendance: [optional item]

Members not in attendance: [optional item]

Approval of minutes: Motion was made by [name], and seconded to approve the minutes of the _____ [date] meeting. **Motion carried.**

Officers' reports:

   President

   Vice president

   Secretary

   Treasurer

Board and committee reports:

Unfinished business:

[Subject title]

   Motion: Moved by [name] that [state motion].

   Motion carried. Motion failed. [leave only one of these]

New business:

[Subject title]

Motion: Moved by [name] that [state motion].

   Motion carried. Motion failed. [leave only one of these]

Announcements:

Adjournment: The meeting was adjourned at _____[time].

_____   _____

    Secretary   Date of approval

[Organization Name]

Skeletal Minutes

Skeletal minutes are minutes prepared in advance of a meeting or convention. They include everything that will be occurring, in the order it will occur, based on the agenda and the script for the meeting. The person in charge of the minutes can fill in the details during the meeting. Skeletal minutes can be used at any type of meeting, but they are probably of greatest assistance at conventions, when a lot of issues will be covered.

Minutes Approval Committee

When you don't meet very often, it might be difficult to recall what happened at the previous meeting, much less what order it was done in. Some of us have trouble remembering what we had for lunch yesterday, much less how the wording ended up on that controversial motion at the annual meeting last year!

When there is going to be at least a few months between meetings, it's probably best for the organization to have a minutes approval committee. Essentially, this is a small group of members who work with the secretary to create an acceptable set of minutes immediately after the meeting. If office equipment is available, they can enter the minutes into a computer, print them out, and make photocopies so that the final copy can be proofed, agreed upon, and signed before the minutes approval committee members go home.

> **Gavel Gaffs**
>
> When there is a minutes approval committee, the minutes don't need to be approved by the membership at the next meeting, because they have already been approved by the minutes approval committee. The minutes approved by the committee are the official minutes of the meeting.

Samples Please!

Since skeletal minutes may be a whole new concept to you, I am including some samples that might be helpful. The first sample is the first few paragraphs of skeletal minutes of the third meeting of a convention. The second is the first few paragraphs of the minutes for that meeting. The third is the sample set of minutes for an organization that meets monthly.

Sample Skeletal Minutes

The third meeting of the Seventeenth Annual Session of the American Association of Fun Loving People was convened on August 9, 20XX, at _____ A.M. President Joyful presided and Harry Happy, secretary, was present.

The report of the Credentials Committee was presented by Geri Glad, Chairman.

Geri Glad submitted the list of delegates and alternates who had registered up until _____ A.M. The number of delegates registered was _____. On behalf of the Credentials Committee, Geri Glad moved that the revised roll of delegates submitted be the official roll of the voting members of the delegate body. **The motion PASSED or FAILED** [circle one]

or

Geri Glad reported there were no changes since the last report of the Credentials Committee and the voting strength remained at _____.

President Joyful declared a quorum present.

Sample Minutes Prepared from Skeletal Minutes

The third meeting of the Seventeenth Annual Session of the American Association of Fun Loving People was convened on August 9, 20XX, at 10:05 A.M. President Joyful presided and Harry Happy, secretary, was present.

The report of the Credentials Committee was presented by Geri Glad, Chairman. Geri Glad reported there were no changes since the last report of the Credentials Committee and the voting strength remained at 555.

President Joyful declared a quorum present.

Sample Minutes of Organization That Meets Monthly

Minutes of the Association of Fun Loving People

Ain't-It-Fun Chapter

Meeting Date: April 1, 2004

Call to Order: A regular meeting of the American Association of Fun Loving People Ain't-It-Fun Chapter, was held at the Fun-Fun-Fun Hotel in Ain't-It-Fun, North

continues

continued

Dakota, on April 1, 20XX. The meeting called to order at 6:00 P.M., by President Sally Never-Sad, and Mary Merry, secretary, was present. President Never-Sad declared a quorum present.

Approval of Minutes: Motion was made by John Jolly to approve the minutes of the March 2, 20XX, meeting. **Motion carried.**

Officers' Reports:

Reports were given by the president and the treasurer.

The treasurer reported the balance on hand at the beginning of the reporting period as $100, receipts of $25 from dues, current disbursements of $25 and a balance on hand of $100. The report was filed.

Committee Reports:

Finance Committee Chairman Sam Smiley reported on the motion to purchase a computer that was referred to the finance committee at the last meeting. The committee recommended that the members approve the motion with the amendment "not to exceed $3,000." After discussion and further amendment the following motion was voted on: "We purchase a PC compatible computer at a price not to exceed $3,000." **Motion carried.**

Program Committee Chairman Gail Glee reported the plans for the program for the remainder of the calendar year.

Unfinished Business:

Paint Headquarters Building

Motion postponed from last month's meeting: "I move that we paint the headquarters building green." After discussion and amendment the following motion was voted on: "I move that we paint the headquarters building white." **Motion carried.**

New Business:

August Fundraiser

Motion: Moved by John Grin that "we sponsor a fundraiser in August. The details are to be worked out by a committee of three appointed by the president." **Motion carried.**

President Never-Sad appointed the following members to the August Fundraiser Committee: Mike Money, Cathy Cash, and Charlie Currency.

Adjournment: The meeting adjourned at 8:45 P.M.

_____   _____
           Secretary   Date of Approval

American Association of Fun Loving People

Ain't-It-Fun Chapter

The Least You Need to Know

◆ The minutes should be a record of the actions taken by the group, not a record of what was said at the meeting.

◆ If your organization makes frequent changes to the minutes, create an unofficial version marked "draft" to send out to members for them to review.

◆ Once minutes are accepted by the membership, they become the official record of the meeting.

◆ Organizations that meet infrequently should consider using a minutes approval committee, which prepares and approves the minutes immediately after the meeting.

Chapter 19

Committees in Action

In This Chapter

- ◆ What committees are really all about
- ◆ Standing committees versus special committees
- ◆ Common committee pitfalls

Ever hear the joke about committees?

They're the only human organisms that have multiple stomachs and no brain.

Unfortunately, this punch line describes many committees that I have worked with. My challenge for you after you have read this chapter is to prove this joke wrong!

What a Committee Is *Supposed* to Be

A committee is a group of one or more persons who are appointed or elected to carry out a charge. The charge can be to investigate, to recommend, or to take action. There are some important components in that definition, so let's break it down:

- ◆ To say that committee members are appointed or elected indicates that the committee is usually not an autonomous group—in other words, they are responsible for and must answer to someone or some body.

◆ The committee's charge is what it was told to do. A committee can only do what it is charged to do—it should do no more and no less than its charge. A committee is charged with a task through the motion to commit or refer (see Chapter 12).

Committees are used when the membership feels that it would be more appropriate to have a smaller group of people research, study, and discuss an issue and report their findings to the parent body rather than leave it up to the entire membership to do this. In some cases, the membership might also ask the committee to recommend an action.

Kinds of Committees

Although committees can have countless names, they all fall into one of two categories: standing or special.

Standing Committees

A standing committee exists from one year to the next, and is typically charged with a continuing function. A typical standing committee is the finance committee. As long as you have money coming in and going out, you will always need a finance committee.

Standing committees are usually established by the bylaws, and the committees' functions are usually laid out there as well.

Parliamentary Pearls

An executive committee is a form of a standing committee. It is usually made up of the officers of the organization. An executive committee only exists if it is authorized in the bylaws. Go to the bylaws to determine if there is an executive committee for your organization, who is on it, and exactly what power it has. The executive committee is usually a subsection of the board of directors and, when it is, it is frequently allowed to act on behalf of the board between meetings of the board.

Special Committees

A special committee is formed to perform a specific task. It comes together, performs the task, gives its final report, and then ceases to exist. It cannot be appointed to perform a task that falls within the assigned function of a standing committee.

A special committee is sometimes referred to as a select committee, an ad hoc committee, a task force, or a work group. No matter what name it goes by, it is still a special committee.

Special committees are formed when a task comes up that doesn't fit the job description of any of the standing committees. Special committees are, or should be, short lived, and specific in focus. For example, if your group decides to have a fundraiser, you might appoint a special committee to take charge of the fundraiser.

> **Gavel Gaffs**
>
> Before you form a special committee, check out the bylaws and make sure that there isn't a standing committee that is assigned that task or a similar task. If there is, the task should be handled by the standing committee.

Committee of the Whole Is Special

A version of a special committee is a committee of the whole and its variations. This is a parliamentary tool that is not used very much in deliberative assemblies. You will find it used more frequently in legislative bodies and governmental bodies. It allows the entire group to discuss an issue with the freedom of a committee.

The committee of the whole comes in the following three versions:

- Committee of the whole
- Quasi committee of the whole
- Informal consideration

How a Committee Works

Unless a committee is so large that it needs to function as a full assembly, a committee can follow the more relaxed rules described in Chapter 2. However, a committee cannot adopt its own rules, unless authorized to do so in the instructions the committee was given or in the bylaws. In addition, committees don't have the power to punish a member. If a member is doing something that he or she shouldn't do, the committee should report that fact to the assembly.

> **Parliamentary Pearls**
>
> The committee chairman is usually named by the same body that named the committee. The chairman of a committee is the leader of the committee, who is responsible for calling and conducting the meetings, and should make sure that people follow up on tasks they volunteered for or were assigned to.

The Committee's Charge

Since a committee is not an autonomous group, it should get its assignment from the parent body, whether that's the board or the membership. The responsibility that goes with the assignment is sometimes referred to as its charge. The charge might entail investigating an issue with no power to act or it might give the committee full power to act. The exact nature of the charge can be spelled out in the motion that creates the committee in the first place or, for standing committees, it can be spelled out in the bylaws.

Whoever has the power to appoint a committee has the power to fill vacancies on the committee and to remove members from the committee. So if a committee member was appointed by the president and that member isn't doing his or her job, the president can remove that person from the committee and appoint someone else to serve on the committee.

Keep Your Mouth Shut

Committee meetings are only open to members of the committee and anyone else the committee invites to attend. Just because you are a member of the organization does not give you the right to attend a committee meeting. The whole idea is to give the assignment to a small, focused group. Allowing everyone to come and go as they wish would defeat the purpose.

In addition, whatever is discussed within the committee is confidential. If a member can't speak up in a committee meeting without fear of everyone in the organization knowing what was said, the freedom of discussion is lost.

Subcommittees: Committees Within Committees

A committee can appoint a subcommittee made up of members of the committee to undertake particular tasks. This is a useful technique for dividing the labor.

Point of Information

Frequently you will find in the bylaws the statement that the president is ex officio a member of all committees (hopefully it adds, "except the nominating committee"). When the president is ex officio a member of all committees, he or she has the right to attend committee meetings, discuss issues, and vote, but isn't required to do an equal share of the work and is not counted in determining a quorum. Note that the rules for a president as ex officio are different from a nonmember being ex officio.

Committee Procedure Manual

It is tough to hit a target if you don't know where the target is located. Similarly, it is difficult for a committee to be successful if it isn't really clear on what its responsibilities are and what is expected of it. That is why I am a firm believer that every committee should have an updated procedures manual.

The committee's procedure manual should be created by the committee, approved by them, and then approved by whomever that committee reports to, usually the board of directors. In Chapter 19, I discussed the nominating committee procedure manual and how helpful it can be. Each committee should have a manual and every member of the committee should have a copy of the manual.

Content of the Procedure Manual

There is no universally accepted manual format for committee procedure manuals. Each committee and each organization has its own needs. The following subjects should be covered in any procedure manual:

♦ Background information

♦ Governing document requirements for the committee

♦ Responsibilities of the committee chairman

♦ Responsibilities of the committee

♦ Forms used by the committee

♦ Information on meetings of the committee

Other options items include the following:

♦ Past reports

♦ Past committee minutes

Committee Pitfalls

All those jokes about committees exist for a reason! Unfortunately, a lot of committees are very ineffective and many organizations use committees inappropriately. Being aware of the following committee pitfalls can help you avoid them:

♦ **The committee does the work, and then the body does the work again.**
This is a terrible waste of time and energy, but it happens all too frequently. A
group gives an assignment to a committee. The committee does the work and
reports back to the group. Then, because the larger group didn't do the work,
they aren't comfortable authorizing the committee to proceed, so they do all of
the work again.

♦ **The committee does its work but doesn't prepare an adequate, succinct
report to the body.** The report is the only evidence that the body will have of
the committee's work, so if the committee doesn't prepare a complete report,
the body won't know what the committee did.
All that work will have been wasted effort.

Parliamentary Pearls

A committee should keep
notes of what was de-
cided, but it usually doesn't
need to keep formal min-
utes. Usually the committee
chairman keeps notes, but it
would be appropriate for the
committee chairman to request
that a member be responsible for
the notes.

♦ **Work, but no recommendation.** The committee prepares a report but fails to include
specific recommendations. The main body
needs to know what action the committee
recommends in order for the committee to
have been effective.

♦ **No work.** The group assigns a committee to
undertake a particular task, but the committee
doesn't do the work it was charged with.

Discharging a Committee

Think of a committee's assignment as an object—for our purposes, we will think of it
as a ball. Only one group of people can be in possession of the ball at a time. If one
group doesn't like the way the other group is handling the ball and thinks they can do
a better job, then in order to do something with it, they must first gain possession of
the ball.

Robert's Says

A **discharge** is a motion
that relieves a committee from further consideration of the task that
has been assigned to it.

Similarly, if an assembly assigns a task to a committee and the assembly doesn't like the way the committee is handling it, or the assembly decides that it
wants to do the task, then the only way that the
assembly can get the task back is to take possession
of it. This is done through a motion to *discharge* a
committee. By using this motion, the assembly can
end the existence of a special committee or take back
the task from a special or standing committee.

The motion to discharge a committee is not necessary in the case of a special committee that has completed its task and has given its final report, because that committee ceases to exist. But if the committee hasn't completed its work and the assembly wants the task back, then the assembly must use the motion to discharge the committee.

Since the motion to discharge is the parliamentary equivalent of getting mad, taking your ball, and going home, this motion should be reserved for special situations.

Parliamentary Pearls

Conventions are a creature all to themselves, and so it makes sense that they have unique committees. I discuss those committees in Chapter 21.

The Least You Need to Know

◆ A committee is a group of one or more persons who are appointed or elected to carry out a charge.

◆ Standing committees' charges are determined by the bylaws; special committees' charges are determined by the membership or board through the motion to commit or refer.

◆ Committees are required to report on their work. If charged to make a recommendation, that recommendation should be included in the report.

20

Officers' and Committee Reports

In This Chapter

- ◆ When officers need to prepare a report
- ◆ The special nature of the treasurer's report
- ◆ What to do when an officer or a committee makes a recommendation
- ◆ How committees prepare and present their reports

Officers and committees must have a system to keep the appointing/ electing body informed of their activities. That information should take the form of a report, which can be given orally or in writing and might or might not include specific recommendations.

Officers' Reports

The bylaws usually require the officers to give an annual report. If so, that report should be done in writing. At all other meetings, officers only report if they have specific information or recommendations to share with the group. It is not unusual for an officer to prepare only the one formal report—the annual report—each year.

Most of the time the officers' reports are informative in nature. If officers wish to include recommendations in their report, they may do so. However, an officer should not make the motion to adopt that recommendation during his or her report. After an officer finishes his or her report, another member may put the recommendation in the form of a motion.

Gavel Gaffs

Frequently officers of the organization are also assigned as chairman of a particular committee. In that situation, the officers' report must be separate from the committee report—sorry, you can't get away with only preparing one report!

Although *Robert's* doesn't specify a format for the officers' reports, it is standard to include the following information in them:

♦ A heading that includes the name of the office, the name of the officer, the date of the report, and the time period the report is covering.

♦ A description of what the officer has done since the last report that fulfils the responsibilities of the office.

♦ Actions that the officer plans to take in the future.

♦ Any recommendations that the officer wants to make to the membership. If there is more than one recommendation, they should be numbered for ease of reference.

Parliamentary Pearls

Even though the secretary is responsible for the minutes, the minutes are not referred to as the secretary's report. They are an agenda item all by themselves and are not considered a part of the secretary's report.

Treasurer's Report

The treasurer's report is so specialized that it warrants a discussion separate from the other officers' reports.

The treasurer usually reports at each meeting. The level of detail to include in the report depends on the kind and size of the organization. Usually the information included in a treasurer's report is very similar to the information you receive from the bank in your monthly account statement. No matter what format, whether it's done by hand or on a fancy spreadsheet, it should include the following items:

♦ Balance on hand at the beginning of the reporting period

♦ Receipts (money that came in)

- ◆ Disbursements (money that went out)

- ◆ Balance on hand at the end of the reporting period

The monthly treasurer's reports on the organization's finances are for informational purposes only, and the report doesn't need to be approved, adopted, or accepted by the organization.

At some point after the report has been received, the organization should arrange to have it reviewed by an auditor or the organization's own audit committee. The purpose of the audit is to certify the accuracy of the report.

The treasurer also must give an annual report. It should include the balance at the beginning of the reporting year, all receipts, all disbursements, and balance at the end of reporting year.

Gavel Gaffs

If you are the presiding officer, be sure to use the right words at the end of the report of the treasurer.

Wrong words: "Is there a motion to approve the report of the treasurer?"

Right words: "Thank you. The report will be filed for audit."

Audit

The purpose of the audit is to certify the correctness of the financial reports. It does not indicate the financial situation of the organization. It makes sure that the proper accounting principles and practices are being used.

Who does the audit is determined by the size of the organization and any state or federal regulations that apply to the organization. If the organization is too small to have a formal audit done by an independent accounting firm, then there should at least be an audit committee whose job it is to review the financial records and certify their correctness.

Whether the audit is done by a committee or an independent audit firm it should include two parts:

- ◆ One part is the certification of the accuracy of the financial records.

- ◆ The second part is more subjective. It is an examination of the current accounting procedures of the organization and recommendations for improvement. If for example, the current reimbursement form does not have all of the information that is needed to practice proper accounting procedures, this part of the audit would recommend a change to the current reimbursement form.

Budget

The treasurer usually works with the finance committee and/or the staff to create and maintain the budget. Just like the preparation of any other budget, the budget of the organization should look first at what amount is reasonable to expect as an income and then how the members want to spend that income.

The budget is usually approved by the board of directors and sometimes by the membership. Once a budget has been approved, expenditure of specific amounts that are within the budgeted amount do not have to be approved.

Committee Report

A committee report is an official statement that is formally adopted by a majority vote of the committee and that is presented to the parent body (either the entire membership or the board of directors) in the name of the committee. It contains information obtained, information regarding action taken, or recommendations on behalf of the committee. Don't worry: It's not as complicated as the definition makes it sound. Let's break it down a bit.

If the committee was charged with obtaining information on an issue, it should report that information to the group that gave it the charge. The report should also include a description of how the committee went about carrying out its assigned task. In addition, sometimes committees are charged with making a recommendation based on their research. If so, the committee's recommendation should be part of the report.

> **Point of Information**
>
> A detailed committee report should include the following elements:
>
> ◆ Description of the way the committee performed task
>
> ◆ Information and facts obtained
>
> ◆ Conclusions drawn from obtained information
>
> ◆ Recommendations of the committee (if there are any)

The Format of the Report

Committee reports are most effective when they are put in writing, although many groups accept oral reports. If the committee submits a written report, the chairman of the committee should sign it and add the word "chairman" after his or her name. The chair's signature indicates that the committee has approved the report and directed the chairman to sign the report on their behalf.

Presenting the Report

The chairman of the committee presents the report to the parent body on behalf of the committee. If the chairman is unable to give the report, another member may present the information.

At the conclusion of the report, the reporting member makes a motion to implement the recommendation of the committee. The suggested wording is: "On behalf of the committee, I move that …." Because the recommendation comes from a committee, no second is needed.

The following is a sample committee report.

Report of the American Association of Fun-Loving People

National Nominating Committee

February 14, 20XX

During the months of November and December the AAFLP nominating committee sought nominations from the membership through the AAFLP Newsletter, *Fun Fun Fun*.

The nominating committee met January 11 and 12, 20XX in Ain't-It-Fun, North Dakota. After deliberation and ballot votes, the committee selected its slate of candidates for office for AAFLP for the upcoming year. The nominating committee's slate of candidates is as follows:

President	Charlie Cheery
Vice President	Joan Jovial
Secretary	Ellen Ecstatic
Treasurer	Einer Elated

The nominating committee will include the slate in the March newsletter, as specified in the AAFLP Bylaws.

The nominating committee also agreed upon the following recommendations:

1. Amend the standing rules by inserting a new 11.03 and renumbering the succeeding subsections:

    11.03 Within six months after its election, the committee shall meet, either in person or by telephone conference call, to develop criteria for offices and a program to encourage candidates to seek office.

2. That the convention standing rules provide that immediately after nominations are completed, each candidate for each office will be given three minutes to address the convention.

Polly Positive, Chairman

AAFLP Nominating Committee

The Least You Need to Know

- ◆ Officers' reports are usually informative in nature, although they can also include recommendations.

- ◆ An officer should not make a motion to adopt one of his or her own recommendations; that should be up to another member after the officer has finished presenting the report.

- ◆ The treasurer's report does not need an approval—it is presented and filed for audit.

- ◆ The committee chair presents the committee report to the parent body on behalf of the entire committee.

Chapter 21

Making the Most of Conventions

In This Chapter

◆ What makes conventions special

◆ Delegates' roles and responsibilities

◆ Convention committees in action

◆ Tips for keeping the convention running smoothly

Every convention is unique. Conventions vary in length, formality, number of attendees, and even the kinds of committees they have. In this chapter, I'm going to explain some of those unique aspects of conventions.

It's Convention Time!

Most conventions are attended by a voting body made up of delegates who are chosen by a subordinate group to represent them. Democratic and Republic national conventions, for instance, fall into this category. Smaller organizations often open their conventions up to all members and give them all the right to vote.

> **Point of Information**
>
> A convention by any other name is still a convention. What I'm referring to as a convention might also be called a conference, congress, house of delegates, delegate assembly, general assembly, house of representatives, and annual meeting. Each group puts its particular spin on the gathering and gives it a name.

Convention FAQs

Members frequently have questions about the convention process. I will try to address those frequently asked questions in the following sections.

What's the Convention Session and When Is It a Meeting?

Earlier in the book we discussed the difference between a meeting and a session. A meeting is an assembly of members gathered to conduct business during which there is no separation of the members except for a short recess. A session is a meeting or a series of connected meetings.

A convention is one session, but usually many meetings. Let's use an example of a convention that runs from Sunday through Thursday. On each of those five days there are two business meetings. That convention has 10 meetings but only one session. Each business meeting is its own meeting, but all the meetings combined make up one session.

Should Delegates Come to a Convention with Their Decisions Already Made?

A delegate is a member who is chosen to represent a particular group of people at a convention. The delegate is a voting member of the convention. Delegates should be sent to the convention informed about how the group they represent feels on issues that are to come up during the convention.

Unfortunately, delegates are often sent to a convention instructed on how to vote on a particular controversial issue. However, doing so is contrary to the basic concept of parliamentary law. Conventions are held to bring everyone together so everyone can hear the same information, discuss the issue together, and then make a group decision. When a delegate is instructed on how to vote ahead of time, all the discussion is wasted. A delegate is a human being with a brain, and that person should be allowed to use his or her brain.

Gavel Gaffs _____

Frequently groups send alternate delegates to conventions. They are sent to take the place of delegates in case those delegates are sick or unable to attend. Unless the rules state otherwise, when an alternate replaces a delegate, it is a permanent replacement. The former delegate can not come back as a delegate.

Some groups abuse the alternate concept by having the alternate sit in the place of the delegate for short periods of time. This happens multiple times during the convention, and it's almost like watching the delegation play musical chairs. Unless the rules indicate otherwise, *Robert's* requires that once an alternate replaces a delegate, there is no coming back!

What Are the Delegates' Responsibilities?

Unfortunately, some delegates treat attendance at a convention as a paid vacation. Being selected as a delegate entails many responsibilities that need to be taken care of before, during, and after the convention.

Before the convention the delegate should fill out and send in all credential and registration forms. Material regarding the business to come before the convention is usually sent out in advance of the convention. The delegate should read all that information in preparation for the convention. The delegate should discuss all controversial issues with the members he or she represents and find out their points of view on the issues.

Gavel Gaffs _____

It's fine for delegates to enjoy themselves and take advantage of being in a different city and all that it has to offer, as long they also fulfill their responsibilities as delegate to their organization.

During the convention the delegate should attend all the business meetings as well as any informative sessions designed to educate delegates on issues to come before the convention. At the business meetings the delegate should take an active role in the deliberations of the convention body. When it is time to vote, the delegate should vote, although the delegate can not be forced to vote.

After the convention the delegate should report back to the group he or she represented. That report may be oral, written, or both. It should be an informative report of key business that transpired at the convention.

Convention Committees

The following four committees that are somewhat convention specific and worth separating out:

- ◆ **Credentials.** Establishes who can vote during the meeting
- ◆ **Rules.** Establishes the rules that the group will follow
- ◆ **Program.** Determines the order of business for the meeting
- ◆ **Resolutions.** Screens, consolidates, and edits resolutions that are to come before the convention body

Let's look at each in turn.

Credentials Committee

The function of the credentials committee is to receive members' credential forms, certify delegates and alternates, and register delegates and alternates at the convention.

In advance of the convention, this committee or the headquarters' staff sends out credentials forms that include the information the committee needs in order to determine whether members are qualified to vote. Then, when members arrive at the convention, they go to the credentials desk to receive their badges, voting cards, or ribbons for the badges that prove that they are voting members.

Point of Information

In Chapter 17, we discussed the role of the tellers' committee in counting the ballots and reporting the count to the members. The tellers' committee, along with the presiding officer and parliamentarian, should determine in advance the best way to conduct a vote count if one is needed. Then, during the convention, the committee should be ready to assist with that count.

Point of Information

At the end of the credentials committee report, the chairman moves the adoption of the report. The report may sound something like this:

"Madam President, attached is the list of the names of the voting delegates who have registered up to this time." [specific statistics would be given here such as number of delegates, alternates, etc.] "On behalf of the committee, I move that the roll of delegates hereby submitted be the official roll of the voting delegates at this time."

After the motion is adopted to approve the credentials report, it is a good idea to remind the body of the number of voting delegates or members.

At the beginning of the convention the credentials committee reports the list of voting members who have registered and the number of voting members. That number is used to determine the total possible number of votes that could be cast on any one motion. This report must be approved by the membership; once it is, the list of voting members becomes the official list for the remainder of the convention.

Rules Committee

Once the credentials committee establishes who can vote, it's time for the rules committee to establish what are called the convention standing rules. These are parliamentary rules as well as other rules that relate to the administration of the convention. Some of the possible subjects covered in the convention standing rules include …

♦ Credentials committee report information.

♦ Any requirements for admission into the convention room, such as badges.

♦ Seating requirements, such as a designated delegates area.

♦ Procedures for an alternate to replace a delegate.

♦ Information on badges and voting cards.

♦ Processes and requirements for presenting motions or resolutions, such as that they must be in writing.

♦ Time limits on individuals speaking in debate.

♦ Debate rules.

♦ Nomination and election rules.

♦ Establishment of a minutes approval committee.

♦ Cell phone and pager regulations.

♦ The parliamentary authority (*Robert's* I hope!).

The rules are usually printed in the convention information and read by the rules committee chairman at the beginning of the meeting.

Parliamentary Pearls

At the end of the report the rules committee chairman moves the adoption of the convention standing rules. It might sound something like this: "Mr. President, on behalf of the rules committee, I move the adoption of the convention standing rules as just read and as printed on page 12 of the convention program."

Program Committee

Once the rules committee completes its report and recommends the adoption of the convention standing rules, the program committee makes its report. The program committee report should include the order of business, the meeting schedule, and any special events. At the end of its presentation the committee chairman, on behalf of the committee, moves its approval.

Resolutions Committee

Every convention handles the resolutions committee and its responsibilities differently. The purpose of the convention resolutions committee is to screen, consolidate, and edit resolutions that are to come before the convention body. Proper use of this committee can significantly reduce the time spent in business meetings because the committee reviews and discusses each resolution and makes its recommendations regarding each resolution to the convention body. Then, at the time of its report, it presents each resolution to the convention body along with its recommendation.

Some resolution committees can originate motions or resolutions, others can choose to not present a resolution to the convention body, still others can't change even a small word without the agreement of the maker of the resolution.

Point of Information

The chairman of the resolutions committee moves the adoption of each resolution and gives the committee's recommendation on how the convention body should vote on the motion. It may make any of the following recommendations:

- ◆ Vote yes, in favor of the resolution.
- ◆ Amend the resolution and then vote yes after the convention body amends it.
- ◆ Vote no, in opposition of the resolution.
- ◆ No recommendation (which means the committee is choosing to avoid giving the convention body a recommendation on how to vote).
- ◆ Referral to a committee (this should be used sparingly).

Little Things That Make a Big Difference at a Convention

There are many little touches at a convention that can ensure that it's run smoothly. The larger the convention, the more important these things become:

◆ **Pages.** Pages are assigned in advance of the meeting and usually wear something to distinguish themselves during the meeting. Before the meeting, pages are responsible for seating delegates in their designated area and other members in their assigned area. During the meeting, pages are responsible for passing notes and messages in the meeting room (all that practice in grade school finally pays off), making sure members who wish to speak can reach a microphone, assisting in the maintenance of order, and being sensitive to and helping fill the needs of the members.

◆ **Timekeepers.** If the convention rules include time limits on the speeches, time-keepers are a must. It is their job to keep time during the business meetings, so they must be familiar with the speaking and debate rules of the convention. Timekeepers should sit so that the presiding officer and the member speaking can both see them.

◆ **Briefings, forums, informational sessions.** There are many different names for these optional, informal meetings, and they can make a huge difference in the success of the meeting. When controversial issues come before the convention body, sessions should be held to give the group the opportunity to discuss the issue a day or two before they have to vote on it. Giving the group that time to process the different sides of the issues not only makes them more informed voters, but usually adds to the quality of their decisions.

> **Parliamentary Pearls**
>
> If speakers get 3 minutes per speech, at the end of 2½ minutes, the time-keeper should hold up a yellow flag. At 3 minutes the timekeeper should hold up a red flag. When the red flag goes up, the presiding officer should allow the speaker to finish his or her sentence and then interrupt the speaker and indicate that the time is up.

The Least You Need to Know

◆ Each group may call its convention something different but they are all conventions by nature.

◆ A convention is one session, but usually many meetings.

◆ Delegates should be sent to the convention informed about how the group that they represent feels on issues that are to come up during the convention. They should not, however, be instructed how to vote on particular issues.

◆ Because of the unique nature of conventions, they often have their own committees and rules of debate.

22

Electronic Meetings

In This Chapter

◆ Why e-meetings can come in handy

◆ Synchronous versus asynchronous meetings

◆ E-meeting venues

◆ Rules for running an e-meeting

Pundits and prognosticators frequently say that the time will come when electronic meetings (e-meetings) will totally replace in-person meetings. I don't agree with such predictions. I believe that the more we are surrounded by technology, the more we will need and want the personal contact of in-person meetings.

I do believe, though, that we will see a significant increase in the use of electronic meetings. As a consequence, it's worth taking a look at this new breed of meetings.

Why E-Meetings?

Why do people use electronic meetings? Here are some of the reasons that e-meetings are becoming more popular:

◆ **Time-sensitive issues.** Some issues need to be addressed before the group can come together for an in-person meeting. Sometimes, if an issue isn't dealt with immediately, it becomes a moot point. For example, say that your group wants to take a stand against a bill that is scheduled to be voted on by your state legislators in two weeks. Your next in-person meeting is three weeks away. If you take a stand on the issue at your next in-person meeting, it will be after the bill has been voted on, and, therefore, a moot point.

◆ **Cost.** If all of the people in your group live in the same area, the cost of conducting a meeting is minimal. But, when the attendees are from all over the country or even the world, you can save everyone money by conducting an e-meeting.

Same Time, Different Place vs. Different Time, Different Place

E-meetings can take place during a set time, just like regular meetings, or they can take place at different times. Meetings that take place at the same time are called *synchronous meetings*. So if you are on a conference call with members from New York, California, Alabama, and Illinois, you are in a synchronous meeting. You are interacting in real time. *Asynchronous* meetings are meetings that occur with the participants in different places at different times. So if your bylaws allow you to debate and take a vote by fax, you are participating in a asynchronous meeting.

Robert's Says

Synchronous meetings occur when participants are in different places at the same time.

Asynchronous meetings occur with the participants in different places at different times.

If you understand these two concepts, you will understand the basis of the rules for your electronic meetings. When you attend a synchronous meeting, you can, for the most part, follow the rules established in *Robert's*, with only a few variations. But, that is not true of asynchronous meetings. Because of the nature of asynchronous meetings, the basic rules of *Robert's* will work, but they must be adapted, sometimes significantly.

You Need Special Rules

Any kind of meeting that is not an in-person meeting must be authorized in the bylaws or the governing documents.

If, in an extreme emergency, you conduct a meeting electronically that is not authorized in the bylaws, the best thing to do is to ratify those actions at the next legal meeting. Be sure to specifically list each action in the minutes of the meeting in which you ratify those actions.

> **Gavel Gaffs** _____
>
> If your bylaws don't authorize an electronic meeting, any action you take during an electronic meeting is not a legal action taken by the group. If your bylaws don't authorize e-meetings and your organization wants to add a clause addressing them, here is some wording that might work for you. These are actual examples from existing bylaws. Notice that each example authorizes particular groups to have specific kinds of electronic meetings.
>
> - "The Board of Directors, Executive Committee, standing committees, and special committees are authorized to meet by telephone conference or through other electronic communications media so long as all the members may simultaneously hear each other and participate during the meeting."
>
> - "The Legislative Council, including its Assemblies or committees, may conduct its business by electronic or conventional means including mail, telephone, fax, computer, or other appropriate means, provided that all members have access to the information and/or debate through one or more of the means listed."
>
> - "The Board of Directors, Executive Committee, standing committees, special committees, and subcommittees of the Board of Directors are authorized to meet by electronic communication media so long as all members may participate."

E-meeting Venues

There are many different formats for electronic meetings. I will list a few here, but by the time you read this chapter, someone will have created at least one new way to meet electronically! The developments in technology are so rapid that it is very difficult to keep up.

Asynchronous meetings include …

- **E-mail.** All members of the meeting are listed in the "to" part of the e-mail. When you reply to a message in the e-mail, you should reply to all, so all of the participants receive the same information.

- **E-mail lists.** These are sometimes referred to as e-mail groups or Listservs. All of the participants in the meeting are on the electronic list and therefore get all of the e-mails. You send an e-mail to the e-mail list and it is automatically sent out to all of the participants in your group.

- **Facsimile/fax.** Although the fax machine is used most frequently as a way of voting electronically, it is sometimes also used as a method of having a "discussion" within a group.

Synchronous meetings include …

- **Telephone conferencing.** This is probably the most frequently used e-meeting venue. Each participant in the phone conference is on a telephone at his or her own location. The advantage of this format is that all members can hear each other; the disadvantage is that they can't see each other. That doesn't seem like much of a disadvantage until you realize that nonverbal communication constitutes more than half of what we communicate.

- **Video conferencing.** This format gives the participants the advantage of being able to hear and see the other meeting participants. It is wonderful technology, but don't let it fool you, it is not the same as being in the same room. It can also be very expensive.

- **Chat rooms.** Some groups use chat rooms and instant messaging to conduct meetings. In order for it to be a synchronous meeting, all attendees must be in the chat room or on instant messaging at the same time. The group must have rules for how members are recognized. For instance, they might require members to type in "hand" when they want to speak, and the chair might recognize a member by typing the word "go" with that individual's name next to it.

E-meeting Rules

Synchronous meetings can rely on the rules already in *Robert's* and need only a few additional rules to account for the unique situation. Asynchronous meetings require detailed new rules, because *Robert's* doesn't cover them.

Rules for Conference Calls

Some of the rules that you might consider including in a set of rules written for conference calls include …

- A conference meeting must be arranged at least 48 hours in advance of the call.

- Each member should seek recognition from the chair before beginning to speak.

- Each member should identify himself or herself prior to speaking.

♦ Motions will be voted on by voice vote. If the chair has a problem determining the vote, he or she may call for a roll call vote. The roll call vote is for determination of the outcome of the vote and shall not be recorded in the minutes.

♦ The minutes of the meeting shall be approved at the next in-person meeting.

Point of Information

Because it might be very difficult to determine a majority or two-thirds vote by voice during a conference call, groups might need to rely on the roll call vote more frequently in those situations. However, it is only appropriate to record each member's vote in the minutes when each member represents a constituency, and even then it's not always appropriate.

Group or E-mail List Meeting Rules

Because *Robert's* was created for synchronous meetings, much of what is contained in *Robert's* must be adapted to asynchronous meetings.

There appear to be at least two different approaches to e-mail list meetings. The first approach is to have a start and stop time/date for the meeting. This start and stop time is similar to the start and stop time of an in-person meeting, but it is much longer because there's no guarantee that people will check their e-mail at the same time.

The second approach is to have the meeting be an ongoing process. In that case, the group establishes a time period for processing each motion. With this approach, it would be possible to have more than one motion being processed at a time. While that is not desirable, it may be the only practical way to be able to deal with multiple motions in a timely manner.

ASHA Electronic Meeting Procedures

The American Speech-Language-Hearing Association (ASHA) has a Legislative Council of 150 members that has been conducting electronic meetings through an e-mail list since 1999 and doing it very effectively. The rules they use were written and adopted in 1999 and have worked so well that they have not needed to change them.

With ASHA's permission, I am including those rules in this chapter. Before I do that, let me tell you a little about the organization, explain the flow of its meetings, and describe how its rules were written. Knowing these three things will assist you in adapting these rules to the needs of your organization, should you decide to do so.

Background on ASHA

ASHA is a national professional, scientific, and credentialing association for speech-language pathologists and audiologists. ASHA is made up of approximately 110,000 professionals. The Legislative Council and the Executive Board share the governance of ASHA.

The rules that I am referring to in this section are the electronic procedures for the Legislative Council (LC). The council is made up of up to 150 councilors. For the most part, the councilors represent the members in their respective states. Frequently the issues dealt with by the LC are time sensitive, such as a bill that is going before Congress that has an effect on the profession. Because of the size of the Legislative Council, it was not cost-effective to have frequent electronic synchronous meetings. Conference calls for a group that size are very expensive.

Flow of the Meeting

It is the flow of the meeting that makes electronic meetings difficult, and so ASHA established meeting rules to control this flow. ASHA rules specify that three different people/groups should be involved in managing the flow of the meeting. The speaker is the chair of the meeting. The administrative assistant to the Legislative Council receives all secondary motions and processes all votes. The committee on resolutions is responsible for placing motions on the e-mail list.

In the in-person meetings of the LC, a resolution/motion is not placed on the floor until after it has been reviewed by the committee on resolutions. That is also true when a resolution/motion goes on the list. Therefore, in the sample rules, you will not find a provision for the making and seconding of a motion. If your group does not utilize a committee like the committee on resolutions, you will want to include in your rules how a motion is made and seconded.

Writing the Rules

A committee was formed to write the rules for ASHA's electronic meetings. Early on in the process the committee agreed that the proposed procedures should replicate the way business is conducted on the floor of the council.

An example might be helpful here. Rule 7 reads: "Each message posted by a Councilor shall be a message written by the Councilor. Forwarding a message from a non-Legislative Council member is prohibited." The committee discussed forwarding messages and whether that should be allowed. To determine the rule, the committee compared that to what happens when a member wants to debate a motion on the floor. In an in-person meeting, the member who is not a councilor cannot just go to the microphone, gain recognition, and speak in debate. Therefore, in an electronic meeting, a member who is not a councilor should not be able to send a message directly to each councilor. In an electronic meeting and an in-person meeting, if a member wants to share a message, it must be first shared with the councilor who then puts the message in his or her own words and includes it in the debate.

Parliamentary Pearls

Be sure to give some thought into how the voting occurs in your e-mail group meetings. If the members have to vote by sending their vote to the entire group, will that affect how they vote? It might be best to have them send their votes to an independent third party who tallies the votes and reports the voting results to the chair.

ASHA Electronic Meeting Procedures

1. The speaker of the Council shall serve as the presiding officer of electronic meetings of the Legislative Council.

2. A proposed timeline for discussing and acting on a resolution/motion shall be established by the committee on resolutions and communicated to the Legislative Council at the beginning of the processing of any resolution/motion based on the following considerations:

   a. The content, urgency for acting on the resolution/motion, and internal and external timing demands;

   b. If there is time and/or need for a draft of the resolution/motion to be made available so Councilors can suggest changes to or request clarification from the Committee on Resolutions. When time does not permit posting of a draft resolution/motion, the committee on resolutions shall forward an explanation to the Council; and

   c. The time when the ASHA membership shall be notified of the resolution/motion using an ASHA communication vehicle available to all members.

   NOTE: The proposed timeline can be modified by the committee on resolutions based on the complexity and number of secondary motions that need to be discussed and voted upon.

3. The process for discussing and acting on resolutions/motions shall include the following:

   a. The resolution/motion shall be posted and discussion shall begin.

   b. At a designated time, discussion on the main motion shall stop and secondary motions shall be presented and acted upon.

   c. After the period for secondary motions has been completed, the resolution in its final form shall be posted for discussion and voting and no additional secondary motions shall be allowed.

4. Proposed secondary motions must be submitted to the administrative assistant to the Legislative Council via the LC Forum Listserv within the required time limits. The committee on resolutions is authorized to consolidate, reword, prioritize and not present to the Legislative Council the secondary motions that are submitted. The committee on resolutions may decide to prioritize and present to the Legislative Council more than one secondary motion at a time. Prioritization shall be based on parliamentary principles and efficient and effective conduct of Legislative Council business. The decision to not present a secondary motion to the Legislative Council can only be made after notification to the Legislative Council with opportunity for Councilors to object. If thirty Councilors object, the secondary motion shall be presented to the Legislative Council.

5. The committee on resolutions shall have the authority to move to postpone a resolution/motion to the next face-to-face meeting of the Legislative Council based upon the following criteria: (a) complexity and number of secondary motions applied to the main motion; (b) determination by the committee on resolutions that it is in the best interest of ASHA to postpone taking action on the resolution/motion.

6. When posting an electronic message related to a resolution/motion, Councilors shall use a format that includes: (a) a heading indicating the resolution/motion number, whether they are speaking for the motion (pro), in opposition to the motion (con), or asking for information (point of information); (b) a closing for each message that includes the Councilor's name and state/delegation.

7. Each message posted by a Councilor shall be a message written by the Councilor. Forwarding a message from a non-Legislative Council member is prohibited.

8. Voting shall be conducted only during the voting period, which shall be a minimum of one week for main motions and three business days for secondary motions.

9. The speaker of the Council shall have the authority to rule that a message is out of order and notify the Council of the ruling.

10. For those resolutions/motions that address issues related to specific ASHA council, boards, committees, and divisions, the Chair of that body shall be subscribed to the Legislative Council e-mail list for the period of discussion of that resolution/motion. The chair shall be able to provide clarification and information to the Council through the speaker of the Council but may not enter into debate or vote.

11. Any appeal from the decision of the chair must be submitted to the administrative assistant to the Legislative Council on the LC Forum e-mail list who shall forward it to the committee on special rules. The committee on special rules shall make the decision on the appeal within three business days and report its decision to the LC on the LC Forum e-mail list.

12. A quorum shall be 51 percent of the members of the LC eligible to vote. The number of votes cast including abstentions determines verification of a quorum.

> **Point of Information**
>
> It is very unusual to count the abstentions when counting votes. But, they are counted in the ASHA rules (rule 12) to determine whether enough members were involved in the decision to make it a binding decision. ASHA didn't want to require members to vote simply to make sure there was a quorum. *Robert's* allows a member to abstain from voting, and this rule does, too.

A Note About Rule 11

Rule 11 was included because if it were not there, two members could defeat a motion that was time-sensitive without that motion coming to a vote. Here is how that would work: Let's say that a motion is pending, and voting on it is scheduled to begin in three days. The motion is that the group support an activity that begins in 10 days. A member makes a point of order, saying that he or she feels that the group should not consider the resolution. The chair rules that the point is not well taken and that the group will proceed to process the resolution.

The same member who made the point of order then moves to appeal from the decision of the chair, and that motion is seconded. There are now only 10 days left until the proposed activity, and the group must now discuss and vote on the appeal and then, if the appeal fails, still discuss and vote on the main motion. There simply isn't enough time to do all of these things. If the group can't quickly resolve the appeal, the motion will not get voted on in time to support the activity, thereby rendering the motion moot. Two people who are against a motion could prevent the majority from voting on it!

To prevent this sort of situation, the appeal from the decision of the chair can be resolved by a committee—the special rules committee. That way it can be resolved in a timely manner, and the vote on the main motion can proceed.

Let's Ease Into This E-mail Group Meeting Thing!

Before your group amends its bylaws to authorize electronic meetings, I strongly encourage you to create an e-mail list and use it for discussion purposes only. Then, after you have had a chance to see how well it works for you, you can write the rules so that you can make your e-meetings decision-making meetings instead of discussion-only meetings.

An organization needs no special rules to discuss issues on an e-mail list—it's similar to discussing issues casually before or after the meeting. However, until you have rules in place, you cannot make decisions on the list. Since the rules for asynchronous meetings are not covered in *Robert's*, you will need to write rules that are specific to your organization. Use the ASHA rules included here as an example or as a starting point for your rules.

Even if you never use the electronic meetings venue to make decisions, it can still be an effective venue for your group. Think about the time you could cut out of in-person meetings if everyone had a chance to "discuss" the issues electronically before the meeting!

The Least You Need to Know

♦ Meetings that are not held in-person must be authorized in the bylaws.

♦ Synchronous meetings occur when participants are in different places at the same time. Asynchronous meetings occur with the participants in different places at different times.

♦ Put serious thought into how the voting will work in your e-meetings.

♦ Have a trial run for your e-meetings before changing your bylaws.

Appendix A

Glossary

abstain   To refrain from voting. Thus giving consent to the decision made by the group.

absentee voting   Voting by mail or by proxy. Absentee voting is not allowed unless expressly authorized in the bylaws.

accept   To adopt or approve a motion or report.

ad hoc   A special committee. The term comes from a Latin term meaning "to this" and refers to a committee formed for a particular purpose.

adjourn   A motion to close the meeting.

adjourned meeting   A meeting that is a continuation of a previous meeting. It occurs when the work was not completed at a regular or special meeting and there was a motion to continue the meeting at a different time. The original meeting and the adjourned meeting make up a single session.

adjournment *sine die*   Pronounced *SIGN-ee DYE-ee*. A Latin term which means "without day." It is the final adjournment of an assembly. The last meeting of the convention is said to adjourn *sine die*.

adopt   To accept or approve a motion or report.

agenda   A predetermined sequence of items of business to be covered at a specific meeting. An order of business.

amend   A motion to modify the pending motion before it is voted on.

amend something previously adopted   A motion that allows the assembly to change an action previously taken. This motion can be applied to any motion previously adopted provided that none of the action involved has been carried out in a way that it is too late to undo.

American Institute of Parliamentarians (AIP)   A professional organization of parliamentarians that emphasizes knowledge of *Robert's*, *Sturgis*, and other parliamentary authorities.

annual meeting   A meeting held yearly usually for the purpose of electing officers and receiving the annual reports of current officers and committees. The annual meeting is usually specified in the bylaws.

appeal from the decision of the chair (appeal)   A motion to take a decision regarding parliamentary procedure out of the hands of the presiding officer and place the final decision in the hands of the assembly.

assembly   A group of people meeting together to openly discuss issues and make decisions that then become the decision of the group. Also referred to as a deliberative assembly.

asynchronous meetings   Electronic meetings that occur with the participants in different places at different times. A meeting conducted on an e-mail list is an example of this kind of electronic meeting.

audit   An examination and verification of the financial records of the association. Depending upon the size of the organization, an audit may be required by federal or state law. The size of the organization also determines whether the audit can be done by an internal group, usually referred to as the audit committee, or an external, independent auditor.

board of directors   A specified group of members who make decisions on behalf of the organization. The membership, authority, and limitations of this group are specified in the bylaws. Meetings of the board are usually only open to members of the board and their invitees.

bylaws   A governing document that, when used without a constitution, comprises the highest body of rules of the organization. In the bylaws, an organization is free to adopt any rules it may wish, subject to higher governing authority such as a parent body or laws, even rules deviating from the organization's established parliamentary authority.

call for the orders of the day   By the use of this motion, a single member can require the assembly to follow the order of business or agenda, or to take up a special order that is scheduled to come up, unless two thirds of the assembly wish to do otherwise.

call of the meeting   The official notice of a meeting given to all members of the organization.

caucus   A meeting to plan strategy toward a particular issue or motion.

chair   The person who is in charge of the meeting. Presiding officer and chair are interchangeable terms. They both are sometimes used to refer to the president of the organization when the president is conducting the meeting.

commit or **refer to a committee**   This motion sends the main motion to a smaller group (a committee) for further examination and refinement before the body votes on it.

committee   A group of one or more persons who are appointed or elected to carry out a charge. The charge can be to investigate, to recommend, or to take action.

committee of the whole   The entire assembly acts as a committee to discuss a motion or issue more informally. The presiding officer vacates the chair and another member is appointed to serve as chairman. This motion is usually reserved for large assemblies, particularly legislative bodies.

committee report   An official statement that is formally adopted by a majority vote of the committee and that is presented to the parent body (either the entire membership or the board of directors) in the name of the committee. It contains information obtained, information regarding action taken, or recommendations on behalf of the committee

consent agenda or **consent calendar**   An agenda category that includes a list of routine, uncontroversial items that are approved with one motion, no discussion, and one vote.

consent calendar   *See* consent agenda.

consideration by paragraph or **seriatim**   The effect of this motion is to debate and amend a long motion paragraph by paragraph. The vote is taken on the whole motion after consideration of each paragraph separately.

constitution   A governing document that contains the highest body of rules of the organization, except rules from a higher governing authority, such as a parent body or laws.

convention   An assembly of delegates usually chosen for one session. The participants frequently attend as representatives of a local, state, or regional association. The convention participants come together to make decisions on behalf of the entire organization.

corresponding secretary   An officer who is responsible for the general correspondence of the organization.

CP   Certified Parliamentarian through the American Institute of Parliamentarians (AIP). To become a CP a person must pass a written examination that covers the rules in various parliamentary authorities and must earn service points.

CPP   Certified Professional Parliamentarian through the American Institute of Parliamentarians (AIP). To become a CPP, a person must pass a rigorous oral examination and demonstrate expertise in presiding.

CPP-T   Certified Professional Teacher of Parliamentary Procedure through American Institute of Parliamentarians (AIP). In addition to being a CPP, the person must complete a teacher education course and must show evidence of successful teaching experience.

CP-T   Certified Teacher of Parliamentary Procedure through American Institute of Parliamentarians (AIP). In addition to being a CP, the person must complete a teacher education course and must show evidence of successful teaching experience.

debate   The discussion of a motion that occurs after the presiding officer has restated the motion and before putting it to a vote.

decorum   To conduct oneself in a proper manner.

defer action   Using specific motions to delay action on a motion.

deliberative assembly   A group of people, meeting together to openly discuss issues and make decisions that then become the decision of the group.

discharge a committee   A motion that relieves a committee from further consideration of the task that has been assigned to it.

discussion   Debate that occurs after the presiding officer restates the motion and before the vote is taken on the motion.

division of the assembly   The effect of this motion is to require a standing vote (not a counted vote). A single member can demand this if he or she feels the vote is too close to declare or unrepresentative. This motion can only be used after the voice vote or hand vote is too close to declare.

division of the question   This motion is used to separate a main motion or amendment into parts to be voted on individually. It can only be used if each part can stand as a separate question.

executive committee   A committee which is generally made up of the officers of the organization. It only exists if expressly authorized in the bylaws.

executive session   A meeting or a portion of a meeting in which the proceedings are secret and the only attendees are members and invited guests.

ex-officio   A person is a member by virtue of an office held. An ex-officio member has full voting and speaking rights, unless otherwise indicated in the bylaws.

fix the time to which to adjourn   This motion sets the time for another meeting to continue business of the session. Adoption of this motion does not adjourn the present meeting or set the time for its adjournment.

friendly amendment   A proposed amendment that is perceived to be a acceptable to the entire assembly. This amendment should be processed just like any other amendment, following the steps of any other motion, even if the maker of the motion "accepts" the amendment.

gavel   A mallet used by the presiding officer to bring order to the meeting.

general consent or **unanimous consent**   A method of voting without taking a formal vote. The presiding officer asks if there are any objections, and if none are expressed, the motion is considered passed.

general orders   A category of the agenda that includes any motion which, usually by postponement, has been made an order of the day without being made a special order. Translated, that means that if an item is postponed until a certain day or after a certain event, it fits into this category.

germane   Related to the subject. An amendment must be germane to the motion it is amending. A secondary amendment must be germane to the primary amendment it is amending.

illegal vote   A vote that is not credited to any candidate or choice, but is counted as a vote cast.

immediately pending   A motion is considered immediately pending when several motions are pending and it is the motion that was most recently stated by the chair and is the one that will be first disposed of.

incidental main motion   A main motion that is incidental to, or related to, the business of the assembly, or its past or future action.

incidental motions   Motions that relate to matters that are incidental to the conduct of the meeting rather than directly to the main motion. They may be offered at any time when they are needed.

informal consideration   A form of committee of the whole. This motion allows the assembly to exchange ideas on an informal basis with more freedom of debate than in a formal assembly.

lay on the table   This motion places in the care of the secretary the pending question and everything adhering to it. If a group meets quarterly or more frequently, the question laid on the table remains there until taken off or until the end of the next regular session. This motion should not be used to kill a motion.

limit or **extend limits of debate**   This motion can reduce or increase the number and length of speeches permitted or limit the length of debate on a specific question.

main motion   A motion that brings before the assembly any particular subject and is made when no other business is pending.

majority   More than half of the votes cast.

mass meeting   An open and informal meeting of a group of people with a common interest.

meeting   An assembly of members gathered to conduct business during which there is no separation of the members except for a short recess.

minutes   The written record of the proceedings of a deliberative assembly. They are a record of what was done at the meeting, not what was said at the meeting.

motion   A proposal that the group take a specific action or stand.

National Association of Parliamentarians (NAP)   A professional organization of parliamentarians that emphasizes *Robert's* as the parliamentary authority.

notice   An official announcement, given verbally or in writing, of an item of business that will be introduced at the meeting. Certain motions require previous notice.

objection to the consideration of a question   The purpose of this motion is to prevent the assembly from considering the question/motion because a member deems the question as irrelevant, unprofitable, or contentious.

old business   An incorrect and misleading term for the part of the agenda properly called unfinished business. Old business is misleading because it indicates that anything that the group once talked about fits here. The only business that fits in unfinished business is business that was started but not yet finished.

on the floor   A motion is considered on the floor when it has been stated by the presiding officer and has not yet been disposed of either permanently or temporarily. Pending and on the floor are interchangeable terms.

order of business   The schedule of business for the meeting; the agenda.

original main motions   Those motions which bring before the assembly a new subject, sometimes in the form of a resolution, upon which action by the assembly is desired.

out of order   A motion, action, request, or procedure that is in violation of the rules of the organization.

ownership of a motion   A concept that refers to whose property the motion is at a given time and, therefore, who has a right to make any changes to it. In the six steps of the motion process, the maker of the motion owns the motion up until the completion of Step 3. After Step 3, the ownership of the motion is transferred to the assembly.

parliamentarian   A person who is an expert in parliamentary procedure and is hired by a person or an organization to give advice on matters of parliamentary law and procedure. Sometimes a parliamentarian is a member of the organization who has some knowledge of parliamentary procedure and is used as a parliamentary resource during the meeting.

parliamentary authority   The parliamentary manual adopted by the organization, usually in its bylaws, to serve as the governing authority.

parliamentary inquiry   A question directed to the presiding officer concerning parliamentary law or the organization's rules as they apply to the business at hand.

parliamentary law   The established rules for the conduct of business in deliberative assemblies. The terms parliamentary law and parliamentary procedure are frequently used interchangeably.

parliamentary procedure   A system of rules for the orderly conduct of business. The terms parliamentary law and parliamentary procedure are frequently used interchangeably.

pending   A motion is considered pending when it has been stated by the presiding officer and has not yet been disposed of either permanently or temporarily. Pending and on the floor are interchangeable terms.

plurality vote   A method of voting in which the candidate or proposition receiving the largest number of votes is elected or selected.

point of information   A nonparliamentary question about the business at hand.

point of order   If a member feels the rules are not being followed, he or she can use this motion. It requires the chair to make a ruling and enforce the rules.

postpone definitely   *See* postpone to a certain time.

postpone indefinitely   This motion, in effect, kills the main motion for the duration of the session without the group having to take a vote on the motion.

postpone to a certain time or **postpone definitely**   If the body needs more time to make a decision or if there is a time for consideration of this question that would be more convenient, this motion may be the answer. If a group meets quarterly or more frequently, the postponement cannot be beyond the next session.

precedence of motions   (pre SEED ens) A rank of motions indicating the order in which specific motions should be processed. When a motion is immediately pending, any motion above it on the precedence of motions is in order and any motion below it is out of order. In this book the terms ladder of motions and precedence of motions are used interchangeably.

presiding officer   The person in charge of the meeting. Presiding officer and chair are interchangeable terms. They both are sometimes used to refer to the president of the organization when the president is conducting the meeting.

prevailing side   The affirmative if the motion passed and the negative if the motion failed. A person is said to have voted on the prevailing side if that member voted yes on a motion that passed or no on a motion that failed.

previous notice   An official announcement, given verbally or in writing, of an item of business that will be introduced at the meeting. Certain motions require previous notice.

previous question   The effect of this motion is to immediately stop debate on the primary motion and any amendments and to move immediately to a vote on the motion. It must be seconded, no debate is allowed, and a two-thirds vote is needed to close debate.

primary amendment   A proposed change to the main motion.

privileged motions   Motions that don't relate to the main motion or pending business but relate directly to the members and the organization. They are matters of such urgency that, without debate, they can interrupt the consideration of anything else.

pro tem   Temporary or for the time being, as in secretary pro tem.

proviso   A provision on when the new bylaws change will take effect. It is not a part of the bylaws. Provisos can be put on a separate sheet of paper or in a footnote and removed after they are no longer in effect.

proxy vote   Written authorization for one member to vote on behalf of another member. Proxy voting is not allowed unless expressly authorized in the bylaws. Many state statutes have rules regarding proxy voting.

PRP   A Professional Registered Parliamentarian; an individual who has been registered by the National Association of Parliamentarians on the basis of passing a course covering advanced knowledge of parliamentary law and procedure according to

Robert's Rules of Order Newly Revised. During the examination the person must demonstrate abilities in presiding, serving as parliamentarian, and teaching parliamentary procedure.

quasi committee of the whole   "As if in" committee of the whole. The entire assembly acts as a committee to discuss a motion or issue more informally. Unlike the committee of the whole, the presiding officer remains in the chair.

question   The business before the assembly. Is used interchangeably with the word motion.

quorum   The number of voting members who must be present in order that business can be legally transacted.

raise a question of privilege   To bring an urgent request or a main motion relating to the rights of either the assembly or an individual up for immediate consideration. It may interrupt business.

ratify   A motion that confirms or validates a previously taken action that needs assembly approval to become legal.

recess   A short interruption which does not close the meeting. After the recess, business resumes at exactly the point where it was interrupted.

recommit   A motion to refer an issue or a motion back to a committee.

reconsider   This motion enables the majority of the assembly to bring back for further consideration a motion that has been voted on. Limitations: Only a member who voted on the prevailing side can make this motion, and in an ordinary meeting of an organization this motion can be made only on the same day the vote to be reconsidered was taken.

refer to a committee or **commit**   This motion sends the main motion to a smaller group (a committee) for further examination and refinement before the body votes on it.

regular meeting   A business meeting of a permanent group that is held at regular intervals (weekly, monthly, quarterly, and so on). The meetings are held when prescribed in the bylaws, the standing rules, or through a motion of the group, usually adopted at the beginning of the administrative year. Each meeting is a separate session.

rescind   This motion allows the assembly to repeal an action previously taken. These motions can be applied to any previously adopted motion, provided that none of the actions involved have been carried out in a way that it is too late to undo.

resolution   A formal motion that usually includes reasons as "whereas" clauses and the action as "resolved" clause(s).

revision of the bylaws   A complete rewrite of the bylaws that is presented as a new document. When presented, the proposed revision can be amended without limitation.

Robert's Rules   A term used to refer to any of the manuals on parliamentary procedure written by Henry M. Robert or based on the manuals he wrote.

RP   A Registered Parliamentarian through the National Association of Parliamentarians (NAP). To become an RP, a person must pass a written examination covering *Robert's Rules of Order Newly Revised.*

ruling   A decision made by the presiding officer. If members of the assembly disagree with the decision, they can appeal the decision.

scope of notice   A concept that applies to motions that require previous notice. It requires that the amendment fall within the range that is created by what currently exists and by what is proposed in the advance notice of the amendmant.

script   Written directions of what is to be said, by whom, and when during the meeting.

second   An indication by a voting member, other than the person who made the motion, that he or she publicly agrees that the proposed motion should be considered.

secondary amendment   A proposed change to the primary amendment.

secondary motion   A motion that may be made while another motion is pending. It includes subsidiary motions, privileged motions, and incidental motions.

seriatim   *See* consider by paragraph.

session   A meeting or a series of connected meetings as in a convention.

skeletal minutes   Minutes prepared in advance of a meeting or convention that include all that will be occurring and the order which it will occur. They contain many blank spaces that are filled in during the meeting by the person(s) in charge of the minutes.

special committee   A committee that is formed to perform a particular function. After it gives its final report, it ceases to exist.

special meeting   A meeting called at a special time for a specific purpose. Notice of the time, place, and purpose of the meeting must be included in the information sent to all of the members regarding the meeting—referred to as the call of the meeting. Only business that was specified in the call of the meeting can be transacted at the meeting.

special orders   This category of the agenda has the effect of setting a certain time when a specified subject will be considered, and of giving it an absolute priority for that time.

standing committee   A permanent committee, usually listed in the bylaws, to perform ongoing functions.

standing rules   Rules adopted by an organization that are administrative in nature rather than procedural. Convention standing rules are rules adopted by the convention's delegates and are procedural in nature.

Sturgis   Another parliamentary authority whose original book *Sturgis Standard Code of Parliamentary Procedure* has been updated by the American Institute of Parliamentarians.

subsidiary motions   Motions that aid the assembly in treating or disposing of a main motion. They are in order only from the time the main motion has been stated by the chair until the chair begins to take a vote on that main motion.

suspend the rules   This motion is used when the assembly wants to do something that violates its own rules. This motion does not apply to the organization's bylaws; local, state, or national law; or fundamental principles of parliamentary law.

synchronous meetings   Electronic meetings that occur when participants are in different places at the same time, such as a conference call.

take from the table   The effect of this motion is to resume consideration of a motion that was laid on the table earlier in the present session or in the previous session of the organization.

tie vote   An equal number of affirmative and negative votes. If a majority vote is needed, the motion fails because it lacks a majority vote.

unanimous consent   *See* general consent.

undebatable   No debate is allowed. Certain motions are undebatable.

unfinished business   A portion of the agenda that includes motions that have been carried over from the previous meeting as a result of that meeting having adjourned without completing its order of business.

vacancy   An office or position which is unfilled or unoccupied.

vacate the chair   To temporarily relinquish the chair so that the presiding officer can participate in debate.

vote   A formal expression of will, opinion or choice by members of an assembly in regard to a matter submitted to it.

withdraw of a motion   A request by the mover of a motion to remove the motion from consideration. After the motion has been stated by the presiding officer, it belongs to the assembly and the assembly's permission (majority vote) is needed to withdraw
the motion.

yielding the floor   A speaker giving part of his or her speaking time to another speaker. While this practice is allowed in some legislative bodies, it is not allowed in deliberative assemblies, unless specifically authorized in the rules.

Robert's Rules of Order, Fourth Edition (Abridged)

Parliamentary law books have been adapted for the ever-changing world we live in, but, for the most part, they do not change the rules that Henry M. Robert had the foresight to write back in 1915. He put together an incredible system of procedures that have truly withstood the test of time.

Here you will find the relevant portions of the last *Rules of Order* book that Henry M. Robert wrote before his death. The sections of his book that follow are the sections that deal with rules regarding specific motions. They supplement my discussion of the rules. I have maintained the section numbers as they are in his book but have left out many of the sections that address areas of parliamentary procedure that aren't relevant to this book. Throughout the book, *Robert's* refers the reader to other sections of his book. You will find those references in brackets.

Part I: Rules of Order

Article I. How Business Is Conducted in Deliberative Assemblies

§1. Introduction of Business {See Chapter 5}

§2. What Precedes Debate {See Chapter 5}

§3. Obtaining the Floor {See Chapter 5}

§4. Motions and Resolutions {See Chapter 5}

§5. Seconding Motions {See Chapter 5}

§6. Stating the Question {See Chapter 5}

§7. Debate {See Chapters 6 & 8}

§8. Secondary Motions {See Chapter 6}

§9. Putting the Question and Announcing the Vote {See Chapter 6}

§10. Proper Motions to Use to Accomplish Certain Objects {See Chapter 6}

10. Proper Motions to Use to Accomplish Certain Objects. {See Chapter 6}
To enable any one to ascertain what motion to use in order to accomplish what is desired, the common motions are arranged in the table below according to the objects to be attained by their use. Immediately after the table is a brief statement of the differences between the motions placed under each object, and of the circumstances under which each should be used. They include all of the Subsidiary Motions [12], which are designed for properly disposing of a question pending before the assembly; and the three motions designed to again bring before the assembly a question that has been acted upon or laid aside temporarily; and the motion designed to bring before another meeting of the assembly a main question which has been voted on in an unusually small or unrepresentative meeting. Motions, as a general rule, require for their adoption only a majority vote—that is, a majority of the votes cast, a quorum being present; but motions to suppress or limit debate, or to prevent the consideration of a question, or, without notice to rescind action previously taken, require a two-thirds vote [48]. The figures and letters on the left in the list below correspond to similar figures and letters in the statement of differences further on. The figures to the right in the list refer to the sections where the motions are fully treated.

The Common Motions Classified According to Their Objects:

(1) To Modify or Amend.

    (a) *Amend*   §33

    (b) *Commit or Refer*   §32

(2) To Defer Action.

    (a) *Postpone to a Certain Time*   §31

    (b) *Make a Special Order* (2/3 Vote)   §20

    (c) *Lay on the Table*   §28

(3) To Suppress or Limit Debate (2/3 Vote).

    (a) *Previous Question* (*to close debate now*) (2/3 Vote)   §29

    (b) *Limit Debate* (2/3 Vote)   §30

(4) To Suppress the Question.

    (a) *Objection to Its Consideration* (2/3 Vote)   §23

    (b) *Previous Question and Reject Question*   §29

    (c) *Postpone Indefinitely*   §34

    (d) *Lay on the Table*   §28

(5) To Consider a Question a Second Time.

    (a) *Take from the Table*   §35

    (b) *Reconsider*   §36

    (c) *Rescind*   §37

(6) To Prevent Final Action on a Question in an
Unusually Small or Unrepresentative Meeting.

    (a) *Reconsider and have Entered on the Minutes*   §36

(1) *To Modify or Amend.* (a) When a resolution or motion is not worded properly, or requires any modification to meet the approval of the assembly, if the changes required can be made in the assembly, the proper motion to make is to *amend* by "inserting," or "adding," or by "striking out," or by "striking out and inserting," or by "substituting" one or more paragraphs for those in the resolution. (b) But if much time will be required, or if the changes required are numerous, or if additional information is required to enable the assembly to act intelligently, then it is usually better to *refer* the question to a committee.

(2) *To Defer Action.* (a) If it is desired to put off the further consideration of a question to a certain hour, so that when that time arrives, as soon as the pending business is disposed of, it shall have the right of consideration over all questions except special orders and a reconsideration, then the proper motion to make is, *to postpone to that certain time*. This is also the proper motion to make if it is desired to defer action simply to another day. As the motion if adopted cannot interrupt the pending question when the appointed time arrives, nor can it suspend any rule, it requires only a majority vote for its adoption. A question postponed to a certain time cannot be taken up before the appointed time except by suspending the rules, which requires a two-thirds vote. (b) If it is desired to appoint for the consideration of a question a certain time

when it may interrupt any pending question except one relating to adjournment or recess, or a question of privilege or a specified order that was made before it was, then the proper course is to move "that the question be made a *special order* for," etc., specifying the day or hour. As this motion, if adopted, suspends all rules that interfere with the consideration of the question at the appointed time, it requires a two-thirds vote for its adoption. A special order cannot be considered before the appointed time except by suspending the rules, which requires a two-thirds vote. (c) If, however, it is desired to lay the question aside temporarily with the right to take it up at any moment when business of this class, or unfinished or new business, is in order and no other question is before the assembly, the proper motion to use is to *lay the question on the table*. When laid upon the table a majority vote may take it up at the same or the next session, as described in 35.

(3) To Suppress Debate. (a) If it is desired to close debate now and bring the assembly at once to a vote on the pending question, or questions, the proper course is to move, or demand, or call for, the previous question on the motions upon which it is desired to close debate. The motion, or demand, for the previous question should always specify the motions upon which it is desired to order the previous question. If no motions are specified, the previous question applies only to the immediately pending question. It requires a two-thirds vote for its adoption. After it has been adopted, privileged and incidental motions may be made, or the pending questions may be laid on the table, but no other subsidiary motion can be made nor is any debate allowed. If it is lost the debate is resumed. (b) If it is desired to limit the number or length of speeches, or the time allowed for debate, the proper course is to move that the speeches or debate be limited as desired, or that the debate be closed and the vote be taken at a specified time. These motions to limit or close debate require a two-thirds vote for their adoption, and are in order, like the previous question, when any debatable question is immediately pending.

(4) To Suppress the Question. A legitimate question cannot be suppressed in a deliberative assembly without free debate, except by a two-thirds vote. If two-thirds of the assembly are opposed to the consideration of the question then it can be suppressed by the following methods: (a) If it is desired to prevent any consideration of the question, the proper course to pursue is *to object to its consideration* before it has been discussed or any other motion stated, and, therefore, it may interrupt a member who has the floor before the debate has begun. It requires no second. On the question of consideration there must be a two-thirds negative vote to prevent the consideration. (b) After the question has been considered the proper way to immediately suppress it is to close debate by ordering the *previous question*, which requires a two-thirds vote, and then to vote down the question. (c) Another method of suppressing a question is to *postpone it indefinitely* (equivalent to rejecting it), which, however, being debatable and

opening the main question to debate, is only of service in giving another opportunity to defeat the resolution should this one fail. For, if the motion to postpone indefinitely is adopted, the main question is dead for that session, and if it is lost, the main question is still pending and its enemies have another opportunity to kill it. When the motion to postpone indefinitely is pending and immediate action is desired, it is necessary to move the previous question as in case (b) above. (d) A fourth method frequently used for suppressing a question is to lay it on the table, though this is an unfair use of the motion, except in bodies like Congress where the majority must have the power to suppress any motion immediately, as otherwise they could not transact business. But in ordinary societies, where the pressure of business is not so great, it is better policy for the majority to be fair and courteous to the minority and use the proper motions for suppressing a question without allowing full debate, all of which require a two-thirds vote. Unless the enemies of a motion have a large majority, laying it on the table is not a safe way of suppressing it, because its friends, by watching their opportunity, may find themselves in a majority and take it from the table and adopt it, as shown in the next paragraph.

(5) To Consider a Question a Second Time. (a) When a question has not been voted on, but has been laid on the table, a majority may *take it from the table* and consider it at any time when no other question is before the assembly and when business of that class, or unfinished or new business, is in order during the same session; or at the next session in ordinary societies having regular meetings as often as quarterly. (b) If a motion has been adopted, or rejected, or postponed indefinitely, and afterwards one or more members have changed their views from the prevailing to the losing side, and it is thought that by further discussion the assembly may modify or reverse its action, the proper course is for one who voted with the prevailing side to move to reconsider the vote on the question. This can be done on the day the vote to be reconsidered is taken, or on the next succeeding day of the same session. (c) If a main motion, including questions of privilege and orders of the day, has been adopted or rejected or postponed indefinitely, and no one is both able and willing to move to reconsider the vote, the question can be brought up again during the same session only by moving to *rescind* the motion. To rescind may be moved by any member, but, if notice of it was not given at a previous meeting, it requires a two-thirds vote or a vote of a majority of the enrolled membership. At any future session, the resolution, or other main motion, may be rescinded in the same way if it had been adopted; or it may be introduced anew if it had been rejected or postponed indefinitely; provided the question cannot be reached by calling up the motion to reconsider which has been made at the previous session. A by-law, or anything else that requires a definite notice and vote for its amendment, requires the same notice and vote to rescind it.

(6) To Prevent Final Action on a Question in an Unusually Small or Unrepresentative Meeting. If an important main motion should be adopted, lost, or postponed indefinitely, at a small or unrepresentative meeting of the society when it was apparent that the action is in opposition to the views of the majority of the members, the proper course to pursue is for a member to vote with the prevailing side and then move to reconsider the vote and have it entered on the minutes. The motion to reconsider, in this form, can be made only on the day the vote was taken which it is proposed to reconsider, and the reconsideration cannot be called up on that day; thus an opportunity is given to notify absent members. The motion to reconsider is fully explained in 36.

Article II. General Classification of Motions

For convenience motions may be classified as follows:

§11. Main or Principal Motions {See Chapter 10}

§12. Subsidiary Motions {See Chapter 12}

§13. Incidental Motions {See Chapter 13}

§14. Privileged Motions {See Chapter 11}

§15. Some Main and Unclassified Motions {See Chapter 14}

Article III. Privileged Motions

§16. Fix the Time to which the Assembly shall Adjourn {See Chapter 11}

§17. Adjourn {See Chapter 11}

§18. Take a Recess {See Chapter 11}

§19. Questions of Privilege {See Chapter 11}

§20. General and Special Orders and a Call for the Orders of the Day {See Chapter 11}

16. To Fix the Time to which the Assembly shall Adjourn. {See Chapter 11} This motion is privileged only when made while another question is pending and in an assembly that has made no provision for another meeting on the same or the next day. The time fixed cannot be beyond the time of the next meeting. If made in an assembly that already has provided for another meeting on the same or the next day, or if made in an assembly when no question is pending, this is a main motion and may be debated and amended and have applied to it the other subsidiary motions, like other main motions. Whenever the motion is referred to in these rules the privileged motion is meant, unless specified to the contrary.

This motion when privileged takes precedence of all others, and is in order even after it has been voted to adjourn, provided the chairman has not declared the assembly adjourned. It can be amended, and a vote on it can be reconsidered. When the assembly has no fixed place for its meetings, this motion should include the place as well as the time for the next meeting, and in this case the place is subject to amendment as well as the time. When the assembly meets at the time to which it adjourned, the meeting is a continuation of the previous session. Thus, if the Annual Meeting is adjourned to meet on another day, the adjourned meeting is a legal continuation of the Annual Meeting. The form of this motion is, "I move that when we adjourn, (or stand adjourned) to 2 P.M. tomorrow."

17. To Adjourn. {See Chapter 11} The motion to adjourn (when unqualified) is always a privileged motion except when, for lack of provision for a future meeting, as in a mass meeting, or at the last meeting of a convention, its effect, if adopted, would be to dissolve the assembly permanently. In any organized society holding several regular meetings during the year, it is, when unqualified, always a privileged motion. When not privileged it is treated as any other main motion, being debatable and amendable, etc.

The privileged motion to adjourn takes precedence of all others, except the privileged motion "to fix the time to which to adjourn," to which it yields. It is not debatable, nor can it be amended or have any other subsidiary motion applied to it; nor can a vote on it be reconsidered. It may be withdrawn.

The motion to adjourn can be repeated if there has been any intervening business, though it is simply progress in debate. The assembly may decline to adjourn in order to hear one speech or to take one vote, and therefore it must have the privilege of renewing the motion to adjourn when there has been any progress in business or debate. But this high privilege is liable to abuse to the annoyance of the assembly, if the chair does not prevent it by refusing to entertain the motion when evidently made for obstructive purposes, as when the assembly has just voted it down, and nothing has occurred since to show the possibility of the assembly's wishing to adjourn.

The motion to adjourn, like every other motion, cannot be made except by a member who has the floor. When made by one who has not risen and addressed the chair and been recognized, it can be entertained only by general consent. It cannot be made when the assembly is engaged in voting, or verifying the vote, but is in order after the vote has been taken by ballot before it has been announced. In such case the ballot vote should be announced as soon as business is resumed. Where much time will be consumed in counting ballots the assembly may adjourn, having previously appointed a time for the next meeting, or, still better, may take a recess as explained in the next section. No appeal, or question of order, or inquiry, should be entertained after the motion to adjourn has been made, unless it is of such a nature that its decision is necessary before an adjournment, or unless the assembly refuses to adjourn, when it would be in order.

Before putting the motion to adjourn, the chair, in most organizations, should be sure that no important matters have been overlooked. If there are announcements to be made they should be attended to before taking the vote, or at least, before announcing it. If there is something requiring action before adjournment, the fact should be stated and the mover requested to withdraw his motion to adjourn. The fact that the motion to adjourn is undebatable does not prevent the assembly's being informed of business requiring attention before adjournment. Members should not leave their seats until the chair has declared the assembly adjourned.

An adjournment *sine die*—that is, without day—closes the session and if there is no provision for convening the assembly again, of course the adjournment dissolves the assembly. But, if any provision has been made whereby another meeting may be held, its effect is simply to close the session. In an assembly, as a convention, which meets regularly only once during its life, but whose bylaws provide for calling special meetings, an adjournment sine die means only the ending of the regular session of the convention, which, however, may be reconvened as provided in the by-laws. If called to meet again the assembly meets as a body already organized.

When the motion to adjourn is qualified in any way, or when its effect is to dissolve the assembly without any provision being made for holding another meeting of the assembly, it loses its privilege and is a main motion, debatable and amendable and subject to having applied to it any of the subsidiary motions.

In committees where no provision has been made for future meetings, an adjournment is always at the call of the chair unless otherwise specified. When a special committee, or the committee of the whole, has completed the business referred to it, instead of adjourning, it rises and reports, which is equivalent to adjournment without day.

The Effect upon Unfinished Business of an adjournment, unless the assembly has adopted rules to the contrary, is as follows:

(a) When the adjournment does not close the session, the business interrupted by it is the first in order after the reading of the minutes at the next meeting, and is treated the same as if there had been no adjournment, an adjourned meeting being legally the continuation of the meeting of which it is an adjournment.

(b) When the adjournment closes a session 9 in an assembly having regular sessions as often as quarterly, the unfinished business should be taken up, just where it was interrupted, at the next succeeding session previous to new business; provided that, in a body elected, either wholly or in part, for a definite time (as a board of directors one-third of whom are elected annually), unfinished business falls to the ground with the expiration of the term for which the board, or any part of it, was elected.

(c) When the adjournment closes a session in an assembly which does not meet as often as quarterly, or when the assembly is an elective body, and this session ends the term of a portion of the members, the adjournment puts an end to all business unfinished at the close of the session. The business may be introduced at the next session, the same as if it had never been before the assembly.

18. Take a Recess. {See Chapter 11} This motion is practically a combination of the two preceding, to which it yields, taking precedence of all other motions. If made when other business is before the assembly, it is a privileged motion and is undebatable and can have no subsidiary motion applied to it except amend. It can be amended as to the length of the recess. It takes effect immediately. A motion to take a recess made when no business is before the assembly, or a motion to take a recess at a future time, has no privilege, and is treated as any other main motion. A recess is an intermission in the day's proceedings, as for meals or for counting the ballots when much time is required; or in the case of meetings like conventions lasting for several days a recess is sometimes taken over an entire day. When a recess is provided for in the order of exercises, or program, the chair, when the time arrives, announces the fact and says the assembly stands adjourned, or in recess, to the specified hour. The assembly by a two-thirds vote can postpone the time for taking a recess, or adjournment. When the hour has arrived to which the recess was taken, the chairman calls the assembly to order and the business proceeds the same as if no recess had been taken. If the recess was taken after a vote had been taken and before it was announced, then the first business is the announcement of the vote. The intermissions in the proceedings of a day are termed recesses, whether the assembly voted to take a recess, or whether it simply adjourned having previously adopted a program or rule providing for the hours of meeting. When an assembly has frequent short regular meetings not lasting over a day, and an adjourned meeting is held on another day, the interval between the meetings is not referred to as a recess.

19. Questions of Privilege. {See Chapter 11} Questions relating to the rights and privileges of the assembly, or to any of its members, take precedence of all other motions except the three preceding relating to adjournment and recess, to which they yield. If the question is one requiring immediate action it may interrupt a member's speech; as, for example, when, from any cause, a report that is being read cannot be heard in a part of the hall. But if it is not of such urgency it should not interrupt a member after he has commenced his speech. Before a member has commenced speaking, even though he has been assigned the floor, it is in order for another member to raise a question of privilege. When a member rises for this purpose he should not wait to be recognized, but immediately on rising should say, "Mr. Chairman,"—and when he catches the chairman's eye, should add, "I rise to a question of privilege affecting the assembly," or "I rise to a question of personal privilege." The chair directs him to state his question, and then decides whether it is one of privilege or not. From this decision any two members may appeal. The chair may decide it to be a question of privilege, but not of sufficient urgency to justify interrupting the speaker. In such a case the speaker should be allowed to continue, and, when he has finished, the chair should immediately assign the floor to the member who raised the question of privilege to make his motion if one is necessary. Whenever his motion is made and stated, it becomes the immediately pending question and is open to debate and amendment and the application of all the other subsidiary motions just as any main motion. Its high privilege extends only to giving it the right to consideration in preference to any other question except one relating to adjournment or recess, and, in cases of great urgency, the right to interrupt a member while speaking. It cannot interrupt voting or verifying a vote. As soon as the question of privilege is disposed of, the business is resumed exactly where it was interrupted; if a member had the floor at the time the question of privilege was raised, the chair assigns him the floor again.

Questions of privilege may relate to the privileges of the assembly or only of a member, the former having the precedence if the two come into competition. Questions of personal privilege must relate to one as a member of the assembly, or else relate to charges against his character which, if true, would incapacitate him for membership. Questions like the following relate to the privileges of the assembly: those relating to the organization of the assembly; or to the comfort of its members, as the heating, lighting, ventilation, etc., of the hall, and freedom from noise and other disturbance; or to the conduct of its officers or employees; or to the punishing of a member for disorderly conduct or other offence; or to the conduct of reporters for the press, or to the accuracy of published reports of proceedings.

Privileged questions include, besides questions of privilege, a call for the orders of the day and the privileged motions relating to adjournment and recess. This distinction between privileged questions and questions of privilege should be borne in mind.

20. Orders of the Day. {See Chapter 11} *A Call for the Orders of the Day* (which, in an ordinary assembly, is a demand that the assembly conform to its program or order of business) can be made at any time when no other privileged motion is pending and the order of business is being varied from, and only then. It requires no second, and is in order when another has the floor, even though it interrupts a speech, as a single member has a right to demand that the order of business be conformed to. It is out of order to call for the orders of the day when there is no variation from the order of business. Thus, the orders of the day cannot be called for when another question is pending, provided there are no special orders made for that time or an earlier time, as general orders cannot interrupt a question actually under consideration. The call must be simply for the orders of the day, and not for a specified one, as the latter has no privilege. When the time has arrived for which a special order has been made, a call for the orders of the day takes precedence of everything except the other privileged motions, namely, those relating to adjournment and recess, and questions of privilege, to which it yields. If there are no special orders a call for the orders of the day cannot interrupt a pending question; but, if made when no question is pending, it is in order even when another has the floor and has made a main motion, provided the chair has not stated the question. Until the time of actually taking up the general orders for consideration this calls yields to a motion to reconsider, or to a calling up of a motion to reconsider, previously made. A call for the orders of the day cannot be debated or amended, or have any other subsidiary motion applied to it.

It is the duty of the chair to announce the business to come before the assembly in its proper order, and if he always performs this duty there will be no occasion for calling for the orders of the day. But there are occasions when the chair fails to notice that the time assigned for a special order has arrived, or he thinks that the assembly is so interested in the pending question that it does not wish yet to take up the special order assigned for that time, and therefore delays announcing it. In such a case, as already stated, any member has a right to call for the orders of the day, and thus compel the chair either to announce the order or else put the question, "Will the assembly proceed to the orders of the day?" To refuse to take up the orders at the appointed time is an interference with the order of business similar to suspending the rules and should require the same vote—namely, two-thirds. In other words, a two-thirds vote in the negative is necessary to prevent proceeding to the orders of the day. If the assembly refuses to proceed to the orders of the day the orders cannot be called for again until the pending business is disposed of.

When the orders of the day are announced, or when they are called for, if it is desired to prolong the discussion of the pending question, some one should move that the time for considering the pending question be extended a certain number of minutes. A two-thirds vote is required for the adoption of this motion as it changes the order of business or program. After the order has been announced and the question is actually pending, it is debatable and may be amended or have any other subsidiary motion applied to it the same as any other main motion. The orders of the day in a mass cannot be laid on the table or postponed, but when an order has been actually taken up it may, by a majority vote, be laid on the table, or postponed, or committed, so that, if there is no other order to interfere, the consideration of the question previously pending will be resumed. Whenever the orders of the day are disposed of, the consideration of the interrupted business is taken up at the point where it was interrupted by the call for the orders of the day. By suspending the rules by a two-thirds vote any question may be taken up out of its proper order.

Orders of the Day. When one or more subjects have been assigned to a particular day or hour (by postponing them to, or making them special orders for, that day or hour, or by adopting a program or order of business), they become the orders of the day for that day or hour, and they cannot be considered before that time, except by a two-thirds vote. They are divided into General Orders and Special Orders, the latter always taking precedence of the former.

A *General Order* is usually made by simply postponing a question to a certain day or hour, or after a certain event. It does not suspend any rule, and therefore cannot interrupt business. But after the appointed hour has arrived it has the preference, when no question is pending, over all other questions except special orders and reconsideration. It cannot be considered before the appointed time except by a reconsideration or by a two-thirds vote. When the order of business provides for orders of the day, questions simply postponed to a meeting, without specifying the hour, come up under that head. If no provision is made for orders of the day, then such postponed questions come up after the disposal of the business pending at the previous adjournment, and after the questions on the calendar that were not disposed of at the previous meeting.

An order of business that specifies the order in which, but not the time when, the business shall be transacted, together with the postponed questions constitutes the general orders. This order cannot be varied from except by general consent or by suspending the rules by a two-thirds vote. If all of this business is not disposed of before adjournment, it becomes "unfinished business," and is treated as unfinished business, as explained in 17 under The Effect Upon Unfinished Business of an Adjournment.

As general orders cannot interrupt the consideration of a pending question, it follows that any general order made for an earlier hour, though made afterwards, by not being disposed of in time may interfere with the general order previously made. Therefore, general orders must take precedence among themselves in the order of the times to which they were postponed, regardless of when the general order was made. If several are appointed for the same time, then they take precedence in the order in which they were made. If several appointed for the same time were made at the same time, then they take precedence in the order in which they were arranged in the motion making the general order.

To *Make a Special Order* requires a two-thirds vote, because it suspends all rules that interfere with its consideration at the specified time, except those relating to motions for adjournment or recess, or to questions of privilege, or to special orders made before it was made. A pending question is made a special order for a future time by "Postponing it and making it a special order for that time." [See Postpone to a Certain Time, 31, which should be read in connection with this section.] If the question is not pending, the motion to make it a special order for a certain time is a main motion, debatable, amendable, etc. The member desirous of making it a special order should obtain the floor when nothing is pending, and business of that class, or new business, is in order, and say, "I move that the following resolution be made the special order for [specifying the time]," and then reads the resolution and hands it to the chair. Or he may adopt this form: "I offer the following resolution, and move that it be made a special order for the next meeting." Or, in case a committee has been appointed to submit a revision of the constitution, the following resolution may be adopted: "Resolved, That the revision of the constitution, be made the special order for Thursday morning and thereafter until it is disposed of." Another way of making special orders is by adopting a program, or order of business, in which is specified the hour for taking up each topic.

Program. It is customary to adopt a program, or order of business, in conventions in session for several days. Since the delegates and invited speakers come from a distance, it is very important that the program be strictly adhered to. No change can be made in it after its adoption by the assembly, except by a two-thirds vote. When the hour assigned to a certain topic arrives, the chair puts to vote any questions pending and announces the topic for the hour. This is done because, under such circumstances, the form of the program implies that the hour, or other time, assigned to each topic is all that can be allowed. But, if any one moves to lay the question on the table, or postpone it to a certain time, or refer it to a committee, the chair should recognize the motion and immediately put it to vote without debate. Should any one move to extend the time allotted the pending question, it should be decided instantly without debate, a two-thirds vote being necessary for the extension. It is seldom that an extension is desirable, as it is unfair to the next topic. When an invited speaker exceeds his time it is extremely discourteous to call for the orders of the day. The chair should have an understanding with invited speakers as to how he will indicate the expiration of their time. This can be done by tapping on a book or a bell. It is usually better to have it understood that the signal will be given one minute before the time expires, or longer if the speaker wishes it, so that he can properly close his address. At the expiration of the time the presiding officer should rise and attract the attention of the speaker and, if he still continues speaking, the chair should say that the time has expired, etc.

A series of special orders made by a single vote is treated the same as a program—that is, at the hour assigned to a particular subject it interrupts the question assigned to the previous hour. If it is desired to continue the discussion of the pending topic at another time, it can be laid on the table or postponed until after the close of the interrupting question, by a majority vote.

Special Orders made at different times for specified hours. When special orders that have been made at different times come into conflict, the one that was first made takes precedence of all special orders made afterwards, though the latter were made for an earlier hour. No special order can be made so as to interfere with one previously made. By reconsidering the vote making the first special order, they can be arranged in the order desired. Suppose, after a special order has been made for 3 P.M., one is made for 2 P.M. and still later one is made for 4 P.M.; if the 2 P.M. order is pending at 3 P.M., the order for 3 P.M., having been made first, interrupts it and continues, if not previously disposed of, beyond 4 P.M., regardless of the special order for that hour. When it, the 3 P.M. order, is disposed of, the special order for 2 P.M. is resumed even if it is after 4 O'clock, because the 2 P.M. order was made before the 4 P.M. order. The only exception to this rule is in the case of the hour fixed for recess or adjournment. When that hour arrives the chair announces it and declares the assembly adjourned, or in recess, even though there is a special order pending that was made before the hour for recess or adjournment was fixed. When the chair announces the hour, any one can move to postpone the time for adjournment, or to extend the time for considering the pending question a certain number of minutes. These motions are undebatable, and require a two-thirds vote.

Special Orders when only the day or meeting is specified. Often subjects are made special orders for a meeting without specifying an hour. If the order of business provides for orders of the day, they come up under that head, taking precedence of general orders. If there is no provision for orders of the day, they come up under unfinished business—that is, before new business. If there is no order of business, then they may be called up at any time after the minutes are disposed of.

The Special Order for a Meeting. Sometimes a subject is made the special order for a meeting, as for Tuesday morning in a convention, in which case it is announced by the chair as the pending business immediately after the disposal of the minutes. This particular form is used when it is desired to devote an entire meeting, or so much of it as is necessary, to considering a special subject, as the revision of the by-laws. This form of a special order should take precedence of the other forms of special orders. It is debatable and amendable.

Article IV. Incidental Motions

§21.   Questions of Order and Appeal {See Chapter 13}

§22.   Suspension of the Rules {See Chapter 13}

§23.   Objection to the Consideration of a Question {See Chapter 13}

§24.   Division of a Question, and Consideration by Paragraph or Seriatim {See Chapter 13}

§25.   Division of the Assembly, and Motions relating to Methods of Voting, or to Closing or Reopening the Polls {See Chapter 13}

§26.   Motions relating to Methods of Making, or to Closing or to Reopening Nominations {See Chapter 13}

§27.   Requests growing out of Business Pending or that has just been pending, as, a Parliamentary Inquiry, a Request for Information, for Leave to Withdraw a Motion, to Read Papers, to be Excused from a Duty, or for any other Privilege {See Chapter 13}

21. Questions of Order and Appeal. {See Chapter 13} A *Question of Order* takes precedence of the pending question out of which it arises; is in order when another has the floor, even interrupting a speech or the reading of a report; does not require a second; cannot be amended or have any other subsidiary motion applied to it; yields to privileged motions and the motion to lay on the table; and must be decided by the presiding officer without debate, unless in doubtful cases he submits the question to the assembly for decision, in which case it is debatable whenever an appeal would be. Before rendering his decision he may request the advice of persons of experience, which advice or opinion should usually be given sitting to avoid the appearance of debate. If the chair is still in doubt, he may submit the question to the assembly for its decision in a manner similar to this: "Mr. A raises the point of order that the amendment just offered [state the amendment] is not germane to the resolution. The chair is in doubt, and submits the question to the assembly. The question is, 'Is the amendment germane to the resolution?" As no appeal can be taken from the decision of the assembly, this question is open to debate whenever an appeal would be, if the chair decided the question and an appeal were made from that decision. Therefore, it is debatable except when it relates to indecorum, or transgression of the rules of speaking, or to the priority of business, or when it is made during a division of the assembly, or while an undebatable question is pending. The question is put thus: "As many as are of opinion that the amendment is germane [or that the point is well taken] say *aye;* as many as are of a contrary opinion say *no.* The ayes have it, the amendment is in order, and the question is on its adoption." If the negative vote is the larger it would be announced thus: "The noes have it, the amendment is out of order, and the question is on the adoption of the resolution." Whenever the presiding officer decides a question of order, he has the right, without leaving his chair, to state the reasons for his decision, and any two members have the right to appeal from the decision, one making the appeal and the other seconding it.

It is the duty of the presiding officer to enforce the rules and orders of the assembly, without debate or delay. It is also the right of every member who notices the breach of a rule, to insist upon its enforcement. In such a case he rises from his seat and says, "Mr. Chairman, I rise to a point of order." The speaker immediately takes his seat, and the chairman requests the member to state his point of order, which he does and resumes his seat. The chair decides the point, and then, if no appeal is taken and the member has not been guilty of any serious breach of decorum, the chair permits him to resume his speech. But, if his remarks are decided to be improper and any one objects, he cannot continue without a vote of the assembly to that effect. [See 43 for a full treatment of this subject of indecorum in debate]. The question of order must be raised at the time the breach of order occurs, so that after a motion has been discussed it is too late to raise the question as to whether it was in order, or for the chair to rule the motion out of order. The only exception is where the motion is in violation of the laws, or the constitution, by-laws, or standing rules of the organization, or of fundamental parliamentary principles, so that if adopted it would be null and void. In such cases it is never too late to raise a point of order against the motion. This is called raising a question, or point, of order, because the member in effect puts to the chair, whose duty it is to enforce order, the question as to whether there is not now a breach of order.

Instead of the method just described, it is usual, when it is simply a case of improper language used in debate, for the chair to call the speaker to order, or for a member to say, "I call the gentleman to order." The chairman decides whether the speaker is in or out of order, and proceeds as before.

Appeal. An appeal may be made from any decision of the chair (except when another appeal is pending), but it can be made only at the time the ruling is made. It is in order while another member has the floor. If any debate or business has intervened it is too late to appeal. An answer to a parliamentary inquiry is not a decision, and therefore cannot be appealed from. While an appeal is pending a question of order may be raised, which the chair decides peremptorily, there being no appeal from this decision. But the question as to the correctness of the ruling can be brought up afterwards when no other business is pending. An appeal yields to privileged motions, and to the motion to lay on the table. The effect of subsidiary motions is as follows: An appeal cannot be amended. If the decision from which an appeal is taken is of such a nature that the reversal of the ruling would not in any way affect the consideration of, or action on, the main question, then the main question does not adhere to the appeal, and its consideration is resumed as soon as the appeal is laid on the table, postponed, etc. But if the ruling affects the consideration of, or action on, the main question, then the main question adheres to the appeal, and when the latter is laid on the table, or postponed, the main question goes with it. Thus, if the appeal is from the decision that a proposed amendment is out of order and the appeal is laid on the table, it would be absurd to come to final action on the main question and then afterwards reverse the decision of the chair and take up the amendment when there was no question to amend. The vote on an appeal may be reconsidered.

An appeal cannot be debated when it relates simply to indecorum, or to transgression of the rules of speaking, or to the priority of business, or if made during a division of the assembly, or while the immediately pending question is undebatable. When debatable, as it is in all other cases, no member is allowed to speak more than once except the presiding officer, who may at the close of the debate answer the arguments against the decision. Whether debatable or not, the chairman when stating the question on the appeal may, without leaving the chair, state the reasons for his decision.

When a member wishes to appeal from the decision of the chair he rises as soon as the decision is made, even though another has the floor, and without waiting to be recognized by the chair, says, "Mr. Chairman, I appeal from the decision of the chair." If this appeal is seconded, the chair should state clearly the question at issue, and his reasons for the decision if he thinks it necessary, and then state the question thus: "The question is, 'Shall the decision of the chair stand as the judgment of the assembly [or society, or club, etc.]?'" or, "Shall the decision of the chair be sustained?" To put the question he would say, "Those in the affirmative say aye," and after the affirmative vote has been taken he would say, "Those in the negative say no. The ayes have it and the decision of the chair is sustained [or stands as the judgment of the assembly]." Or, "The noes have it and the decision of the chair is reversed." In either case he immediately announces what is before the assembly as the result of the vote. If there is a tie vote the chair is sustained, and if the chair is a member of the assembly he may vote to make it a tie, on the principle that the decision of the chair stands until reversed by a majority, including the chairman if he is a member of the assembly. In stating the question, the word "assembly" should be replaced by "society," or "club," or "board," etc., as the case may be. The announcement of a vote is not a decision of the chair. If a member doubts the correctness of the announcement he cannot appeal, but should call for a "Division" [25].

22. Suspension of the Rules. {See Chapter 13} The motion to suspend the rules may be made at any time when no question is pending; or while a question is pending, provided it is for a purpose connected with that question. It yields to all the privileged motions (except a call for the orders of the day), to the motion to lay on the table, and to incidental motions arising out of itself. It is undebatable and cannot be amended or have any other subsidiary motion applied to it, nor can a vote on it be reconsidered, nor can a motion to suspend the rules for the same purpose be renewed at the same meeting except by unanimous consent, though it may be renewed after an adjournment, even if the next meeting is held the same day.

When the assembly wishes to do something that cannot be done without violating its own rules, and yet it is not in conflict with its constitution, or by-laws, or with the fundamental principles of parliamentary law, it "suspends the rules that interfere with" the proposed action. The object of the suspension must be specified, and nothing else can be done under the suspension. The rules that can be suspended are those relating to priority of business, or to business procedure, or to admission to the meetings, etc., and would usually be comprised under the heads of rules of order. Sometimes societies include in their by-laws some rules relating to the transaction of business without any intention, evidently, of giving these rules any greater stability than is possessed by other rules of their class, and they may be suspended the same as if they were called rules of order. A standing rule as defined in 67 may be suspended by a majority vote. But sometimes the term "standing rules" is applied to what are strictly rules of order, and then, like rules of order, they require a two-thirds vote for their suspension. Nothing that requires previous notice and a two-thirds vote for its amendment can be suspended by less than a two-thirds vote.

No rule can be suspended when the negative vote is as large as the minority protected by that rule; nor can a rule protecting absentees be suspended even by general consent or a unanimous vote. For instance, a rule requiring notice of a motion to be given at a previous meeting cannot be suspended by a unanimous vote, as it protects absentees who do not give their consent. A rule requiring officers to be elected by ballot cannot be suspended by a unanimous vote, because the rule protects a minority of one from exposing his vote, and this he must do if he votes openly in the negative, or objects to giving general consent. Nor can this result be accomplished by voting that the ballot of the assembly be cast by the secretary or any one else, as this does away with the essential principle of the ballot, namely, secrecy, and is a suspension of the by-law, and practically allows a viva voce vote. If it is desired to allow the suspension of a by-law that cannot be suspended under these rules, then it is necessary to provide in the by-laws for its suspension.

The *Form* of this motion is, "to suspend the rules that interfere with," etc., stating the object of the suspension, as, "the consideration of a resolution on …," which resolution is immediately offered after the rules are suspended, the chair recognizing for that purpose the member that moved to suspend the rules. Or, if it is desired to consider a question which has been laid on the table, and cannot be taken up at that time because that class of business is not then in order, or to consider a question that has been postponed to another time, or that is in the order of business for another time, then the motion may be made thus, "I move to suspend the rules and take up [or consider] the resolution …" When the object is not to take up a question for discussion but to adopt it without debate, the motion is made thus: "I move to suspend the rules and adopt [or agree to] the following resolution," which is then read: or, "I move to suspend the rules, and adopt [or agree to] the resolution on …" The same form may be used in a case like this: "I move to suspend the rules, and admit to the privileges of the floor members of sister societies," which merely admits them to the hall.

Instead of a formal motion to suspend the rules, it is more usual to ask for general consent to do the particular business that is out of order. As soon as the request is made the chair inquires if there is any objection, and if no one objects, he directs the member to proceed just as if the rules had been suspended by a formal vote. [See General Consent 48.]

23. Objection to the Consideration of a Question. {See Chapter 13} An objection may be made to the consideration of any original main motion, and to no others, provided it is made before there is any debate or before any subsidiary motion is stated. Thus, it may be applied to petitions and to communications that are not from a superior body, as well as to resolutions. It cannot be applied to incidental main motions, such as amendments to by-laws, or to reports of committees on subjects referred to them, etc. It is similar to a question of order in that it can be made when another has the floor, and does not require a second; and as the chairman can call a member to order, so he can put this question, if he deems it advisable, upon his own responsibility. It cannot be debated, or amended, or have any other subsidiary motion applied to it. It yields to privileged motions and to the motion to lay on the table. A negative, but not an affirmative vote on the consideration may be reconsidered.

When an original main motion is made and any member wishes to prevent its consideration, he rises, although another has the floor, and says, "Mr. Chairman, I object to its consideration." The chairman immediately puts the question, "The consideration of the question has been objected to: Will the assembly consider it? [or, Shall the question be considered?]" If decided in the negative by a two-thirds vote, the whole matter is dismissed for that session; otherwise, the discussion continues as if this objection had never been made. The same question may be introduced at any succeeding session.

The *Object* of this motion is not to cut off debate (for which other motions are provided) but to enable the assembly to avoid altogether any question which it may deem irrelevant, unprofitable, or contentious. If the chair considers the question entirely outside the objects of the society, he should rule it out of order, from which decision an appeal may be taken.

Objection to the consideration of a question must not be confounded with objecting where unanimous consent, or a majority vote, is required. Thus, in case of the minority of a committee desiring to submit their views, a single member saying, "I object," prevents it, unless the assembly by a majority vote grants them permission.

24. Division of a Question, and Consideration by Paragraph. {See Chapter 13} *Division of a Question.* The motion to divide a question can be applied only to main motions and to amendments. It takes precedence of nothing but the motion to postpone indefinitely, and yields to all privileged, incidental, and subsidiary motions except to amend and to postpone indefinitely. It may be amended but can have no other subsidiary motion applied to it. It is undebatable. It may be made at any time when the question to be divided, or the motion to postpone indefinitely, is immediately pending, even after the previous question has been ordered. But it is preferable to divide the question when it is first introduced. When divided each resolution or proposition is considered and voted on separately, the same as if it had been offered alone. The motion to adopt, which was pending when the question was divided, applies to all the parts into which the question has been divided and should not, therefore, be repeated. The formality of a vote on dividing the question is generally dispensed with, as it is usually arranged by general consent. But if this cannot be done, then a formal motion to divide is necessary, specifying the exact method of division.

When a motion relating to a certain subject contains several parts, each of which is capable of standing as a complete proposition if the others are removed, it can be divided into two or more propositions to be considered and voted on as distinct questions, by the assembly's adopting a motion to divide the question in a specified manner. The motion must clearly state how the question is to be divided, and any one else may propose a different division, and these different propositions, or amendments, should be treated as filling blanks; that is, they should be voted on in the order in which they are made, unless they suggest different numbers of questions, when the largest number is voted on first. If a resolution includes several distinct propositions, but is so written that they cannot be separated without its being rewritten, the question can not be divided. The division must not require the secretary to do more than to mechanically separate the resolution into the required parts, prefixing to each part the words "Resolved, That," or "Ordered, That," and dropping conjunctions when necessary, and replacing pronouns by the nouns for which they stand, wherever the division makes it necessary. When the question is divided, each separate question must be a proper one for the assembly to act upon, if none of the others is adopted. Thus, a motion to "commit with instructions" is indivisible; because, if divided, and the motion to commit should fail, then the other motion, to instruct the committee, would be absurd, as there would be no committee to instruct. The motion to "strike out certain words and insert others" is strictly one proposition and therefore indivisible.

If a series of independent resolutions relating to different subjects is included in one motion, it must be divided on the request of a single member, which request may be made while another has the floor. But however complicated a single proposition may be, no member has a right to insist upon its division. His remedy is to move that it be divided, if it is capable of division, or, if not, to move to strike out the objectionable parts. A motion to strike out a name in a resolution brings the assembly to a vote on that name just as well as would a division of the question, if it were allowed to go to that extent, which it is not. If a series of resolutions is proposed as a substitute for another series, such a motion is incapable of division; but a motion can be made to strike out any of the resolutions before the vote is taken on the substitution. After they have been substituted it is too late to strike out any of them. When a committee reports a number of amendments to a resolution referred to it, one vote may be taken on adopting, or agreeing to, all the amendments provided no one objects. But if a single member requests separate votes on one or more of the amendments, they must be considered separately. The others may all be voted on together.

Consideration by Paragraph or Seriatim. Where an elaborate proposition is submitted, like a series of resolutions on one subject, or a set of by-laws, the parts being intimately connected, it should not be divided. The division would add greatly to the difficulty of perfecting the different paragraphs or by-laws by amendments. If the paragraphs are adopted separately, and amendments to succeeding paragraphs make it necessary to amend a preceding one, it can be done only by first reconsidering the vote on the preceding paragraph. In the case of by-laws the trouble is increased, because each by-law goes into effect as soon as adopted, and its amendment is controlled by any by-law or rule that may have been adopted on the subject. When the paragraphs are voted on separately no vote should be taken on the whole. But in all such cases the proper course is to consider the proposition by paragraph, or section, or resolution, or, as it is often called, *seriatim*. The chair should always adopt this course when the question consists of several paragraphs or resolutions, unless he thinks the assembly wishes to act on them immediately as a whole, when he asks if they shall be taken up by paragraph, and the matter is settled informally. Should the chair neglect to take up the proposition by paragraph, any one may move that the proposition be considered by paragraph, or seriatim.

The method of procedure in acting upon a complicated report, as, a set of by-laws, or a series of resolutions that cannot well be divided, is as follows, the word "paragraph" being used to designate the natural subdivisions, whether they are paragraphs, sections, articles, or resolutions. The member submitting the report, having obtained the floor, says that such and such a committee submits the following report; or, that the committee recommends the adoption of the following resolutions. In either case he reads the report, or resolutions, and moves their adoption. Should he neglect to move their adoption, the chair should call for such a motion, or he may assume the motion and state the question accordingly. The chairman, or the secretary, or the member who reported it, as the chair decides is for the best interest of the assembly, then reads the first paragraph, which is explained by the reporting member, after which the chair asks, "Are there any amendments to this paragraph?" The paragraph is then open to debate and amendment. When no further amendments are proposed to this paragraph, the chair says, "There being no further amendments to this paragraph the next will be read." In a similar manner each paragraph in succession is read, explained if necessary, debated, and amended, the paragraphs being amended but not adopted. After all the paragraphs have been amended, the chair says the entire by-law, or paper, or resolution is open to amendment, when additional paragraphs may be inserted and any paragraph may be further amended. When the paper is satisfactorily amended, the preamble, if any, is treated the same way, and then a single vote is taken on the adoption of the entire paper, report, or series of resolutions. If the previous question is ordered on a resolution, or series of resolutions, or on a set of by-laws, before the preamble has been considered it does not apply to the preamble, unless expressly so stated, because the preamble cannot be considered until after debate has ceased on the resolutions or by-laws. It is not necessary to amend the numbers of the sections, paragraphs, etc., as it is the duty of the secretary to make all such corrections where changes are rendered necessary by amendments.

25. Division of the Assembly and other Motions relating to Voting. {See Chapter 13} *A Division of the Assembly* may be called for, without obtaining the floor, at any time after the question has been put, even after the vote has been announced and another has the floor, provided the vote was taken viva voce, or by show of hands, and it is called for before another motion has been made. This call, or motion, is made by saying, "I call for a division," or "I doubt the vote," or simply by calling out, "Division." It does not require a second, and cannot be debated, or amended, or have any other subsidiary motion applied to it. As soon as a division is called for, the chair proceeds again to take the vote, this time by having the affirmative rise, and then when they are seated having the negative rise. While any member has the right to insist upon a rising vote, or a division, where there is any question as to the vote being a true expression of the will of the assembly, the chair should not permit this privilege to be abused to the annoyance of the assembly, by members constantly demanding a division where there is a full vote and no question as to which side is in the majority. It requires a majority vote to order the vote to be counted, or to be taken by yeas and nays (roll call) or by ballot. These motions are incidental to the question that is pending or has just been pending, and cannot be debated. When different methods are suggested they are usually treated not as amendments, but like filling blanks, the vote being taken first on the one taking the most time. In practice the method of taking a vote is generally agreed upon without the formality of a vote.

When the vote is taken by ballot during a meeting of the assembly, as soon as the chair thinks all have voted who wish to, he inquires if all have voted, and if there is no response he declares the polls closed, and the tellers proceed to count the vote. If a formal motion is made to close the polls it should not be recognized until all have presumably voted, and then it requires a two-thirds vote like motions to close debate or nominations. If members enter afterwards and it is desired to reopen the polls it can be done by a majority vote. None of these motions are debatable.

26. Motions relating to Nominations. {See Chapter 13} If no method of making nominations is designated by the by-laws or rules, and the assembly has adopted no order on the subject, any one can make a motion prescribing the method of nomination for an office to be filled. If the election is pending, this motion is incidental to it; if the election is not pending, it is an incidental main motion. It is undebatable and when it is an incidental motion it can have no subsidiary motion applied to it except to amend. It yields to privileged motions. The motion may provide for nominations being made by the chair; or from the floor, or open nominations as it is also called; or for a nominating committee to be appointed; or for nominations to be made by ballot; or by mail.

Closing and Reopening Nominations. Before proceeding to an election, if nominations have been made from the floor or by a committee, the chair should inquire if there are any further nominations. If there is no response he declares the nominations closed. In very large bodies it is customary to make a motion to close nominations, but until a reasonable time has been given, this motion is not in order. It is a main motion, incidental to the nominations and elections, cannot be debated, can be amended as to the time, but can have no other subsidiary motion applied to it. It yields to privileged motions, and requires a two-thirds vote as it deprives members of one of their rights.

If for any reason it is desired to reopen nominations it may be done by a majority vote. This motion is undebatable. It can be amended as to the time, but no other subsidiary motion can be applied to it. It yields to privileged motions.

27. Requests Growing out of the Business of the Assembly. {See Chapter 13}
During the meetings of a deliberative assembly there are occasions when members wish to obtain information, or to do or to have done things that necessitate their making a request. Among these are the following, which will be treated separately:

   (a) Parliamentary Inquiry;

   (b) Request for Information;

   (c) Leave to Withdraw a Motion;

   (d) Reading Papers;

   (e) To be Excused from a Duty;

   (f) For any other Privilege.

(a) Parliamentary Inquiry. A parliamentary inquiry, if it relates to a question that requires immediate attention, may be made while another has the floor, or may even interrupt a speech. It should not, however, be permitted to interrupt a speaker any more than is necessary to do justice to the inquirer. It yields to privileged motions, if they were in order when the inquiry was made, and it cannot be debated or amended or have any other subsidiary motion applied to it. The inquirer does not obtain the floor, but rises and says, "Mr. Chairman, I rise to a parliamentary inquiry." The chairman asks him to state his inquiry, and if he deems it pertinent, he answers it. Or, if the inquiry is made when another has the floor, and there is no necessity for answering it until the speech is finished, the chair may defer his answer until the speaker has closed his remarks. While it is not the duty of the chairman to answer questions of

parliamentary law in general, it is his duty when requested by a member, to answer any questions on parliamentary law pertinent to the pending business that may be necessary to enable the member to make a suitable motion or to raise a point of order. The chairman is supposed to be familiar with parliamentary law, while many of the members are not. A member wishing to raise a point of order and yet in doubt, should rise to a parliamentary inquiry and ask for information. Or, for instance, he may wish to have the assembly act immediately on a subject that is in the hands of a committee, and he does not know how to accomplish it—his recourse is a parliamentary inquiry.

(b) Request for Information. A request for information relating to the pending business is treated just as a parliamentary inquiry, and has the same privileges. The inquirer rises and says, "Mr. Chairman, I rise for information," or, "I rise to a point of information," whereupon the chair directs him to state the point upon which he desires information, and the procedure continues as in case of a parliamentary inquiry. If the information is desired of the speaker, instead of the chair, the inquirer upon rising says, "Mr. Chairman, I should like to ask the gentleman a question." The chairman inquires if the speaker is willing to be interrupted, and if he consents, he directs the inquirer to proceed. The inquirer then asks the question through the chair, thus, "Mr. Chairman, I should like to ask the gentleman," etc. The reply is made in the same way, as it is not in order for members to address one another in the assembly. While each speaker addresses the chair, the chair remains silent during the conversation. If the speaker consents to the interruption the time consumed is taken out of his time.

(c) Leave to Withdraw or Modify a Motion. A request for leave to withdraw a motion, or a motion to grant such leave, may be made at any time before voting on the question has commenced, even though the motion has been amended. It requires no second. It may be made while incidental or subsidiary motions are pending, and these motions cease to be before the assembly when the question to which they are incidental or subsidiary is withdrawn. It yields to privileged motions, and cannot be amended or have any other subsidiary motion applied to it. It is undebatable. When it is too late to renew it, the motion to reconsider cannot be withdrawn without unanimous consent. When a motion is withdrawn, the effect is the same as if it had never been made. Until a motion is stated by the chairman, the mover may withdraw or modify it without asking consent of any one. If he modifies it the seconder may withdraw his second. After the question has been stated it is in possession of the assembly, and he can neither withdraw nor modify it without the consent of the assembly. When the mover requests permission to modify or withdraw his motion, the chair asks if there is any objection, and if there is none he announces that the motion is withdrawn or modified in such and such a way, as the case may be. If any one objects the chair puts the question on granting the request, or a motion may be made to grant it. In case

the mover of a main motion wishes to accept an amendment that has been offered, without obtaining the floor, he says, "Mr. Chairman, I accept the amendment." If no objection is made the chair announces the question as amended. If any one objects, the chair states the question on the amendment, as it can be accepted only by general consent. A request for leave to do anything is treated the same as a motion to grant the leave except that the request must be made by the maker of the motion it is proposed to modify, while the motion to grant the leave is made by some one else and therefore requires no second as it is favored by the one making the request.

(d) Reading Papers. If any member objects, a member has no right to read, or have the clerk read, from any paper or book, as a part of his speech, without the permission of the assembly. The request or the motion to grant such permission yields to privileged motions. It cannot be debated, or amended, or have any other subsidiary motion applied to it. It is customary, however, to allow members to read printed extracts as parts of their speeches, as long as they do not abuse the privilege.

Where papers are laid before the assembly, every member has a right to have them read once, or if there is debate or amendment he has the right to have them read again, before he can be compelled to vote on them. Whenever a member asks for the reading of any such paper evidently for information, and not for delay, the chair should direct it to be read, if no one objects. But a member has not the right to have anything read (excepting as stated above) without permission of the assembly. If a member was absent from the hall when the paper under consideration was read, even though absent on duty, he cannot insist on its being again read, as the convenience of the assembly is of more importance than that of a single member.

(e) To be Excused from a Duty. If a member is elected to office, or appointed on a committee, or has any other duty placed on him, and he is unable or unwilling to perform the duty, if present he should decline it immediately, and if absent he should, upon learning of the fact, at once notify the secretary *or* president orally or in writing that he cannot accept the duty. In most organizations members cannot be compelled to accept office or perform any duties not required by the by-laws, and therefore they have the right to decline office. But if a member does not immediately decline, by his silence he accepts the office, and is under obligation to perform the duty until there has been a reasonable opportunity for his resignation to be accepted. The secretary, for instance, cannot relieve himself from the responsibility of his office by resigning. His responsibility as secretary does not cease until his resignation is accepted, or, at least, until there has been a reasonable time for its acceptance. It is seldom good policy to decline to accept a resignation. As a member has no right to continue to hold an office the duties of which he cannot or will not perform, so a society has no right to force an office on an unwilling member. When a member declines an office, no motion is necessary, unless the by-laws of the society make the performance of such

duties obligatory upon members. If the member is present at the election, the vacancy is filled as if no one had been elected. If the member was not present at the election, when the chair announces his refusal to take the office, as it is a question of privilege relating to the organization of the society, the election to fill the vacancy may take place at once unless notice is required, or other provision for filling vacancies is provided by the by-laws. In the case of a resignation, the chair may at once state the question on accepting it, or a motion to that effect may be made. In either case it is debatable and may have any subsidiary motion applied to it. It yields to privileged and incidental motions.

(f) Request for Any Other Privilege. When any request is to be made the member rises and addresses the chair, and as soon as he catches the eye of the chairman, states at once why he rises. He should rise as soon as a member yields the floor, and, though the floor is assigned to another, he still makes his request. He should never interrupt a member while speaking unless he is sure that the urgency of the case justifies it. As a rule all such questions are settled by general consent, or informally, but, if objection is made, a vote is taken. An explanation may be requested or given, but there is no debate. As these requests arise, they should be treated so as to interrupt the proceedings as little as is consistent with the demands of justice.

Article V. Subsidiary Motions

§28.   Lay on the Table {See Chapter 12}

§29.   The Previous Question {See Chapter 12}

§30.   Limit or Extend Limits of Debate {See Chapter 12}

§31.   Postpone Definitely, or to a Certain Time {See Chapter 12}

§32.   Commit or Refer, or Recommit {See Chapter 12}

§33.   Amend {See Chapter 12}

§34.   Postpone Indefinitely {See Chapter 12}

28. To Lay on the Table. {See Chapter 12} This motion takes precedence of all other subsidiary motions and of such incidental questions as are pending at the time it is made. It yields to privileged motions and such motions as are incidental to itself. It is undebatable and cannot have any subsidiary motion applied to it. It may be applied to any main [11] motion; to any question of privilege or order of the day, after it is before the assembly for consideration; to an appeal that does not adhere to the main question, so that the action on the latter would not be affected by the reversal of the chair's decision; or to the motion to reconsider when immediately pending, in which case the question to be reconsidered goes to the table also. No motion that has another motion adhering to it can be laid on the table by itself; if laid on the table it carries with it everything that adheres to it. When a motion is taken from the table [35] everything is in the same condition, as far as practicable, as when the motion was laid on the table, except that if not taken up until the next session the effect of the previous question is exhausted. If debate has been closed by ordering the previous question, or otherwise, up to the moment of taking the last vote under the order, the questions still before the assembly may be laid on the table. Thus, if, while a resolution and an amendment and a motion to commit are pending, the previous question is ordered on the series of questions, and the vote has been taken and lost on the motion to commit, it is in order to lay on the table the resolution, which carries with it the adhering amendment.

This motion cannot be applied to anything except a question actually pending, therefore it is not in order to lay on the table a class of questions, as the orders of the day, or unfinished business, or reports of committees, because they are not pending questions, as only one main motion can be pending at a time.

To accomplish the desired object, which is evidently to reach a special subject or class of business, the proper course is to suspend the rules by a two-thirds vote and take up the desired question or class of business. Sometimes when it is desired to pass over the next order or class of business, that business is "passed," as it is called, by general consent. In such case, as soon as the business for which it was "passed" is disposed of, it is then taken up. By general consent, the business to come before the assembly may be considered in any order the assembly desires.

If a motion to lay on the table has been made and lost, or if a question laid on the table has been taken from the table, it shows that the assembly wishes to consider the question now, and therefore a motion made the same day to lay that question on the table is out of order until there has been material progress in business or debate, or unless an unforeseen urgent matter requires immediate attention. The assembly cannot be required to vote again the same day on laying the question on the table unless there is such a change in the state of affairs as to make it a new question. Motion relating to adjournment or recess, made and lost, are not business justifying the renewal of the motion to lay on the table, but the renewal of the motion might be justified after a vote on an important amendment, or on the motion to commit. A vote on laying on the table cannot be reconsidered, because, if lost the motion may be renewed as soon as there has been material progress in debate or business, or even before if anything unforeseen occurs of such an urgent nature as to require immediate attention; and if adopted the question may be taken from the table as soon as the interrupting business has been disposed of and while no question is pending, and business of this class, or new or unfinished business, is in order.

The *Form* of this motion is, "I move to lay the question on the table," or, "That the question be laid on the table," or, "That the question lie on the table." It cannot be qualified in any way; if it is qualified, thus, "To lay the question on the table until 2 P.M.," the chair should state it properly as a motion to postpone until 2 P.M., which is a debatable question, and not the motion to lay on the table.

The *Object* of this motion is to enable the assembly, in order to attend to more urgent business, to lay aside the pending question in such a way that its consideration may be resumed at the will of the assembly as easily as if it were a new question, and in preference to new questions competing with it for consideration. It is to the interest of the assembly that this object should be attained instantly by a majority vote, and therefore this motion must either apply to, or take precedence of, every debatable motion whatever its rank. It is undebatable, and requires only a majority vote, notwithstanding the fact that if not taken from the table the question is suppressed. These are dangerous privileges which are given to no other motion whose adoption would result in final action on a main motion. There is a great temptation to make an improper use of them, and lay questions on the table for the purpose of instantly suppressing them by a majority vote, instead of using the previous question, the legitimate motion to bring the assembly to an immediate vote. The fundamental principles of parliamentary law require a two-thirds vote for every motion that suppresses a main question for the session without free debate. The motion to lay on the table being undebatable, and requiring only a majority vote, and having the highest rank of all subsidiary motions, is in direct conflict with these principles, if used to suppress a question. If habitually used in this way, it should, like the other motions to suppress without debate, require a two-thirds vote.

The minority has no remedy for the unfair use of this motion, but the evil can be slightly diminished as follows: The person who introduces a resolution is sometimes cut off from speaking by the motion to lay the question on the table being made as soon as the chair states the question, or even before. In such cases the introducer of the resolution should always claim the floor, to which he is entitled, and make his speech. Persons are commonly in such a hurry to make this motion that they neglect to address the chair and thus obtain the floor. In such case one of the minority should address the chair quickly, and if not given the floor, make the point of order that he is the first one to address the chair, and that the other member, not having the floor, was not entitled to make a motion.

As motions laid on the table are merely temporarily laid aside, the majority should remember that the minority may all stay to the moment of final adjournment and then be in the majority, and take up and pass the resolutions laid on the table. They may also take the question from the table at the next meeting in societies having regular meetings as frequently as quarterly. The safer and fairer method is to object to the consideration of the question if it is so objectionable that it is not desired to allow even its introducer to speak on it; or, if there has been debate so it cannot be objected to, then to move the previous question, which, if adopted, immediately brings the assembly to a vote. These are legitimate motions for getting at the sense of the members at once as to whether they wish the subject discussed, and, as they require a two-thirds vote, no one has a right to object to their being adopted.

The *Effect* of the adoption of this motion is to place on the table, that is, in charge of the secretary, the pending question and everything adhering to it; so, if an amendment is pending to a motion to refer a resolution to a committee, and the question is laid on the table, all these questions go together to the table, and when taken from the table they all come up together. An amendment proposed to anything already adopted is a main motion, and therefore when laid on the table, does not carry with it the thing proposed to be amended. A question of privilege may be laid on the table without carrying with it the question it interrupted. In legislative bodies, and all others that do not have regular sessions as often as quarterly, questions laid on the table remain there for that entire session, unless taken up before the session closes. In deliberative bodies with regular sessions as frequent as quarterly, the sessions usually are very short and questions laid on the table remain there until the close of the next regular session, if not taken up earlier; just as in the same assemblies a question can be postponed to the next session, and the effect of the motion to reconsider, if not called up, does not terminate until the close of the next session. The reasons for any one of these rules apply with nearly equal force to the others. While a question is on the table no motion on the same subject is in order that would in any way affect the question that is on the table; it is necessary first to take the question from the table and move the new one as a substitute, or to make such other motion as is adapted to the case.

29. The Previous Question {See Chapter 12} takes precedence of all subsidiary motions except to lay on the table, and yields to privileged and incidental motions, and to the motion to lay on the table. It is undebatable, and cannot be amended or have any other subsidiary motion applied to it. The effect of an amendment may be obtained by calling for, or moving, the previous question on a different set of the pending questions (which must be consecutive and include the immediately pending question), in which case the vote is taken first on the motion which orders the previous question on the largest number of questions. It may be applied to any debatable or amendable motion or motions, and if unqualified it applies only to the immediately pending motion. It may be qualified so as to apply to a series of pending questions, or to a consecutive part of a series beginning with the immediately pending question. It requires a two-thirds vote for its adoption. After the previous question has been ordered, up to the time of taking the last vote under it, the questions that have not been voted on may be laid on the table, but can have no other subsidiary motions applied to them. An appeal made after the previous question has been demanded or ordered and before its exhaustion, is undebatable. The previous question, before any vote has been taken under it, may be reconsidered, but not after its partial execution. As no one would vote to reconsider the vote ordering the previous question who was not opposed to the previous question, it follows that if the motion to reconsider prevails, it will be impossible to secure a two-thirds vote for the previous question, and, therefore, if it is voted to reconsider the previous question it is considered as rejecting that question and placing the business as it was before the previous question was moved. If a vote taken under the previous question is reconsidered before the previous question is exhausted, there can be no debate or amendment of the proposition; but if the reconsideration is after the previous question is exhausted, then the motion to reconsider, as well as the question to be reconsidered, is divested of the previous question and is debatable. If lost, the previous question may be renewed after sufficient progress in debate to make it a new question.

The *Form* of this motion is, "I move [or demand, or call for] the previous question on [here specify the motions on which it is desired to be ordered]." As it cannot be debated or amended, it must be voted on immediately. The form of putting the question is, "The previous question is moved [or demanded, or called for] on [specify the motions on which the previous question is demanded]. As many as are in favor of ordering the previous question on [repeat the motions] will rise." When they are seated he continues, "Those opposed will rise. There being two-thirds in favor of the motion, the affirmative has it and the previous question is ordered on [repeat the motions upon which it is ordered]. The question is [or recurs] on [state the immediately pending question]. As many as are in favor," etc. If the previous question is ordered the chair immediately proceeds to put to vote the questions on which it was ordered until all the votes are taken, or there is an affirmative vote on postponing definitely or indefinitely, or committing, either of which exhausts the previous question. If there can be the slightest doubt as to the vote the chair should take it again immediately, counting each side. If less than two-thirds vote in the affirmative, the chair announces the vote thus: "There not being two-thirds in favor of the motion, the negative has it and the motion is lost. The question is on," etc., the chair stating the question on the immediately pending question, which is again open to debate and amendment, the same as if the previous question had not been demanded.

The question may be put in a form similar to this: "The previous question has been moved on the motion to commit and its amendment. As many as are in favor of now putting the question on the motion to commit and its amendment will rise; those opposed will rise. There being two-thirds in favor of the motion, the debate is closed on the motion to commit and its amendment, and the question is on the amendment," etc. While this form is allowable, yet it is better to conform to the regular parliamentary form as given above.

The *Object* of the previous question is to bring the assembly at once to a vote on the immediately pending question and on such other pending questions as may be specified in the demand. It is the proper motion to use for this purpose, whether the object is to adopt or to kill the proposition on which it is ordered, without further debate or motions to amend.

The *Effect* of ordering the previous question is to close debate immediately, to prevent the moving of amendments or any other subsidiary motions except to lay on the table, and to bring the assembly at once to a vote on the immediately pending question, and such other pending questions as were specified in the demand, or motion. If the previous question is ordered on more than one question, then its effect extends to those questions and is not exhausted until they are voted on, or they are disposed of as shown below under exhaustion of the previous question. If the previous question is voted down, the discussion continues as if this motion had not been made. The effect of the previous question does not extend beyond the session in which it was adopted. Should any of the questions upon which it was ordered come before the assembly at a future session they are divested of the previous question and are open to debate and amendment.

The previous question is *Exhausted* during the session as follows:

(1) When the previous question is unqualified, its effect terminates as soon as the vote is taken on the immediately pending question.

(2) If the previous question is ordered on more than one of the pending questions its effect is not exhausted until all of the questions upon which it has been ordered have been voted on, or else the effect of those that have been voted on has been to commit the main question, or to postpone it definitely or indefinitely.

If, before the exhaustion of the previous question, the questions on which it has been ordered that have not been voted on are laid on the table, the previous question is not exhausted thereby, so that when they are taken from the table during the same session, they are still under the previous question and cannot be debated or amended or have any other subsidiary motion applied to them.

30. Limit or Extend Limits of Debate. {See Chapter 12} Motions, or orders, to limit or extend the limits of debate, like the previous question, take precedence of all debatable motions, may be applied to any debatable motion or series of motions, and, if not specified to the contrary, apply only to the immediately pending question. If it is voted to limit the debate, the order applies to all incidental and subsidiary motions and the motion to reconsider, subsequently made, as long as the order is in force. But an order extending the limits of debate does not apply to any motions except the immediately pending one and such others as are specified. They are undebatable, and require a two-thirds vote for their adoption. These motions may be amended, but can have no other subsidiary motion applied to them. They yield to privileged and incidental motions, and to the motions to lay on the table and for the previous question. They may be made only when the immediately pending question is debatable. When one of them is pending, another one that does not conflict with it may be moved as an amendment. After one of these motions has been adopted it is in order to move another one of them, provided it does not conflict with the one in force. This motion to limit or extend the limits of debate may be reconsidered even though the order has been partially executed, and if lost it may be renewed after there has been sufficient progress in debate to make it a new question.

After an order is adopted closing debate at a certain hour, or limiting it to a certain time, the motions to postpone and to commit cannot be moved until the vote adopting the order has been reconsidered; but the pending question may be laid on the table, and if it is not taken from the table until after the hour appointed for closing the debate and taking the vote, no debate or motion to amend is allowed, as the chair should immediately put the question. After the adoption of an order limiting the number or length of the speeches, or extending these limits, it is in order to move any of the other subsidiary motions on the pending question.

An order modifying the limits of debate on a question is in force only during the session in which it was adopted. If the question in any way goes over to the next session it is divested of this order and is open to debate according to the regular rules.

The various *Forms* of this motion are as follows:

(1) To fix the hour for closing debate and putting the question, the form is similar to this: "I move that debate close and the question be put on the resolution at 9 P.M."

(2) To limit the length of the debate, the motion may be made thus: "I move that debate on the pending amendment be limited to twenty minutes."

(3) To reduce or increase the number and length of speeches, the motion should be made in a form similar to one of these: "I move that debate on the pending resolution and its amendments be limited to one speech of five minutes from each member;" "I move that Mr. A's time be extended ten minutes;" "I move that Messrs. A and B (the leaders on the two sides) be allowed twenty minutes each, to be divided between their two speeches at their pleasure, and that other members be limited to one speech of two minutes each, and that the question be put at 9 P.M."

31. To Postpone to a Certain Time or Definitely {See Chapter 12} takes precedence of the motions to commit, to amend, and to postpone indefinitely, and yields to all privileged [14] and incidental motions, and to the motions to lay on the table, for the previous question, and to limit or to extend the limits of debate. It allows of a limited debate which must not go into the merits of the main question any more than is necessary to enable the assembly to determine the propriety of the postponement. It may be amended as to the time, and also by making the postponed question a special order. The previous question and the motions limiting or extending the limits of debate may be applied to it. It cannot be laid on the table alone, but when it is pending the main question may be laid on the table which carries with it the motion to postpone. It cannot be committed or postponed indefinitely. It may be reconsidered. When it makes a question a special order it requires a two-thirds vote.

The time to which a question is postponed must fall within the session or the next session, † and, if it is desired to postpone it to a different time, which must not be beyond the next regular session, it is necessary first to fix the time for an adjourned meeting, and then the question may be postponed to that meeting. Some societies have frequent meetings for literary or other purposes at which business may be transacted, while they hold every month or quarter a meeting especially for business. In such societies these rules apply particularly to the regular business meetings, to which questions may be postponed from the previous regular business meeting or from any of the intervening meetings. Neither the motion to postpone definitely nor an amendment to it, is in order when it has the effect of an indefinite postponement; that is, to defeat the measure, as, for instance, to postpone until tomorrow a motion to accept an invitation to a banquet tonight. If the motion to postpone indefinitely is in order at the time, the chair may treat it as such at his discretion, but it cannot be recognized as a motion to postpone definitely. It is not in order to postpone a class of business, as reports of committees; as each report is announced or called for, it may be postponed, or the rules may be suspended by a two-thirds vote and the desired question be taken up. A matter that is required by the by-laws to be attended to at a specified time or meeting as the election of officers cannot, in advance, be postponed to another time or meeting, but when that specified time or meeting arrives the assembly may postpone it to an adjourned meeting. This is sometimes advisable as in case of an annual meeting for the election of officers occurring on a very stormy night so that a bare quorum is present. After an order of the day or a question of privilege is before the assembly for action, its further consideration may be postponed, or any other subsidiary motion may be applied to it. When a question has been postponed to a certain time, it becomes an order of the day for that time and cannot be taken up before that time except by a reconsideration, or by suspending the rules for that purpose, which requires a two-thirds vote. [See Orders of the Day, 20, for the treatment of questions that have been postponed definitely.]

The *Form* of this motion depends upon the object sought.

(1) If the object is simply to postpone the question to the next meeting, when it will have precedence of new business, the form of the motion is "to postpone the question [or, that the question be postponed] to the next meeting." It then becomes a general order for that meeting.

(2) If the object is to specify an hour when the question will be taken up as soon as the question then pending, if there is any, is disposed of, the form is similar to this: "I move that the question be postponed to 3 P.M."

(3) If it is desired to postpone the question until after a certain event, when it shall immediately come up, the form is, "To postpone the question until after the address on Economics."

(4) If the object is to insure its not being crowded out by other matters there should be added to the motion to postpone as given in the first two cases above, the words, "and be made a special order." Or the motion may be made thus: "I move that the question be postponed and made a special order for the next meeting [or, for 3 P.M. tomorrow]." The motion in this form requires a two-thirds vote, as it suspends the rules that may interfere with its consideration at the time specified as explained under Orders of the Day [20].

(5) If it is desired to postpone a question to an adjourned meeting and devote the entire time, if necessary, to its consideration, as in case of revising by-laws, after providing for the adjourned meeting the motion should be made in this form: "I move that the question be postponed and made the special order for next Tuesday evening." Or, a question may be postponed and made the special order for the next regular meeting.

The *Effect* of postponing a question is to make it an order of the day for the time to which it was postponed, and if it is not then disposed of, it becomes unfinished business. Postponing a question to a certain hour does not make it a special order unless so specified in the motion. The motion to postpone definitely may be amended by a majority vote so as to make the amended motion one to make the question a special order. If this is done the amended motion will require a two-thirds vote. [Orders of the Day, 20, should be read in connection with this section.]

32. To Commit or Refer. {See Chapter 12} (All the rules in regard to this motion, except where stated to the contrary, apply equally to the motions to Go into Committee of the Whole, to Consider Informally, and to Recommit as it is called when a question is committed a second time.) This motion takes precedence of the motions to amend and to postpone indefinitely, and yields to all the other subsidiary motions and to all privileged and incidental motions. It cannot be applied to any subsidiary motion, nor can it be laid on the table or postponed except in connection with the main question. The previous question, and motions to limit or extend the limits of debate, and to amend, may be applied to it without affecting the main question. It is debatable but only as to the propriety of committing the main question. If the motion to postpone indefinitely is pending when a question is referred to a committee, it is lost, and is not referred to the committee. Pending amendments go with the main motion to the committee. The motion to commit may be reconsidered, but after the committee has begun the consideration of the question referred to it, it is too late to move to reconsider the vote to commit. The committee may, however, then be discharged as shown below.

The motion to commit (that is, to refer to a committee) may vary in form all the way from the simple form of, "That the question be referred to a committee," to the complete form of referring to question "to a committee of five to be appointed by the chair, with instructions to report resolutions properly covering the case, at the next regular business meeting." If the motion is made in the complete form the details may be changed by amendments, though they are usually treated not as ordinary amendments, but as in filling blanks.

If the motion is made in the simple form of merely referring the pending question to a committee there are three courses that may be pursued in completing the details, the one to be chosen depending upon the circumstances of the case. (1) The simple, or skeleton, motion may be completed by moving amendments, or making suggestions, for adding the required details as stated below. (2) The chair on his own initiative may call for suggestions to complete the motion, first inquiring as to what committee the question shall be referred, and continuing in the order shown hereafter. (3) The motion in its simplest form may be put to vote at once by its enemies' ordering the previous question, and where the motion to commit is almost certain to be lost this is sometimes done to save the time that would be uselessly spent in completing the details. If it should happen that the motion to commit is adopted, which is improbable, then the details are completed before any new business, except privileged matters, can be taken up. These details are taken up in the order given below, the chair calling for the several items much as if he were completing the motion before it was voted on.

In completing a motion simply to refer to a committee, the first question the chair asks is, "To what committee shall the question be referred?" If different ones are suggested, the suggestions are not treated as amendments of those previously offered, but are voted on in the following order until one receives a majority vote: Committee of the whole; as if in committee of the whole; consider informally; standing committee, in the order in which they are proposed; special (select) committee (largest number voted on first). If the question has already been before a standing or special committee the motion becomes the motion to recommit, and the committees would be voted on in the above order except the old committee would precede other standing and select committees. In suggesting or moving that the committee be a special one, the word "special" is not generally used, the motion being made to refer the question to a committee of five, or any other number, which makes it a special committee; that is, not a standing committee. If any committee except a special one is decided upon, the chair should then put the question on referring the question to that committee. But any one may interrupt him and move to add instructions, or he, himself, may suggest them, or instructions may be given after the vote has been taken on committing the question. Instructions may be given to the committee by a majority vote at any time before it submits its report, even at another session.

If the committee is to be a special one, it is necessary in addition to its number to decide how it is to be appointed. If different methods are suggested, or moved, they are voted on in the following order: Ballot; nominations from the floor (or open nominations); nominations by the chair; and lastly, appointment by the chair, the method that should usually be adopted in very large assemblies. When this is decided the completed motion to commit is put to vote. Instructions as heretofore stated may be added before the vote is taken on the motion to commit, or they may be given afterwards. If the motion to commit is adopted, no new business, except privileged matters, can intervene until the appointment of the committee by the method prescribed, except that when the chair appoints the committee he may wish time to make his selections, which, however, must be announced to the assembly.

If nominations are made from the floor no one can nominate more than one, if objection is made. The member making a nomination in a large assembly rises, and, addressing the chair without waiting to be recognized, says, "I nominate Mr. A." In small assemblies the nominations for committees are frequently made by members from their seats suggesting names. The chair repeats each name as he hears it, and if no more than the prescribed number is suggested, he puts the question on the members named constituting the committee. If more names than the prescribed number are suggested, the chair puts the question on each name in succession, beginning with the first named, until enough are chosen to fill the committee. The negative must be put as well as the affirmative, a majority vote being required for each member of the committee. If the committee is nominated by the chair he states the question thus: "The question is, 'Shall these members constitute the committee?'" It is now in order to move to strike out any of the names, and if such a motion is adopted the chair replaces them with other names. When he appoints the committee no vote is taken, but he must announce the names of the committee to the assembly, and until such announcement is made the committee cannot act. If it is desired to permit the chair to appoint a committee after adjournment, it must be authorized by a vote. The power to appoint a committee carries with it the power to appoint its chairman and to fill any vacancy that may arise in the committee. The resignation of a member of a committee should be addressed to the appointing power.

The *Forms* of this motion are as follows: "To refer the question to a committee;" "To recommit the resolution;" "That the subject be referred to a committee of three to be appointed by the chair, and that it report by resolution at the next meeting;" "That it be referred to a committee with power;" "That the assembly do now resolve itself into [or, go into] committee of the whole, to take under consideration," etc., specifying the subject; "That the resolution be considered as if in committee of the whole"; "That the resolution be considered informally."

The *Object* of the motion to refer to a standing or special committee is usually to enable a question to be more carefully investigated and put into better shape for the assembly to consider, than can be done in the assembly itself. Where an assembly is large and has a very large amount of business it is safer to have every main question go to a committee before final action on it is taken. A special committee to investigate and report upon a subject should consist of representative members on both sides of the question, so that both parties in the assembly may have confidence in the report, or reports in case there is disagreement and a minority report is submitted. By care in selecting committees in ordinary assemblies, debates upon delicate and troublesome questions can be mostly confined to the committees. It is not at all necessary to appoint on the committee the member who makes the motion to refer, but it is usual, and the courteous thing to do, when he is specially interested or informed on the subject. If the appointing power does not designate a chairman of the committee, the member first named acts as such unless the committee elects its own chairman. Consequently it is very important that the first named should be an efficient person, especially in a committee for action.

Sometimes a question is referred to a committee with full power to act in the case. When the duty assigned it has been performed, it should report what it has done, and when this report has been made the committee ceases to exist. When the assembly has decided a question and appoints a committee to take certain action (such as a committee of arrangements for holding a public meeting), then the committee should be small, and all should be favorable to the action to be taken. If any one is appointed on such a committee who is not in sympathy with the proposed action, he should say so and ask to be excused. Sometimes such a committee is given power to add to its number.

The object of going into committee of the whole, or considering a question as if in committee of the whole, or informally, is to enable the assembly to discuss a question with perfect freedom, there being no limit to the number of speeches. The first method is used in the United States House of Representatives, and the second in the United States Senate. The last one is the simplest, and is best adapted to ordinary societies that are not very large. If any form of the motion to commit is made with reference to a question not pending, it becomes a main motion. Thus, a motion to go into committee of the whole on a question not pending, or to appoint a committee upon a subject not pending, or to appoint a committee to take certain action, is a main motion.

To Discharge a Committee. When a committee has made its final report and it has been received by the assembly, the committee ceases to exist without any motion being made to that effect. If, for any reason, the assembly wishes to take a question out of the hands of a committee, and it is too late to reconsider the vote on the committal, it is necessary to "discharge the committee from further consideration" of the resolution or other matter referred to it, for as long as the matter is in the hands of the committee, the assembly cannot consider anything involving practically the same question. If the committee has not yet taken up the question referred to it, the proper motion on the day or the day after it was referred, is to reconsider the vote to commit, which requires only a majority vote. If the motion to reconsider cannot be made, a motion to discharge the committee should be made, which, if adopted, practically rescinds action taken, and therefore requires a two-thirds vote, or a vote of a majority of the membership, unless previous notice of the motion has been given, when it requires only a majority vote. When the committee is discharged its chairman returns to the secretary all papers that have been entrusted to him. It requires a motion to bring the matter referred before the assembly, and this motion may be combined with the motion to discharge, thus: "I move that the committee to whom was referred the resolution on immigration be discharged, and that the resolution be now taken up for consideration [or, be considered at some other specified time]."

33. To Amend {See Chapter 12} takes precedence of the motion to postpone indefinitely, and yields to all other subsidiary motions and to all privileged and incidental motions, except the motion to divide the question. It can be applied to all motions except those in the *List of Motions that Cannot be Amended* [33]. It can be amended itself, but this "amendment of an amendment" (an amendment of the second degree) cannot be amended. The previous question and motions to limit or extend the limits of debate may be applied to an amendment, or to only an amendment of an amendment, and in such case they do not affect the main question, unless so specified. An amendment is debatable in all cases except where the motion to be amended is undebatable. An amendment of a pending question requires only a majority vote for its adoption, even though the question to be amended requires a two-thirds vote. An amendment of a constitution or by-laws, or rules of order, or order of business, previously adopted, requires a two-thirds vote; but an amendment of that amendment requires only a majority vote. When a motion or resolution is under consideration only one amendment of the first degree is permitted at a time, and one amendment of that amendment—that is, an amendment of the second degree—is allowed also. An amendment of the third degree would be too complicated and is not in order. Instead of making it, a member may say that if the amendment of the amendment is voted down, he will offer such and such an amendment of the amendment. While there can be only one amendment of each degree pending at the same time, any number of them may be offered in succession. An amendment must be germane to the subject to be amended—that is, it must relate to it, as shown further on. So an amendment to an amendment must be germane to the latter.

Form. An amendment may be in any of the following forms: (a) to *insert* or *add* (that is, place at the end); (b) to *strike out*; (c) to *strike out* and *insert*, or to *substitute*, as it is called, when an entire paragraph or resolution is struck out and another is inserted. The third form is a combination of the other two and cannot be divided, though, as shown hereafter, for the purposes of amendment the two motions are treated separately, the words to be struck out being first amended and then the words to be inserted. No amendment is in order the effect of which is to convert one of these forms into another.

The motion to amend is made in a form similar to this: "I move to amend the resolution by inserting the word 'very' before the word 'good;'" or, it may be reduced to a form as simple as this: "I move to insert 'very' before 'good.'" The motion to insert should always specify the word before or after which the insertion is to be made. The motion to strike out should also locate the word, provided it occurs more than once. When the chair states the question on the amendment he should repeat the motion in detail so that all may understand what modification is proposed. Unless the effect of the amendment is very evident, he should, in putting the question, show clearly the effect of its adoption, even though it requires the reading of the entire resolution, and then the words to be inserted, or struck out, or struck out and inserted, and finally the resolution as it will stand if the amendment is adopted. He then says, "As many as are in favor of the amendment [or, of striking out, etc., or of inserting, etc.] say *aye*; those opposed, say *no*. The ayes have it, the amendment is adopted, and the question is on the resolution as amended, which is, '*Resolved*, That,'" etc., reading the resolution as amended. If the vote is taken by show of hands or by rising, the question is put and the vote announced thus: "As many as are in favor of the amendment will rise [or, will raise the right hand]; those opposed will rise [or, will manifest it in the same way]. The affirmative has it and the amendment is adopted. The question is on the resolution," etc. The instant the amendment is voted, on, whether it is adopted or lost, the chair should announce the result of the vote and state the question that is then before the assembly.

To Insert or Add Words. When a motion to *insert [or add]* certain words is made, the words to be inserted should be perfected by amendments proposed by their friends before the vote is taken on inserting or adding them. After words have been inserted or added, they cannot be changed or struck out except by a motion to strike out the paragraph, or such a portion of it as shall make the question an entirely different one from that of inserting the particular words; or by combining such a motion to strike out the paragraph or a portion of it with the motion to insert other words. The principle involved is that when the assembly has voted that certain words shall form a part of a resolution, it is not in order to make another motion that involves exactly the same question as the one it has decided. The only way to bring it up again is to move to reconsider [36] the vote by which the words were inserted. If the motion to insert is lost, it does not preclude any other motion to insert these words together with other words, or in place of other words, provided the new motion presents essentially a new question to the assembly.

To *Strike out Words.* The motion to strike out certain words can be applied only to consecutive words, though, as the result of amendments, the words may be separated when the final vote is taken. If it is desired to strike out separated words, it is necessary to strike out the separated words by separate motions, or still better, a motion may be made to strike out the entire clause or sentence containing the words to be struck out and insert a new clause or sentence as desired. The motion to strike out certain words may be amended only by striking out words from the amendment, the effect of which is to retain in the resolution the words struck out of the amendment provided both motions are adopted. If the motion to strike out certain words is adopted, the same words cannot be again inserted unless the place or the wording is so changed as to make a new proposition. If the motion to strike out fails, it does not preclude a motion to strike out the same words and insert other words, or to strike out a part of the words, or to strike out a part and insert other words; or to strike out these words with others, or to do this and insert other words. In each of these cases the new question is materially different from the old one. For striking out all, or a part, of something that has been previously adopted, see "Rescind, etc." [37].

To *Strike Out* and *Insert Words* is a combination of the two preceding motions, and is indivisible. For purposes of amendment it is resolved into its constituent elements, and the words to be struck out are first amended, after which the words to be inserted are amended. After their amendment the question is put on the motion to strike out and insert. If it is adopted, the inserted words cannot be struck out, nor can the words struck out be inserted, unless the words or place are so changed as to make the question a new one, as described above. If the motion is lost, it does not preclude either of the single motions to strike out or to insert the same words, nor another motion to strike out and insert, provided there is any material change in either the words to be struck out or the words to be inserted, so that the questions are not practically identical. When it is desired to strike out or modify separated words, a motion may be made to strike out so much of the resolution as is necessary to include all the words to be struck out or changed, and to insert the desired revision including these words. If the words are inserted in the place previously occupied by the words struck out, they may differ materially from the latter, provided they are germane to it. If the words are to be inserted at a different place, then they must not differ materially from those struck out, as it must be in the nature of a transfer. The combined motion to strike out words in one place and to insert different words in another place is not in order. Either the place or the words must be substantially the same. If there are several changes to be made, it is usually better to rewrite the paragraph and offer it as a substitute, as shown further on.

Amendments Affecting an Entire Paragraph. A motion to insert (or add) or to strike out a paragraph, or to substitute one paragraph for another, is an amendment of the first degree, and therefore cannot be made when an amendment is pending. The friends of the paragraph to be inserted or struck out should put it in the best possible shape by amending it before it is voted on. After a paragraph has been inserted it cannot be amended except by adding to it; and it cannot be struck out except in connection with other paragraphs so as to make the question essentially a new one. If a paragraph is struck out, it cannot be inserted afterwards unless it is so changed in wording or place as to present an essentially new question. If the motion to insert or to strike out a paragraph is lost, it does not preclude any other motion except one that presents essentially the same question as the one that the assembly has already decided, as shown above in the case of amending words of a paragraph. Thus, when a motion to insert a paragraph has been lost, it is in order to move to insert a part of the paragraph or the entire paragraph if materially altered. So, though the assembly has refused to strike out a paragraph, it is in order to strike out a part of the paragraph or otherwise to amend it, though it is safer for its friends to make it as nearly perfect as possible before the vote is taken on striking it out, with a view to defeating that motion.

A motion to *substitute* one paragraph for another (which is a combination of the two preceding motions) after being stated by the chair is resolved into its two elements for the purpose of amendment, the chair at first entertaining amendments only to the paragraph to be struck out, these amendments being of the second degree. After it is perfected by its friends, the chair asks if there are any amendments proposed to the paragraph to be inserted. When both paragraphs have been perfected by amendments the question is put on substituting one paragraph for the other. Even though the paragraph constitutes the entire resolution and the motion to substitute is carried, it is necessary afterwards to vote on adopting the resolution, as it has only been voted to substitute one paragraph for another. A paragraph that has been substituted for another cannot be amended afterwards, except by adding to it, like any other paragraph that has been inserted. The paragraph that has been replaced cannot be again inserted unless so modified as to constitute a new question, as with any paragraph that has been struck out. If the motion to substitute is lost, the assembly has only decided that that particular paragraph shall not replace the one specified. It may be willing that it replace some other paragraph, or that it be inserted, or that the paragraph retained in the resolution be further amended, or even struck out. But no amendment is in order that presents to the assembly practically a question that it has already decided.

In parliamentary language it is not correct to speak of "substituting" one word or part of a paragraph for another, as the term is applied to nothing less than a paragraph. When a question is being considered by section, it is in order to move a substitute for the pending section. A substitute for the entire resolution, or report, cannot be moved until the sections have all been considered and the chair has announced that the entire paper is open to amendment. When a resolution with amendments of the first and second degree pending, is referred to a committee, they may report it back with a substitute for the resolution which they recommend, even though two amendments are pending. In such a case the chair states the question first on the amendments that were pending when the resolution was committed. When they are disposed of, he states the question on the substitute recommended by the committee and proceeds as in case of any other substitute motion.

Improper Amendments. An amendment is not in order which is not germane to the question to be amended; or merely makes the affirmative of the amended question equivalent to the negative of the original question; or is identical with a question previously decided by the assembly during that session; or changes one form of amendment to another form; or substitutes one form of motion for another form; or strikes out the word *Resolved* from a resolution; or strikes out or inserts words which would leave no rational proposition before the assembly; or is frivolous or absurd. An amendment of an amendment must be germane to—that is, must relate to—the subject of the amendment as well as the main motion. No independent new question can be introduced under cover of an amendment. But an amendment may be in conflict with the spirit of the original motion and still be germane, and therefore in order.

Illustrations: A resolution of censure may be amended by striking out the word "censure" and inserting the word "thanks," for both relate to opinion of certain conduct; refusing to censure is not the same as expressing thanks. A resolution to purchase some books could not be amended by striking out the words relating to books and inserting words relating to a building. Suppose a resolution pending directing the treasurer to purchase a desk for the secretary, and an amendment is offered to add the words, "and to pay the expenses of the delegates to the State Convention;" such an amendment is not germane to the resolution, as paying the expenses of the delegates is in no way related to purchasing a desk for the secretary, and is therefore out of order. But if an amendment were offered to insert the words "and a permanent record book" after the word "desk," it would be in order, because both are articles to enable the secretary to perform his duties. If a resolution were pending condemning certain things, it could be amended by adding other things that were similar or in some way related to them. Suppose a resolution commending A and B for heroism is pending; if the acts of heroism were not connected, amendments are in order adding other names for other acts of heroism; but if the commendation is for an act of heroism in which A and B were joined, then no names can be added to the resolution unless the parties were connected with A and B in that act. Suppose the following resolution pending: "*Resolved*, That the Secretary be instructed to notify our representative in Congress that we do approve of his course in regard to the tariff." A motion to amend by inserting *not* after the word *be* would be out of order, because an affirmative vote on "not instructing" is identical in effect with a negative vote on "instructing." But the motion to insert the word *not* after *do* is in order, for an affirmative vote on disapproving of a certain course is not the same as a negative vote on a resolution of approval, as the latter may mean nothing but an unwillingness to express an opinion on the subject. If a resolution is pending and a member makes the motion, "*I move to strike out the words* 'pine benches' *and insert the words* 'oak chairs,' " it is an amendment of the first degree, and no other amendment of that degree is in order until this is acted upon. All the words in italics are necessary for this form of motion, and are not subject to amendment. The only amendments in order are those that change the words "pine benches" or "oak chairs"—that is, first those to be struck out, and when they are perfected, then those to be inserted. Suppose the motion to "*strike out* 'pine' " is pending, and it is moved to amend by adding "*and insert* 'oak.' " This motion is out of order, as it changes one form of amendment to another form. It is not in order to move to strike out the word "adopt" in a motion and insert the word "reject," as "adopt" is a formal word necessary to show the kind of motion made. Practically, however, the same result may be attained by moving to postpone indefinitely—that is, to reject, the main question. The chair should never rule an amendment out of order unless he is perfectly sure that it is so. If he is in doubt he should admit the amendment, or submit the question as to its being in order to the assembly as described in 21.

Every original main motion may be amended. All others may be amended, except those contained in the following list of

Motions That Cannot Be Amended

To adjourn (except when it is qualified, or when made in an assembly with no provision for a future meeting)   §17

Call for the orders of the day   §20

Question of order, and appeal   §21

To object to consideration of a question   §23

Call for a division of the assembly   §25

To grant leave to withdraw a motion	§27
To grant leave to speak after indecorum	§21
A request of any kind	§27
To take up a question out of its proper order	§22
To suspend the rules	§22
To lay on the table	§28
To take from the table	§35
To reconsider	§36
The previous question	§39
To postpone indefinitely	§34
To amend an amendment	§33
To fill a blank	§33
A nomination	§66

A motion to adopt a resolution or a by-law may be amended by adding, "and that it be printed and that members be supplied with copies," or, "that they go into effect at the close of this annual meeting," or anything of a similar kind. Under each of the privileged, incidental, and subsidiary motions, it is stated whether or not the motion may be amended, and, when necessary, the way in which it may be amended is explained. An amendment to anything already adopted is not a subsidiary motion. The matter to be amended is not pending and is therefore not affected by anything done with the amendment, provided it is not adopted. Such an amendment is a main motion subject to amendments of the first and second degrees. If the motion is to strike out an entire resolution that has been adopted, it is usually called to *Rescind* and is explained under that head [37]. If the motion is to amend a by-law, etc., it will be found under Amendments of Constitutions, By-laws, etc. Minutes are usually amended (corrected) informally, the chair directing the correction to be made when suggested. But if objection is made, a formal vote is necessary for the amendment. The minutes may be corrected whenever the error is noticed regardless of the time which has elapsed; but after their adoption, when too late to reconsider the vote, they require a two-thirds vote for their amendment, unless previous notice of the proposed amendment has been given, when only a majority vote is required for its adoption, the same as with the motion to rescind [37]. This is necessary for the protection of the records, which otherwise would be subject to the risk of being tampered with by temporary majorities. The numbers prefixed to paragraphs, articles, etc., are only marginal indications and should be corrected by the secretary, if necessary, without any motion to amend. For amending a long paper, such as a series of resolutions, or a set of by-laws, which should be considered and amended by paragraph, see 24.

Filling Blanks. Propositions for filling blanks are treated somewhat differently from other amendments, in that any number of members may propose, without a second, different names or numbers for filling the blanks, no one proposing more than one name or number for each place, unless by general consent. These are treated not as amendments, one of another, but as independent propositions to be voted on successively. If the blank is to be filled with a name, the chair repeats the names as they are proposed so all may hear them, and finally takes a vote on each name, beginning with the first proposed, until one receives a majority vote. If the blank is to be filled with several names and no more names are suggested than required, the names may be inserted without a vote. If more names than required are suggested, a vote is taken on each, beginning with the first, until enough to fill the blank have received a majority vote. If the number of names is not specified, a vote is taken on each name suggested, and all that receive a majority vote are inserted.

If the blank is to be filled with a number or a date, then the largest sum, or the longest time, or the most distant date, is put first, unless it is evident to the chair that the reverse order is necessary to enable the first vote to be taken on the proposition that is least likely to be adopted. Suppose a committee is being instructed to purchase a building for a blank amount: the voting on filling the blank should begin with the largest sum proposed; if that is lost, all who voted for it, and some others, would favor the next largest sum, so that the vote would be greater, and so on down to the largest sum that is favored by a majority. If the voting began with the smallest sum, every one would be willing to pay that amount, and it might be adopted and thus cut off voting on the other propositions, whereas a majority would prefer authorizing the committee to spend a larger amount. On the other hand, suppose the committee was being authorized to sell a building for a blank amount: here it is evident that there would be more in favor of the large sum than of the small one. So to get at the wish of the assembly the voting should begin with the smallest sum proposed; all who are willing to sell for that amount, and some additional ones, will be willing to sell for the next larger sum; and so the smallest sum for which the majority is willing to sell will be gradually reached.

It is sometimes convenient to create a blank, as in the following example: A resolution is pending requesting the proper authorities to prohibit the erection of wooden buildings north of A street, and an amendment to strike out A and insert B, and an amendment of the second degree to strike out B and insert C, have been made. The debate developing the fact that several other streets have their advocates, the best course is for the chair to state that, if there is no objection, the motion would be treated as having a blank for the name of the street, and that A, B, and C have been proposed for filling the blank. In this way other names could be suggested and they would be voted on successively beginning with the one that made the prohibited area the largest, and continuing down until one was reached that could get a majority in its favor. If objection is made to leaving a blank for the name, the chair may put the question without waiting for a motion, or any one may move, as an incidental motion, that a blank be created for the name of the street. This motion is undebatable, and cannot be amended, but it may be moved to fill the blank by ballot or in any other way.

The blanks in a resolution should be filled usually before voting on the resolution. But sometimes, when a large majority is opposed to the resolution, the previous question is ordered without waiting for the blanks to be filled, thus stopping debate and further amendment, and bringing the assembly at once to a vote on the resolution. Under such circumstances the resolution would usually be rejected. But should it be adopted, it would be necessary to fill the blanks in the skeleton resolution before any other than privileged business would be in order.

The method adopted in filling blanks has sometimes a great advantage over ordinary amendment. In amending, the last one proposed is the first one voted on, whereas in filling blanks the first one proposed, or nominated, is voted on first, except where, from the nature of the case, another order is preferable, and then that order is adopted as explained above.

Nominations are treated like filling blanks; any number may be pending at the same time, not as amendments of each other, but as independent propositions to be voted on in the order in which they were made until one receives a majority vote.

34. To Postpone Indefinitely {See Chapter 12} takes precedence of nothing except the main motion to which it is applied, and yields to all privileged , incidental , and other subsidiary motions. It cannot be amended or have any other subsidiary motion applied to it except the previous question and motions limiting or extending the limits of debate. It is debatable and opens the main question to debate. It can be applied to nothing but main questions, which include questions of privilege and orders of the day after they are before the assembly for consideration. An affirmative vote on it may be reconsidered, but not a negative vote. If lost it cannot be renewed. It is simply a motion to reject the main question. If a main motion is referred to a committee while to postpone indefinitely is pending, the latter motion is ignored and does not go to the committee.

The *Object* of this motion is not to postpone, but to reject, the main motion without incurring the risk of a direct vote on it, and it is made only by the enemies of the main motion when they are in doubt as to their being in the majority.

The *Effect* of making this motion is to enable members who have exhausted their right of debate on the main question, to speak again, as, technically, the question before the assembly is different, while, as far as the subject of discussion is concerned, there is no difference caused by changing the question from adopting to rejecting the measure, because the merits of the main question are open to debate in either case. If adopted, its effect is to suppress the main motion for that session, unless the vote is reconsidered. As this motion does not suppress the debate on the main question, its only useful effect is to give the opponents of the pending measure a chance of killing the main motion without risking its adoption in case of failure. For, if they carry the indefinite postponement, the main question is suppressed for the session; if they fail, they still have a vote on the main question, and, having learned their strength by the vote taken, they can form an opinion of the advisability of continuing the struggle.

Article VI. Some Main and Unclassified Motions

§35.   Take from the Table {See Chapter 14}

§36.   Reconsider {See Chapter 14}

§37.   Rescind {See Chapter 14}

§38.   Renewal of a Motion {See Chapter 5}

§39.   Ratify {See Chapter 2}

§40.   Dilatory, Absurd, or Frivolous Motions {See Chapter 10}

§41.   Call of the House

35. To Take from the Table {See Chapter 14} takes precedence of no pending question, but has the right of way in preference to main motions if made during the session in which it was laid on the table while no question is actually pending, and at a time when business of this class, or unfinished business, or new business, is in order; and also during the next session in societies having regular business meetings as frequently as quarterly. It yields to privileged and incidental motions, but not to subsidiary ones. It is undebatable, and no subsidiary motion can be applied to it. It is not in order unless some business has been transacted since the question was laid on the table, nor can it be renewed until some business has been transacted since it was lost. The motion to take from the table cannot be reconsidered, as it can be renewed repeatedly if lost, and, if carried, the question can be again laid on the table after progress in debate or business.

In ordinary deliberative assemblies, a question is supposed to be laid on the table only temporarily with the expectation of its consideration being resumed after the disposal of the interrupting question, or at a more convenient season. As soon as the question that was introduced when the first question was laid on the table, is disposed of, any one may move to take this first question from the table. When he rises to make the motion, if the chair recognizes some one else as having first risen, he should at once say that he rises to move to take a question from the table. The chair then assigns him the floor if the other member has risen to make a main motion. If the new main motion has been stated by the chair before he claims the floor, he must wait until that question is disposed of before his motion will be in order. When taken up, the question with everything adhering to it is before the assembly exactly as when it was laid on the table. Thus, if a resolution has amendments and a motion to commit pending at the time it was laid on the table, when it is taken from the table the question is first on the motion to commit. If a motion to postpone to a certain time is pending when the question is laid on the table, and it is taken from the table after that time, then the motion to postpone is ignored when the question is taken up. If the question is taken up on the day it was laid on the table, members who have exhausted their right of debate cannot again speak on the question. But if taken up on another day, no notice is taken of speeches previously made. The previous question is not exhausted if the question upon which it was ordered is taken from the table at the same session, even though it is on another day.

36. Reconsider. {See Chapter 14} This motion is peculiar in that the making of the motion has a higher rank than its consideration, and for a certain time prevents anything being done as the result of the vote it is proposed to reconsider. It can be made only on the day the vote to be reconsidered was taken, or on the next succeeding day, a legal holiday or a recess not being counted as a day. It must be made by one who voted with the prevailing side. Any member may second it. It can be made while any other question is pending, even if another member has the floor, or after it has been voted to adjourn, provided the chair has not declared the assembly adjourned. It may be made after the previous question has been ordered, in which case it and the motion to be reconsidered are undebatable.

While the making of the motion to reconsider has such high privilege, its consideration has only the rank of the motion to be reconsidered, though it has the right of way in preference to any new motion of equal rank, as illustrated further on; and the reconsideration of a vote disposing of a main question either temporarily or permanently may be called up, when no question is pending, even though the general orders are being carried out. The motion to reconsider cannot be amended, postponed indefinitely, or committed. If the reconsideration is laid on the table or postponed definitely, the question to be reconsidered and all adhering questions go with it. The previous question and the motions limiting or extending the limits of debate may be applied to it when it is debatable. It is undebatable only when the motion to be reconsidered is undebatable. When debatable it opens to debate the merits of the question to be reconsidered. It cannot be withdrawn after it is too late to renew the motion. If the motion to reconsider is lost it cannot be repeated except by general consent. No question can be twice reconsidered unless it was materially amended after its first reconsideration. A reconsideration requires only a majority vote, regardless of the vote necessary to adopt the motion reconsidered.

The motion to reconsider *cannot be applied* to a vote on a motion that may be renewed within a reasonable time; or when practically the same result may be attained by some other parliamentary motion; or when the vote has been partially executed (except in case of the motion to limit debate), or something has been done as the result of the vote that the assembly cannot undo; or to an affirmative vote in the nature of a contract, when the other party to the contract has been notified of the vote; or to a vote on the motion to reconsider. In accordance with these principles, votes on the following motions *cannot be reconsidered*: Adjourn; Take a Recess; Lay on the Table; Take from the Table; Suspend the Rules or Order of Business; and Reconsider. Affirmative votes on the following cannot be reconsidered: Proceed to the Orders of the Day; Adopt, or after they are adopted, to Amend, or Repeal, or Rescind, the Constitution, By-laws, or Rules of Order or any other rules that require previous notice for their amendment; Elect to membership or office if the member or officer is present and does not decline, or if absent and has learned of his election in the usual way and has not declined; to Reopen Nominations. A negative vote on the motion to Postpone Indefinitely cannot be reconsidered as practically the same question comes up again when the vote is taken on the main question. After a committee has taken up the matter referred to it, it is too late to reconsider the vote committing it, though the committee may be discharged. But after debate has proceeded under an order limiting or extending the limits of debate, the vote making that order may be reconsidered, as the debate may develop facts that make it desirable to return to the regular rules of debate. The minutes, or record of proceedings, may be corrected at any time without reconsidering the vote approving them.

If the main question is pending and it is moved to reconsider the vote on any subsidiary [12], incidental [13], or privileged motion, the chair states the question on the reconsideration the moment the motion to be reconsidered is in order if it were made then for the first time. Thus, if while the motions to commit, for the previous question, and to lay on the table are pending, it is moved to reconsider a negative vote on postponing to a certain time, the chair proceeds to take the vote on laying on the table and, if that is lost, next on the previous question, and then on reconsidering the vote on the postponement, and if that is adopted, then on the postponement, and if that is lost, then on to commit. If the motion to lay on the table had been carried, then when the question was taken from the table the same method of procedure would be followed; that is, the question would be first on ordering the previous question, and next on reconsidering the vote on the postponement, etc. If the reconsideration of an amendment of the first degree is moved while another amendment of the same degree is pending, the pending amendment is first disposed of and then the chair announces the question on the reconsideration of the amendment. If the reconsideration of an amendment to an immediately pending question is moved the chair at once announces the question on the reconsideration.

If the reconsideration is moved while another subject is before the assembly, it cannot interrupt the pending business, but, as soon as that has been disposed of, if called up it has the preference over all other main motions and general orders. In such a case the chair does not state the question on the reconsideration until it is called up.

If the motion to reconsider is made at a time when the reconsideration could be called up if it had been previously made, the chair at once states the question on the reconsideration, unless the mover adds to his motion the words, "and have it entered on the minutes," as explained further on.

If, after the vote has been taken on the adoption of a main motion, it is desired to reconsider the vote on an amendment, it is necessary to reconsider the vote on the main question also, and one motion should be made to cover both votes. The same principle applies in case of an amendment to an amendment, whether the vote has been taken on the resolution, or only on the amendment of the first degree. When the motion covers the reconsideration of two or three votes, the debate is limited to the question that was first voted on. Thus, if the motion is to reconsider the votes on a resolution and amendments of the first and second degree, the debate is limited to the amendment of the second degree. If the motion to reconsider is adopted the chair states the question on the amendment of the second degree and recognizes the mover of the reconsideration as entitled to the floor. The question is now in exactly the same condition it was in just previous to taking the original vote on that amendment.

The *Forms* of making this motion are as follows: "I move to reconsider the vote on the resolution relating to a banquet." "I move to reconsider the vote on the amendment to strike out 'Wednesday' and insert 'Thursday.'" [This form is used when the resolution is still pending.] "I move to reconsider the votes on the resolution relating to a banquet and on the amendment to strike out 'Wednesday' and insert 'Thursday.'" [This form is used when the vote has been taken on the resolution, and it is desired to reconsider the vote on an amendment.] When the motion to reconsider is made the chair states the question, if it can then be considered, and proceeds as with any other question. If it cannot be considered at that time, he says, "Mr. A moves to reconsider the vote on … The secretary will make a note of it," and proceeds with the pending business. The reconsideration, after being moved, is brought before the assembly for action as explained in the previous paragraph. If it is *called up* by a member, he simply says, after obtaining the floor, "I call up the motion to reconsider the vote on …" This call requires no second or vote. If the call is in order, as previously explained, the chair says, "The motion to reconsider the vote [or votes] on … is called up. The question is, 'Will the assembly reconsider the vote [or votes] on …? Are you ready for the question?'" If the reconsideration is one that the chair states the question on as soon as it can be considered (as when it is moved to reconsider an amendment while another amendment is pending), as soon as the proper time arrives the chair states the question on the reconsideration the same as if the motion to reconsider were made at this time.

When the debate, if there is any, is finished, he *puts the question* thus: "As many as are in favor of reconsidering the vote on the resolution relating to a banquet, say *aye*; those opposed say *no*. The ayes have it and the votes on the resolution is reconsidered. The question is now on the resolution, which is," etc. Or, the question may be put thus: "The question is, Will the assembly reconsider the votes on the resolution relating to a banquet, and on the amendment to strike out 'Wednesday' and insert 'Thursday?' As many as are in favor of the reconsideration say *aye*; those opposed say *no*. The ayes have it and the votes on the resolution and the amendment are reconsidered. The question is now on the amendment, which is," etc. If the motion to reconsider is adopted the business is in exactly the same condition it was in before taking the vote, or the votes, that have been reconsidered, and the chair instantly states the question on the immediately pending question, which is then open to debate and amendment as before.

The *Effect of Making* this motion is to suspend all action that the original motion would have required until the reconsideration is acted upon; but if it is not called up, this effect terminates with the session [63], except in an assembly having regular meetings as often as quarterly, when, if not called up, its effect does not terminate till the close of the next regular session. As long as its effect lasts, any one at an adjourned, or a special, or a regular meeting, may call *up* the motion to reconsider and have it acted upon, though it is not usual for any one but the mover to call it up on the day it is made if the session lasts beyond that day and there is no need of prompt action.

The *Effect of the Adoption* of this motion is to place before the assembly the original question in the exact position it occupied before it was voted upon; consequently no one, after the reconsideration is adopted, can debate the question reconsidered who had on that day exhausted his right of debate on that question; his only recourse is to discuss the question while the motion to reconsider is before the assembly. If the question is not reconsidered until a later day than that on which the vote to be reconsidered was taken, then it is open to free debate regardless of speeches made previously. When a vote taken under the operation of the previous question is reconsidered, the question is then divested of the previous question, and is open to debate and amendment, provided the previous question had been exhausted by votes taken on all the questions covered by it, before the motion to reconsider was made.

In standing and special committees a vote may be reconsidered regardless of the time elapsed since the vote was taken, provided the motion is made by one who did not vote with the losing side, and that all members who voted with the prevailing side are present, or have received due notice that the reconsideration would be moved at this meeting. A vote cannot be reconsidered in committee of the whole.

Reconsider and Have Entered on the Minutes. The motion to reconsider, as previously explained in this section, provides means for correcting, at least on the day on which it occurred, errors due to hasty action. By using the same motion and having it entered on the minutes so that it cannot be called up until another day, a means is provided for preventing a temporary majority from taking action that is opposed by the majority of the society. This is needed in large societies with frequent meetings and small quorums, the attendance in many cases not exceeding ten percent of the membership. It enables a society with a small quorum to protect itself from injudicious action by temporary majorities, without requiring previous notice of main motions and amendments as is done in the English Parliament. To accomplish this, however, it is necessary to allow this form of the motion to be applied to a vote finally disposing of a main motion, regardless of the fact that the motion to reconsider has already been made. Otherwise it would be useless, as it would generally be forestalled by the motion to reconsider, in its simple form, which would be voted down, and then this motion could not be made. As this form of the motion is designed only to be used when the meeting is an unrepresentative one, this fact should be very apparent, and some members of the temporary minority should vote with the temporary majority on adopting or postponing indefinitely a main motion of importance, when they think the action is in opposition to the wishes of the great majority of the society. One of them should then move "to reconsider the vote on the resolution [or motion] and have it [or, request that it be] entered on the minutes," which has the effect of suspending all action required by the vote it is proposed to reconsider, as previously explained, and thus gives time to notify absent members of the proposed action. If no member of the temporary minority voted with the majority, and it is too late for any one to change his vote so as to move to reconsider, then some one should give notice of a motion to rescind the objectionable vote at the next meeting, which may be done by a majority vote after this notice has been given.

Should a minority make an improper use of this form of the motion to reconsider by applying it to a vote which required action before the next regular business meeting, the remedy is at once to vote that when the assembly adjourns it adjourns to meet on another day, appointing a suitable day, when the reconsideration could be called up and disposed of. The mere making of this motion would probably cause the withdrawal of the motion to reconsider, as it would defeat the object of that motion if the majority of the society is in favor of the motion to be reconsidered. If the motion to reconsider is withdrawn, of course the other would be.

This form of the motion to reconsider and have entered on the minutes differs from the simple form to reconsider in the following respects:

(1) It can be made only on the day the vote to be reconsidered is taken. If a meeting is held on the next day the simple form of the motion to reconsider, made then, accomplishes the object of this motion by bringing the question before the assembly on a different day from the one when the vote was taken.

(2) It outranks the simple form of the motion to reconsider, and may be made even after the vote has been taken on the motion to reconsider, provided the result of the vote has not been announced. If made after the simple form of the motion to reconsider, it supersedes the latter, which is thereafter ignored.

(3) It can be applied only to votes which finally dispose of the main question. They are as follows: an affirmative or negative vote on adopting, and an affirmative vote on postponing indefinitely, a main question. And it may be applied to a negative vote on the consideration of a question that has been objected to, provided the session extends beyond that day.

(4) In an assembly not having regular business meetings as often as quarterly, it cannot be moved at the last business meeting of a session.

(5) It cannot be called up on the day it is made, except when it is moved on the last day of a session of an assembly not having regular business sessions as often as quarterly, when any one can call it up at the last business meeting of the session.

After it is called up there is no difference in the treatment of the two forms of the motion.

37. Rescind, Repeal, or Annul. {See Chapter 14} Any vote taken by an assembly, except those mentioned further on, may be rescinded by a majority vote, provided notice of the motion has been given at the previous meeting or in the call for this meeting; or it may be rescinded without notice by a two-thirds vote, or by a vote of a majority of the entire membership. The notice may be given when another question is pending, but cannot interrupt a member while speaking. To rescind is identical with the motion to amend something previously adopted, by striking out the entire by-law, rule, resolution, section, or paragraph, and is subject to all the limitations as to notice and vote that may be placed by the rules on similar amendments. It is a main motion without any privilege, and therefore can be introduced only when there is nothing else before the assembly. It cannot be made if the question can be reached by calling up the motion to reconsider which has been previously made. It may be made by any member; it is debatable, and yields to all privileged and incidental motions; and all of the subsidiary motions may be applied to it. The motion to rescind can be applied to votes on all main motions, including questions of privilege and orders of the day that have been acted upon, and to votes on an appeal, with the following *exceptions*: votes cannot be rescinded after something has been done as a result of that vote that the assembly cannot undo; or where it is in the nature of a contract and the other party is informed of the fact; or, where a resignation has been acted upon, or one has been elected to, or expelled from, membership or office, and was present or has been officially notified. In the case of expulsion, the only way to reverse the action afterwards is to restore the person to membership or office, which requires the same preliminary steps and vote as is required for an election.

Where it is desired not only to rescind the action, but to express very strong disapproval, legislative bodies have, on rare occasions, voted to rescind the objectionable resolution and expunge it from the record, which is done by crossing out the words, or drawing a line around them, and writing across them the words, "Expunged by order of the assembly," etc., giving the date of the order. This statement should be signed by the secretary. The words expunged must not be so blotted as not to be readable, as otherwise it would be impossible to determine whether more was expunged than ordered. Any vote less than a majority of the total membership of an organization is certainly incompetent to expunge from the records a correct statement of what was done and recorded and the record of which was officially approved, even though a quorum is present and the vote to expunge is unanimous.

Article VII. Debate

§42.   Debate {See Chapter 8}

§43.   Decorum in Debate {See Chapter 8}

§44.   Closing and Preventing Debate {See Chapter 8}

§45.   Principles of Debate and Undebatable Motions {See Chapter 8}

45. Principles of Debate and Undebatable Motions. {See Chapter 8} All main motions are debatable, and debate is allowed or prohibited on other motions in accordance with the following principles:

(a) High privilege is, as a rule, incompatible with the right of debate of the privileged motion: and, therefore, all highly privileged motions are undebatable, except those relating to the privileges of the assembly or a member. Questions of privilege [19] rarely arise, but when they do, they are likely to be so important that they must be allowed to interrupt business, and yet they cannot generally be acted upon intelligently without debate, and, therefore, they are debatable. The same is true of appeals from the decision of the chair which are debatable, unless they relate to indecorum, or to transgression of the rules of speaking, or to priority of business, or are made while an

undebatable question is pending; in which cases there is not sufficient need of debate to justify making them an exception to the rule, and therefore an appeal under any of these circumstances is undebatable.

(b) Motions that have the effect of suspending a rule are not debatable. Consequently motions to suppress, or to limit, or to extend the limits of, debate are undebatable, as they suspend the ordinary rules of debate.

(c) Appeals made after the previous question has been ordered are undebatable, as it would be manifestly improper to permit debate on them when the assembly by a two-thirds vote has closed debate on the pending question. So any order limiting debate on the pending question applies to questions arising while the order is in force.

(d) To Amend, or to Reconsider, an undebatable question is undebatable, whereas to amend, or to reconsider, a debatable question is debatable.

(e) A Subsidiary Motion is debatable to just the extent that it interferes with the right of the assembly to take up the original question at its pleasure. *Illustrations*: To "Postpone Indefinitely" a question places it out of the power of the assembly to again take it up during that session, except by reconsideration, and consequently this motion allows of free debate, even involving the whole merits of the original question. To "Commit" a question only delays the discussion until the committee reports, when it is open to free debate, so it is only debatable as to the propriety of the commitment and as to the instructions, etc. To "Postpone to a Certain Time" prevents the consideration of the question till the specified time, except by a reconsideration or suspension of the rules, and therefore allows of limited debate upon the propriety of the postponement. To "Lay on the Table" leaves the question so that the assembly can consider it at any time that that question or that class of business is in order, and therefore to lay on the table should not be, and is not, debatable.

Because a motion is undebatable it does not follow that while it is pending the chair may not permit a question or an explanation. The distinction between debate and asking questions or making brief suggestions, should be kept clearly in mind, and when the latter will aid the assembly in transacting business, the chair should permit it before taking the vote on an undebatable question. He should, however, remain standing during the colloquy to show that he has the floor, and he should not allow any more delay in putting the question than he feels is helpful to the business.

The following lists of motions that open the main question to debate, and of those that are undebatable, are made in accordance with the above principles:

Motions That Open the Main Question to Debate

Undebatable Motions

Art. VIII. Vote

48. Motions requiring more than a Majority Vote. {See Chapter 9} *Majority Vote.* Any legitimate motion not included among those mentioned below as requiring more than a majority vote, requires for its adoption only a majority; that is, more than half of the votes cast, ignoring blanks, at a legal meeting where a quorum is present, unless a larger vote for its adoption is required by the rules of the assembly.

General Consent or Unanimous Vote. By general, or unanimous, or silent, consent the assembly can do business with little regard for the rules of procedure, as they are made for the protection of the minority, and when there is no minority to protect, there is little use for the restraint of the rules, except such as protect the rights of absent members, or the right to a secret vote. In the former case the consent of the absentees cannot be given, and in the latter case the consent cannot be withheld by the minority without exposing their votes, which they cannot be compelled to do. When the election is not by ballot and there are several candidates one of whom receives a majority vote, sometimes a motion is made to make the vote unanimous. It should never be made except by the candidate with the largest number of votes after the successful one, or his representative, and even then its propriety is doubtful. One negative vote defeats a motion to make a vote unanimous, as a single objection defeats a request for general consent.

By the legitimate use of the principle that the rules are designed for the protection of the minority, and generally need not be strictly enforced when there is no minority to protect, business may be greatly expedited. When there is evidently no opposition, the formality of voting can be avoided by the chair's asking if there is any objection to the proposed action, and if there is none, announcing the result. The action thus taken is said to be done by general consent, or unanimous or silent consent. Thus, after an order has been adopted limiting the speeches to two minutes each, if a speaker is so interesting that when his time has expired there is a general demand for him to go on, the chair, instead of waiting for a motion and taking a vote, could accept it as the will of the assembly that the speaker's time be extended, and would direct him to proceed. Or, he might say that if there is no objection the member's time will be extended two minutes, or some other time.

Two-thirds Vote. A two-thirds vote means two-thirds of the votes cast, ignoring blanks which should never be counted. This must not be confused with a vote of two-thirds of the members present, or two-thirds of the members, terms sometimes used in by-laws. To illustrate the difference: Suppose 14 members vote on a question in a meeting of a society where 20 are present out of a total membership of 70, a two-thirds vote would be 10; a two-thirds vote of the members present would be 14; and a vote of two-thirds of the members would be 47.

There has been established as a compromise between the rights of the individual and the rights of the assembly the principle that a two-thirds vote is required to adopt any motion that suspends or modifies a rule of order previously adopted; or prevents the introduction of a question for consideration; or closes, or limits, or extends the limits of debate; or limits the freedom of nomination or voting; or closes nominations or the polls; or deprives one of membership or office. It will be found that every motion in the following list belongs to one of the classes just mentioned.

Motions Requiring a Two-thirds Vote

Amend (Annul, Repeal, or Rescind) any part of the Constitution, By-laws, or Rule, of Order, previously adopted; it also requires previous notice	§68
Amend or Rescind a Standing Rule, a Program or Order of Business, or a Resolution, previously adopted, without notice being given at a previous meeting or in the call for the meeting	§37
Take up a Question out of its Proper Order	§22
Suspend the Rules	§22
Make a Special Order	§20
Discharge an Order of the Day before it is pending	§20
Refuse to Proceed to the Orders of the Day	§20
Sustain an Objection to the Consideration of a Question	§23
Previous Question	§29
Limit, or Extend the Limits, of Debate	§30
Extend the Time Appointed for Adjournment or for Taking a Recess	§20
Close Nominations [26] or the Polls	§25
Limit the Names to be Voted for	
Expel from Membership: it also requires previous notice and trial	§75
Depose from Office: it also requires previous notice	
Discharge a Committee when previous notice has not been given	§32
Reconsider in Committee when a member of the majority is absent and has not been notified of the proposed reconsideration	§36

Article IX. Committees and Boards

Article X. The Officers and the Minutes

Article XI. Miscellaneous

Part II

Article XII. Organization and Meetings

Article XIII. Legal Rights of Assemblies and Trial of Their Members

Basic Information on Motions

Here's a handy table covering the basic characteristics of motions. Feel free to copy it and refer to it during meetings. The motions in bold constitute the ladder of motions.

Motion	Purpose	Interrupt speaker?	Second Needed?	Debatable?	Amendable?	Vote Needed
Fix the time to which to adjourn	Sets the time for a continued meeting	No	Yes	No[1]	Yes	Majority
Adjourn	Closes the meeting	No	Yes	No	No	Majority
Recess	Establishes a brief break	No	Yes	No[2]	Yes	Majority
Raise a Question of Privilege	Asks urgent question regarding to rights	Yes	No	No	No	Ruled by chair
Call for orders of the day	Requires that the meeting follow the agenda	Yes	No	No	No	One member
Lay on the table	Puts the motion aside for later consideration	No	Yes	No	No	Majority
Previous question	Ends debate and moves directly to the vote	No	Yes	No	No	Two thirds
Limit or extend limits of debate	Changes the debate limits	No	Yes	No	Yes	Two thirds
Postpone to a certain time	Puts off the motion to a specific time	No	Yes	Yes	Yes	Majority[3]
Commit or refer	Refers the motion to a committee	No	Yes	Yes	Yes	Majority
Amend an amendment (secondary amendment)	Proposes a change to an amendment	No	Yes	Yes[4]	No	Majority
Amend a motion or resolution (primary amendment)	Proposes a change to a main motion	No	Yes	Yes[4]	Yes	Majority
Postpone indefinitely	Kills the motion	No	Yes	Yes	No	Majority
Main motion	Brings business before the assembly	No	Yes	Yes	Yes	Majority
Point of order	Requests that the rules be followed; requires chair to rule	Yes	No	No	No	Ruled by chair

Motion					
Appeal from the decision of the chair Challenges a ruling of the chair	Yes	Yes	Depends[4]	No	Majority[5]
Suspend the rules Allows the group to violate the rules (not bylaws)	No	Yes	No	No	Two thirds
Objection to consideration Keeps the motion from being considered	Yes[6]	No	No	No	Two thirds[7]
Division of the question Separates consideration of the motion	No	Yes	No	Yes	Majority
Division of the assembly Requires a standing vote	Yes	No	No	No	One member
Parliamentary inquiry or point of information Allows a member to ask a question about business at hand	Yes	No	No		Responded to by chair
Withdraw a motion (after stated by chair) Removes a motion from consideration	Yes	Depends[8]	No	No	Majority
Take from the table Resumes considering a motion that was laid on the table	No	Yes	No	No	Majority
Reconsider Considers a motion again	Yes[9]	Yes	Depends[10]	No	Majority
Rescind or amend something previously adopted Repeals a previously adopted motion or amends it after it has been adopted	No	Yes	Yes	Yes	Depends[11]

1 Is debatable when another meeting is scheduled for the same or next day, or if the motion is made while no question is pending

2 Unless no question is pending

3 Majority, unless it makes question a special order

4 If the motion it is being applied to is debatable

5 Majority in negative required to reverse chair's decision

6 When another member has been assigned the floor, until debate has begun or a subsidiary motion has been stated by the chair

7 Two thirds against consideration sustains objection

8 Yes, if motion is made by person requesting permission; no, if made by another member

9 When another has been assigned the floor, but not after he has begun to speak

10 Only if motion to be reconsidered is debatable

11 a) a majority with notice; b) two thirds; or c) majority of entire membership

Index

N

O

P

T

U-V

W-X-Y-Z